Sumerian Hymnology:
The Eršemma

HEBREW UNION COLLEGE ANNUAL SUPPLEMENTS

NUMBER 2

Sumerian Hymnology: The Eršemma

Mark E. Cohen

CINCINNATI, 1981

Published with the assistance of
The Neumann Memorial Publication Fund
established by Sidney Neumann as a memorial to his parents,
Abraham and Emma Neumann
and the
Henry Englander—Eli Mayer Publication Fund
established in their honor by
Esther Straus Englander and Jessie Straus Mayer

Library of Congress Cataloging in Publication Data
Main entry under title:

Sumerian hymnology, the eršemma.

(Hebrew Union College annual supplements ; no. 2)
Includes bibliographical references and index.
1. Hymns, Sumerian. 2. Hymns, Sumerian—Translations into English. 3. Hymns, English—Translations from Sumerian. I. Cohen, Mark E. II. Title: Eršemma. III. Series: Hebrew Union College annual. Supplements ; no. 2.
PJ4083.S9 299'.92 81-2422
ISBN 0-87820-601-9 AACR2
ISSN 0275-9993

Printed in the United States of America by
KTAV Publishing House, Inc.

To my lovely wife Rochelle

Table of Contents

Acknowledgments

For permission to collate or publish tablets in their care, I am grateful to Dr. E. Sollberger and the Trustees of the British Museum; Prof. W. W. Hallo, Curator of the Yale Babylonian Collection; Prof. Å. W. Sjöberg, Curator of the University Museum Collection; Prof. M. Civil of the Oriental Institute; Prof. Dr. G. R. Meyer, Director-General, Staatliche Museen zu Berlin, Vorderasiatische Abteilung; Dr. Ira Spar and the Metropolitan Museum.

I am indebted to Prof. Å. W. Sjöberg, not only for the valuable suggestions and advice freely offered, but also for the sincere concern he has continually shown for me. I thank Prof. M. Civil for guidance and for always informing me of texts he had identified as belonging to this corpus. I am grateful to Prof. S. N. Kramer, who was eager to help me with this manuscript and whose ideas and suggestions proved most valuable to me throughout this work. I also express my appreciation to Prof. W. G. Lambert, who kindly informed me of tablets and fragments belonging to this corpus.

For his painstaking care in editing this volume, I am indebted to Professor David B. Weisberg, without whose concern this work could not have been published.

Abbreviations

Abbreviations are according to the standard abbreviations of The Assyrian Dictionary of the University of Chicago with the exception of the following:

ANET	J. Pritchard, Ancient Near Eastern Texts, 3rd ed., Princeton, Princeton University Press, 1969.
A. Salonen Festschrift	Studia Orientalia 46, Amsterdam, N. Holland Publishing, 1975.
Cal K	K.2742+K.8207 (S. Langdon, AJSL 42 110).
Das Lugalbandaepos	C. Wilcke, Das Lugalbandaepos, Wiesbaden, Otto Harrassowitz, 1969.
Dumuzi's Dream	B. Alster, Dumuzi's Dream, Copenhagen, Akademisk Vorlag, 1972.
ELA	S. Cohen, Enmerkar and the Lord of Aratta, Dissertation, U. of Pa., 1973.
Falkenstein Festschrift	Heidelberger Studien zum Alten Orient, Wiesbaden, Otto Harrassowitz, 1967.
Gilgameš	A. Shaffer, Sumerian Sources of Tablet XII of the Epic of Gilgameš, Dissertation, U. of Pa., 1963.
Götterepitheta	K. Tallquist, Akkadische Götterepitheta, Hildesheim, Georg Olms Verlag, 1974.
GSG	A. Poebel, Grundzüge der sumerischen Grammatik, Rostock, 1923.
Image of Tammuz	Th. Jacobsen, Toward the Image of Tammuz and Other Essays on Mesopotamian History and Culture, Cambridge, Harvard University Press, 1970.
Königshymnen	W. H. Römer, Sumerische 'Königshymnen' der Isin-Zeit, Leiden, E. J. Brill, 1965.

Kultlyrik	J. Krecher, Sumerische Kultlyrik, Wiesbaden, Otto Harrassowitz, 1966.
Menschenbild	G. Pettinato, Das altorientalische Menschenbild und die sumerischen und akkadischen Schöpfungsmythen, Heidelberg, Carl Winter's Universitätsbuchhandlung, 1971.
Mondgott	Å. Sjöberg, Der Mondgott Nanna-Suen in der sumerischen Überlieferung, Uppsala, Almqvist and Wiksell, 1960.
Nanna-Suen's Journey	A. Ferrara, Nanna-Suen's Journey to Nippur, Biblical Institute Press, Rome, 1973.
Sacred Marriage	S. N. Kramer, The Sacred Marriage Rite: Aspects of Faith, Myth, and Ritual in Ancient Sumer, Bloomington and London, Indiana University Press, 1969.
SAHG	A. Falkenstein, W. von Soden, Sumerische und Akkadische Hymnen und Gebete, Stuttgart, Carl Winter's Universitätsbuchhandlung, 1953.
SGL	A. Falkenstein, J. van Dijk, Sumerische Götterlieder I-II, Heidelberg, Carl Winter's Universitätsbuchhandlung, 1959–1960.
Studies Albright	H. Goedicke, Near Eastern Studies in Honor of William Foxwell Albright, Baltimore, Johns Hopkins Press, 1971.
Studies Gelb	Orientalia NS 42 1–2, Pontifical Institute Press, 1973.
Studies Kramer	AOAT 25, NeuKirchen-Vluyn, Butzon and Bercker Kevelaer, 1976.
Studies Oppenheim	Studies Presented to A. Leo Oppenheim, Chicago, University of Chicago Press, 1964.
Tierbilder	W. Heimpel, Tierbilder in der sumerischen Literatur, Rome, Pontifical Biblical Institute, 1968.
YNER	Yale Near Eastern Researches 1–6, New Haven, Yale University Press, 1967–1975.

PART I

Introduction

The greatest quantity of Sumerian literature extant today derives from tablets dating to the Old Babylonian period (ca. 2000–1600 B.C.E.). During this period, which witnessed the hegemony of such cities as Isin, Larsa, Mari, Eshnunna, Asshur and finally Babylon, Sumerian was no longer the vernacular; Akkadian had finally succeeded in replacing Sumerian. Yet Sumerian remained pre-eminent as the literary language in the southern area known as Sumer. Akkadian was probably just beginning to be used in this capacity. Many of the Sumerian compositions preserved from this period were unquestionably composed much earlier, as for example the Keš-temple Hymn, the Instructions of Šuruppak, the Temple Hymns[1] and a cycle of hymns to the goddess Inanna which tradition ascribed to Enḫedu-anna, the daughter of Sargon of Akkad.[2] Also included in this pre-Old Babylonian literature are the numerous royal hymns in honor of the kings of the Ur III Empire (ca. 2120–2000 B.C.E.). In addition other works are cited in literary catalogues presumed to date to the Ur III period.[3] So, too, we believe that a great many other texts, particularly those referred to as "myths" and "epics," were authored before the Old Babylonian period. In the literary tablets from this period two Sumerian dialects occur. The first we shall refer to as "main dialect" and the other as Emesal. The Emesal dialect occurs in most of the lamentations, in songs with the rubric eršemma, several incantation-hymns, a few proverbs and in several other texts, particularly those involving the goddess Inanna.[4] Basically all other Sumerian literary texts are in the main dialect.[5]

(1)Å. W. Sjöberg and E. Bergmann, The Collection of Sumerian Temple Hymns, TCS 3, New York (1973).

(2)See W. W. Hallo and J. J. A. van Dijk, The Exaltation of Inanna, YNER 3 (1968) pp. 1–11.

(3)See W. W. Hallo, "On the antiquity of Sumerian literature", JAOS 83 (1963) 167ff.

(4)For the use of the Emesal dialect see J. Krecher, Kultlyrik 11ff.

(5)Occasionally a main dialect composition contains an Emesal term. Note Civil, "The

A razzia into Babylonia by the Hittites (ca. 1595 B.C.E.) coupled with a takeover by invading Kassites brought the Old Babylonian period to an abrupt end. Moreover, this may have had a profound effect upon the transmission of Sumerian literature. Three basic lines of development seem to have occurred. First, with but few exceptions, the main dialect compositions ceased to be tradited.[6] Secondly, eventually bilingual compositions employing main dialect Sumerian with an Akkadian interlinear translation were authored.[7] And thirdly, from the corpus of the Old Babylonian Emesal material the lamentations and some of the eršemmas continued to be tradited. The eršaḫunga, probably attested in the Old Babylonian period without a rubric, along with the šuilla, blossomed by the middle of the First Millennium B.C.E. In addition an Akkadian interlinear translation was developed for these Emesal texts. However, some other Old Babylonian Emesal works did not survive.

What caused the ill-fate of most of the main dialect compositions? The scribes in their schools copied these main dialect compositions, recopying older texts, while composing new ones for their own pleasure or at the command of the king or other important personages. At some point under the Kassites most of these main dialect texts were no longer being copied. What had occurred? Benno Landsberger had suggested that due to political developments scribal schools may have been forced to close, noting in particular that the breaking away of southern Sumer during the reign of Hammurapi's son, Samsuiluna, may have cost the northern schools the loss of Sumerian literature.[8] William Hallo has recently proposed a conscious scribal selection process, traditing compositions whose themes met the needs and taste of the moment, while discarding all others.[9]

By the close of the Old Babylonian period and the beginning of the

---

Homes of the Fish", Iraq 23 (1961) p. 164 line 152 and W. G. Lambert, "The Fable of the Fox", BWL 186ff. obverse 11.

(6)Some main dialect compositions which continued to be tradited through the Kassite period are The Lugalbanda Epic (see C. Wilcke, Das Lugalbandaepos lines 1–20, 59–70a); lugal-e; an-gim; Enki and Ninmah; Examination Text D (Å. W. Sjöberg, JCS 24 (1972) 126ff.); Examination Text A (Å. W. Sjöberg, ZA 64 (1975) 137 ff.); proverbs (see W. G. Lambert, BWL 225 ff.); possibly The Fable of the Fox (W. G. Lambert, BWL 186 ff.); possibly the Ninurta Hymn SLTN 61 (M. E. Cohen, WO 8 22 ff.); possibly the creation myth KAR 4.

(7)Just a few examples of bilingual texts composed after the Old Babylonian period are the series *utukki lemnuti;* a Nebuchadnezzar I inscription (W. G. Lambert, JCS 21 126 and CRRA 19 (1971) 434 ff.); Marduk's chariot (W. G. Lambert, Symbolae Biblicae et Mesopotamicae, Leiden (1973) 271 ff.); a bilingual hymn to Ninurta (W. G. Lambert, BWL 118 ff.).

(8)B. Landsberger, "Scribal Concepts of Education," *City Invincible* (Chicago, 1958); p. 101 ff.

(9)W. W. Hallo, "Toward a History of Sumerian Literature," *Sumerological Studies in Honor of Thorkild Jacobsen* (*Assyriological Studies* no. 20), (Chicago, 1976) p. 181 ff.

Kassite domination the scribal schools may have been subjected to strong administrative pressure to de-emphasize Sumerian for the more practical Akkadian. Also, and perhaps even more significant, with the burgeoning of the vernacular Akkadian as *the* literary medium, there may have been a wholesale abandonment of Sumerian. If one doubts the possibility and likelihood that a switch in language emphasis could lead to the almost total extinction of a culture's literary heritage, he need but be reminded of the fate of Greek literature in the Middle Ages, when the emphasis upon Latin caused the disappearance of many Greek works forever, while endangering the transmission of others. That such a devastating shift in literary emphasis may have occurred in the Kassite period is quite possible. In the secular life of the state, Sumerian no longer played any part and therefore, aside from curiosity and antiquity's sake, there was little reason for a future hireling of the administrative apparatus to know Sumerian. Akkadian met both the administrative and literary needs of the country. Several centuries later, amidst a revival of nationalistic spirit to recapture past glories before the Kassite domination, Sumerian was once more intensely studied, but as would happen with Greek literature in the Renaissance, many of the works had disappeared. Whether the survival of the few main dialect compositions was a matter of luck or intention we cannot be sure, though we believe chance to be more likely. But these texts were studied, recopied and provided with Akkadian interlinear translations. In addition, new bilingual compositions were composed, uniting the old medium of Sumerian with the popular Akkadian.

Why then did the uninterrupted transmission of much of the Emesal material occur? Whereas Sumerian main dialect had been used for the literary needs of the royal court, Emesal was almost totally rooted in a specific religious institution and thus less dependent upon the administration. Of all society's institutions the one most impervious to change has been religion. Religion attempts to provide man with a constant, secure relationship with the world about him and thus, in an attempt to impart this feeling of constancy, religious institutions hold precious that which is oldest in their tradition, the greatest symbol of constancy. Sumerian was just such a symbol. The more the centuries passed and life changed, the more important became the use of Sumerian for liturgical purposes. There had been, of course, a great number of main dialect Sumerian religious compositions in the Old Babylonian period. Yet we suspect that these main dialect texts were commissioned by the king for various occasions or were written for public festivals and events. Probably they weren't used more than a few times and were then "discarded" into the scribal school curricula.[10] These compositions probably never became part of a religious

(10)Note W. W. Hallo, *CRRA* 17 (1969) 120–121: "The divine hymn was not, however, simply

institution's liturgy and therefore, in the absence of a religious institution to perpetuate them, gave way to Akkadian compositions.

What was the religious institution that perpetuated the Emesal literature? A catalogue of Emesal compositions compiled for the famous "library" of the neo-Assyrian monarch, Asshurbanipal (668–627 B.C.E), states in its colophon that these works were the province of the gala-priest.[11] Ritual texts from First Millennium B.C.E. Uruk detail ritual ceremonies of the gala-priest, citing known Emesal compositions as being part of his liturgy.[12] Also, many copies of the Emesal texts divulge in their colophons that the tablets were owned and copied by gala-priests.[13] Thus, that the Emesal compositions were the liturgy of the gala-priest by the First Millennium B.C.E. is clear. In the Second Millennium B.C.E., the only evidence clearly linking the Emesal material with the gala-priest is from Mari. A ritual of the gala-priest[14] has been preserved in which the gala-priest is instructed to recite an Emesal composition. Two other possible indicators of the gala-priest's recitations of Emesal texts are first, that the gala-priest is frequently mentioned in Emesal compositions and secondly, the gala-priest is known to have played the balag, an instrument which accompanied the Emesal lamentations. Thus, the Emesal texts seem to have constituted the liturgy of the gala-priest in the Second Millennium B.C.E. as well as in the First Millennium B.C.E.

Unfortunately our knowledge of the religious duties of the gala-priest in the Third and Second Millennia B.C.E. is scant and therefore, of course, very little about the role of Emesal literature in the cult can be known with any degree of certainty. It is clear from evidence dating to the Third Millennium B.C.E. that the gala-priest participated in funerary activities, one of

---

used at the dedication of the statue, and then forgotten, any more than the statue remained forever sheltered from general view in the niche of its sanctuary. On the great festivals, the statue left its throne-dais and was carried in public procession to be admired by all, and on these occasions, it may be suggested, the mouth of the statue was once more formally opened and the hymn in its honor again recited. In this manner, a text that began as a dedicatory inscription, of virtually monumental character, was transformed into a canonical composition, copied and recopied in temple and school." Hallo cites the enuma eliš as "late evidence for the perpetuation of the cultic life situation here sugested for the divine hymns." Yet we wonder if, in most cases, the relegating of the hymn to the school curriculum spelled the end of the work in cultic life.

(11)4R^2 53

(12)F. Thureau-Dangin, *Rituels accadiens,* Paris 1921.

(13)See H. Hunger, "Babylonische und assyrische Kolophone," *AOAT* 2, Kevelaer 1968.

(14)See Krecher, *Kultlyrik,* p. 34.

his duties involving the playing of the balag-instrument (a harp or drum). An inscription of Gudea, governor of Lagash (ca. 2140 B.C.E.) states that formerly "in the graveyard of the city the hoe was not placed, the corpse was not buried, the gala-priest did not bring the balag-instrument—no wail came out of it."[15] Also a funerary composition preserved on an Old Babylonian tablet states that as part of the burial ceremony the gala-priest "calls out" to Utu, the judge of the netherworld, thereby indicating the recitation of an actual composition by the gala-priest at a funeral.[16]

From economic tablets we also know that gala-priests could be associated with specific deities and temples. But we cannot speak with any certainty as to their specific duties within the temple's cult.[17]

Lastly, the Mari Ritual mentions the gala-priest's reciting Emesal compositions in a ritual involving the king during a ceremony for the beginning of the month.[18]

Basically, this is all we know with certainty concerning the gala-priest's religious activities in the Third and Second Millennia B.C.E. However, the fact that such a large corpus of Emesal compositions exists in Old Babylonian copies indicates that the gala-priest must have had a wide range of activities necessitating the different genres. If we choose to extrapolate from the Emesal texts themselves and from information provided by First Millennium B.C.E. ritual instructions and calendars, we may suggest the following minimum schedule of religious activities for the gala-priest in the Second Millennium B.C.E.:

1) the recitation of compositions at funerals
2) the recitation of incantation-hymns to keep away evil demons on such occasions as the onset of a journey or the dedication of buildings and objects[19]
3) the recitation of lamentations and possibly eršemmas during the razing of dilapidated buildings in order to assuage the anger of the gods at seeing

(15)Gudea St.B v 1 ff.: ki-maḫ-uru-ka al nu-gar ad_x ki nu-túm gala-e balag nu-túm ér nu-ta-è.

(16)M. E. Cohen, "Another Utu Hymn," *ZA* 67 (1977) 1 ff.

(17)For a discussion of the gala-priest and his activities, see H. Hartmann, *Die Musik der sumerischen Kultur,* Frankfurt am Main (1960) 129 ff.; J. Krecher, *Kultlyrik* 35 ff.; J. Renger, "Untersuchungen zum Priestertum der altbabylonischen Zeit," *ZA* 59 187 ff.

(18)For the Mari ritual of the *kalû*-priest, see below sub, "The cultic setting of the eršemma."

(19)For a discussion of the širnamšub(ba), see M. E. Cohen, *JAOS* 95 (1975) 592 ff. Another širnamšubba is UM 29-15-242, a composition concerning Inanna with the incipit u_4-ru u_4-ru, (courtesy, Å. W. Sjöberg, Curator).

their holy shrines being torn down. This may well have extended to the renovation of sacred objects.
4) the recitation of specific lamentations and eršemmas on a cyclical basis on certain days of each month as a constant vigil to prevent the anger of the gods over acts unknowingly committed by the city or king.

It is this last item which we believe proved so significant for the preservation of certain genres of Emesal literature. The recitation of compositions at funerals, for dedications, for journeys and for the razing of buildings could have involved compositions composed specifically for the occasion, texts which may never have been recited again. And even if reused, this was dependent upon the discretion of the gala-priest. That is to say, he decided whether to chant an existing work or to compose a new one. However, once a fixed liturgy in which specific texts were to be recited every year on certain days of the month had been established, once such a cultic calendar had been developed, failure to recite that certain, specific text on the appropriate day would have unleashed the fury of the gods upon the city. In other words, it was no longer a question of an appropriate text for the occasion, but rather of a specific, irreplaceable composition. This, we suggest, was the determining factor in the survival of certain Emesal compositions and similarly the reason for the disappearance of others.

Two Emesal genres attested in the Old Babylonian period, the lamentation and the eršemma, and possibly a third, the eršaḫunga, survived to the very end of the First Millennium B.C.E., presumably because they constituted this fixed liturgy. This book is an examination of one of these genres, the eršemma.

Catalogue of the Eršemmas

The following catalogue of incipits of eršemmas was jointly prepared by Prof. Miguel Civil and myself. Catalogues B_2 and B_3 were published by S. N. Kramer, A. Salonen Festschrift,[20] and the identifications listed below in these two catalogues are according to the identifications made by Kramer in his article.

Catalogue: B_1: VAT 6481 (VAS 10 216)
B_2: BM 23771 (S. N. Kramer, A. Salonen Festschrift (text A))
B_3: BM 23701 (S. N. Kramer, A. Salonen Festschrift (text B))
B_4: Ni 9925 (ISET I pl.203)
K_1: K.2; K.2529($4R^2$ 53)+K.2376(BL 103; RA 18 158); BM 82-3-23,5220 (BL 151)
NB_2: A.3513

1. dilmun^{ki} nigin-na[21]	B_3 17[22]; K_1 ii 2, 23[23], 24[24], 38, iii 22; NB_2 7
2. [. . .]⌜x⌝ zu[25]	K_1 ii 3
3. ušum gùd nú-a[26]	K_1 ii 4, 21
4. [ù-li-li] en-zu sá-mar-mar[27]	K_1 ii 5

(20)Two British Museum iršemma "Catalogues," *Studia Orientalia* (1975) 46 pp. 141–166.

In the footnotes, references will be made to K.3635+K.11979, a ritual tablet belonging to Asshur-napišta-uṣur; BM 79-7-8, 343, possibly part of the previous tablet.

(21)BM 79-7-8, 70 (BL 80); BM 29623 (*CT* 15 pl. 12–13); K.2003+K.3466 (*$4R^2$* 28* 4) rev. 5–70; K.2789+K.4964+K.4966 1–21; K.3506 1–17; K.5273 (BL 93) 1–13; K.6084 (BL 144) 1–7; K.8646 5–10; Sm. 47 1–8; Sm. 528 6; *UET* 6/2 207 16–24; VAT 37+ (*SBH* 70) obv. 1–14; VAT 245+(*SBH* 46) rev. 27–30; VAT 2173+(*SBH* 85) 1–10; VAT 6427 (*VAS* 17 55) obv. 1–10; Cal K obv. 5, 8, 27, 31; *R. Acc.* 14:14, 34:13, 40:11, 44(o.174):9: the incipit is cited in R. Caplice, *OrNS* 39 119 "Ritual for the Royal Army" line 40; cited in K. 3635 obv. 14 as dilmun^{ki} nigín-na to be recited with the ér umun-še-er-ma-al-la-an-ki-a..

(22)-ù instead of -na

(23)nigín-na-àm

(24)nigín-na 7-àm; perhaps this is a different eršemma.

(25)BM 121072 (*CT* 51 no. 189); K.3480; VAT 215 (*SBH* 45) rev.; VAT 14486 (*LKU* 10) rev.

(26)Cal K obv. 3

(27)AO.6495 (*TCL* 6 no. 56); Cal K obv. 10; *R. Acc.* 40:6 (m[ar-ma]r instead of sá-mar-mar)

5.	[umun]-bára-kù-ga[28]	K_1 ii 6
6.	[ur-sag] abzu-ta[29]	K_1 ii 7
7.	[. . .] ér i-si-iš	K_1 ii 8
8.	a [še-eb]-é-kur-ra[30]	K_1 ii 9
9.	ù-[u$_8$]-a-ba mu-un-ḫul[31]	K_1 ii 10
10.	me-er-[ra]-mu-dè[32]	K_1 ii 11
11.	é-zi ⌜AN⌝ [x] ⌜x⌝	K_1 ii 12
12.	a mu-un-ga-mu	K_1 ii 12
13.	umun-mu za-e[33]	K_1 ii 13
14.	alim-ma umun-gìr-[ra][34]	K_1 ii 14
15.	e-lum gu$_4$-sún e-lum gu$_4$-sún[35]	K_1 ii 14
16.	gakkul-àm-ma al-šú	K_1 ii 15, 53, iii 28
17.	[x]-dam kur-ra mú-a[36]	K_1 ii 17
18.	⌜x x⌝ e$^!$-ne-èm-mà-ni gakkul-àm-ma al-šú	K_1 ii 18
19.	šà-ba-ni ga-an-ḫun[37]	K_1 ii 19, 37
20.	[a]-ab-ba-ḫu-luḫ-ḫa še-⌜ša$_4$⌝	K_1 ii 20
21.	umun-aga-kù-ga	K_1 ii 25
22.	^{d}Utu è-ma-ra[38]	K_1 ii 26
23.	gu$_4$-maḫ pa-è-a[39]	K_1 ii 27

(28)BM 85197 (*CT* 42 no. 9 obv. ii 12 ff.); VAT 1512 (*VAS* 10 211); Cal K obv. 14; *R. Acc.* 42:5

(29)Cal K obv. 18

(30)BM 79-7-6,26 (5*R*^{2} 52 no. 2 obv. 47 ff.); K. 2701b; incipit cited in R. Caplice, *op. cit.*, 118 line 19.

(31)*R. Acc.* 34:6 has mu-ḫul instead of mu-un-ḫul

(32)K.2442 (*SBH* 49a); k.4629 (*SBH* III) col. iv; Rm. 132 (5*R*^{2} 52 no. 1) col. iii 30 to iv 3; VAT 16+VAT 409 (*SBH* 49); BM 79037 rev. 1–5 (this tablet contains the near end of mu-tin nu-nuz dím-ma, the very end of its eršemma and the first few lines of another composition).

(33)*STT* 155; cf. NBC 1315 (*RA* 16 208) rev. 15–23

(34)K.3315 (BL 163); K.9154 (*BA* 10/1 12; BL 15); VAT 283+(*SBH* 22) obv.

(35)VAT 283+(*SBH* 22) rev. with incipit: gu$_4$-sún-na e-lum gu$_4$-sún-e

(36)Cal K rev. 4

(37)Cal K obv. 22, 33, rev. 1

(38)L.1486 (*ISET* 1 p. 219; *R. Sem.* 9 172 ff.; *Bab.* 3 75 ff.); N. 1760; VAT 1314 (*VAS* 2 70); VAT 1323 (*VAS* 2 73); VAT 1557 (*VAS 2 71); VAT 3538 (VAS* 10 152).

(39)BM 29631 (*CT* 15 pl.15–16); BM 96927 rev. v 38' to vi 16

24. ù-ma gul-gul-e[40]	K_1 ii 28, iii 20
25. ur-sag zà-zu-ta	K_1 ii 29
26. umun urú-mu in-di-bi maḫ-a[40a]	K_1 ii 30
27. ur-sag a-má-ru$_X$-ḫu-luḫ-ḫa[41]	K_1 ii 31
28. ur-sag a-má-ru$_X$-gal[42]	K_1 ii 33
29. nam-mu-un-šub-bé-en[43]	K_1 ii 22, 35
30. TUM$_{10}$ kur-ra šèg-gá[44]	B_2 52; K_1 ii 36
31. umun-ra a-ra-zu-a	K_1 ii 41
32. a é-an-na a gi$_6$-pàr-kù[45]	B_3 35; K_1 ii 43
33. me-e gašan-mu	K_1 ii 46
34. an-sù-ud-ág izi-gin$_7$[46]	K_1 ii 51
35. urú a-še-er-ra èn-šè ba-gul-e[47]	B_2 57[48]; K_1 iii 2
36. lugal nam-ta-[è][49]	K_1 iii 3
37. ur-sag urú ur$_4$-[ur$_4$][50]	K_1 iii 4
38. in-di in-[di]	K_1 iii 5

(40)BM 82–5–22, 541; Cal K obv. 37 has just one gul

(40a)Incipit cited in K.11979 obv. 6

(41)K.11211 (*Studies Albright* 352); K.17611

(42)Incipit cited in R. Caplice, *op. cit.*, 119 line 25: ur-sag mar-ru$_x$ -gal

(43)K.4630 (BL 192)+K.10205 (BL 193; *BA* 10/1 4b); K.5160 (*BA* 10/1 4a) rev.; K.13534 (BL 125); Cal K obv. 7(?), 16; to be recited with the balag en-zu sá-mar-mar according to K.3653 obv. 3; cited in BM 79–7–8,343:3

(44)BM 82–7–14, 1157 (reference courtesy, E. Sollberger and the Trustees of the British Museum); BM 29615 (*CT* 15 pl.7–9); Liverpool City Museum 56.5.1 (C. Wilcke, *AfO* 24 15–17); *PRAK* B 307; *PRAK* C 57; cf. *PRAK* C 97 obv. 5–12

(45)L.1492 (*ISET* 1 pp. 221–222)

(46)K.7670; K.16740; MLC 1881 (*BRM* 4 10); Sm. 954 (Delitsch *AL*[3] pp. 34–36); VAT 159+(*SBH* 53) rev.; VAT 613+(*VAS* 2 4 obv. ii 21 ff.); Cal K obv. 29

(47)BM 132094 (*CT* 42 21); K.3801 (BL 94); K.8608 (BL 162); K.9309 (BL 63); LB1823 (*TLB* 2 6) ii 14 to iii; *UET* 6/2 205 obv. 8–14; VAT 14486 (*LKU* 10) obv. i

(48)a-še-er-re instead of a-še-er-ra

(49)This is the eršemma catchline in BM 132094 (*CT* 42 21): lugal nam-ta-è lugal nam-ta-è; cf. *VAS* 2 51 obv. 8: lú nam-ta-e lú-nam-ta-e lú nam-ta-e da-ga-na-ab

(50)Cf. BM 34813 (*CT* 51 105) obv.; either a Sammeltafel or this incipit is shared with this šu-íl-lá.

39.	nir-gál lú-è-dè[51]	B_1 rev. 17[52]; K_1 iii 6[53]
40.	umun urú ku_4-ku_4[54]	K_1 iii 7
41.	umun nir urú in-ga-te	K_1 iii 8
42.	umun àm-di-di	K_1 iii 9
43.	é- abzu-ta	K_1 iii 10
44.	é šà-ab ḫun-gá-ta[55]	K_1 iii 11
45.	ur-sag ᵈUt-u_x-lu[56]	B_1 rev. 16[57]; K_1 iii 12
46.	ur-sag è-ni-ta[58]	K_1 iii 13
47.	an-na za-e maḫ-me-en[59]	K_1 iii 14
48.	e-lum za-e maḫ-me-en	K_1 iii 15
49.	ᵈUtu-gin_7 è-ta	K_1 iii 16
50.	ur-sag-gal me-ni še-er-ma-al-la íl-la[60]	K_1 iii 17
51.	me-ni še-er-ma-al-la e-ne-èm-mà-ni gú-è	K_1 iii 18
52.	ur-sag-gal me-ni še-er-ma-al-la e-ne-èm-mà-ni maḫ-àm	K_1 iii 19[61]
53.	kur-gal a-a ᵈMu-ul-líl[62]	K_1 iii 23
54.	umun mu-e-ši-in-DU	K_1 iii 24

(51)K.4956 (BL 9a); K.9315 (BL 9b); VAT 268+(SBH 74); VAT 10977 (*KAR* 305): lú-è-NI instead of lú-è-dè; also occurs as the incipit of a balag-lamentation in Cal K obv. 23 and *4R₂* 53 i 30

(52)[nir-gal lú-è-dè] lú ta-zu mu-un-zu

(53)lu- instead of lú-

(54)This is the eršemma catchline in K.4956 (BL 9a): umun-e urú ku_4-ku_4 [dìm(?)]-me-er-ka-na-ág-gá mu-un-da-ḫúl-le-eš

(55)Cal K obv. 24, rev. 17; *R. Acc.* 34:13, 40:12, 42:7 (é-šà-ab-ḫun-gá-e-ta)

(56)BM 132093 (*CT* 42 12) obv. 1–26; Metropolitan Museum 86.11.288 obv. 1–24; Cal K obv. 23

(57)[. . . -l]u a-ma-ru-na-nam

(58)BM 42274 (*CT* 42 24); K.5983 (*OECT* 6 pl. 21); K.9863

(59)K.5201 (*BA* 5 p. 396); Cal K obv. 13

(60)AO.5377 (*TCL* 15 no. 11) obv. 21 to rev.; this incipit occurs as the incipit of a balag-lamentation in Cal K obv. 12

(61)ur-sag-NI.GAL.ME instead of ur-sag-gal me-ni

(62)BM 132093 (*CT* 42 12) rev. 7 ff.; K.3506 19–23; Metropolitan Museum 86.11.288 rev. 1–18.

55.	dé-a-na-ni dé-a-na-ni[63]	K$_1$ iii 25
56.	umun é àm-di-di-ni-ta	K$_1$ iii 26
57.	egí-maḫ-dìm-me-er-an-ki-a	K$_1$ iii 27
58.	gašan-maḫ-Kèš^{ki}-àm-ta	K$_1$ iii 29
59.	i-lu-ke$_4$ i-lu-ke$_4$[64]	B$_3$ 6[65]; K$_1$ iii 30, 35
60.	am mur-ra nu-un-ti[66]	K$_1$ iii 31
61.	a-a-zu eden-na ér pà-da-zu	K$_1$ iii 32
62.	egí-mèn du-a-mu te-e-a	K$_1$ iii 33
63.	egí in-di-di urú a-še-er-ra	K$_1$ iii 34
64.	gakkul-àm-ma al-šú e-ne-èm-^{d}Mu-ul-líl-lá	K$_1$ iii 21
65.	an-na mu-un-dúb	K$_1$ iii 36
66.	urú gašan-zu-šè	K$_1$ iii 37
67.	in-di tu-ra[67]	K$_1$ iii 38
68.	šà-ba-a-ni dè-èm-mà-ḫun-gá	K$_1$ iii 39
69.	egí-maḫ ^{d}A-ru-ru	K$_1$ iii 40
70.	egí-maḫ gašan-an-ki-a[67a]	K$_1$ iii 41
71.	an-e usan-e	B$_2$ 1[68], 28[69], 65[70]; B$_3$ 1[71]

(63)Perhaps *PRAK* C 130 rev.

(64)BM 132093 (*CT* 42 12) obv. 29 ff.; MLC 382 obv. 1–12; Metropolitan Museum 86.11.288 obv. 25–33

(65)Just i-lu-ke$_4$

(66)BM 15821 (*CT* 15 pl. 18)

(67)VAT 7760 (*VAS* 10 201): in-di du-ra in-di du-ra with duplicate BM 79-7-8,87:

in-di tu-ra in-[
a-lak-ti šum-ru-[
in-di tu-ra [
a-lak-ti šum-[
ur$_5$-ra-na n[am-
qid-da-[
še-eb-é(?)-[

cf. Ni13236 (*ISET* 1 p. 209)

(67a)K.7076: 3 ff.

(68)an-e AN.GU.AN-e

(69)an-e GÚ.AN!-e

(70)an GÚ.AN-e

(71)an ú-sa$_{11}$(?)-an-na

72.	su$_8$-ba-dè ta an-ak[72]	B$_2$ 2; B$_3$ 2
73.	i-bí-kù a-lu-lu šà-kù a-še-er-sù	B$_2$ 4, 20; B$_3$ 3[73]
74.	ám-mu-lu-ke$_4$ en-na	B$_2$ 5, 14[74]; B$_3$ 66[75]
75.	na-ám-dam-a-na gig-ga[76]	B$_2$ 6, 15
76.	ám-mà mà-e-me-en[77]	B$_2$ 7, 16; B$_3$ 63[78]
77.	ám-ma-ma-al-la ám-nu-zu-a	B$_2$ 8, 17[79]
78.	šà-zu a-gin$_7$ dù[80]	B$_2$ 9, 18
79.	ul-e pa-pa-al-ta[81]	B$_2$ 10, 19; B$_3$ 51
80.	a-nigín-an-na[82]	B$_2$ 11; B$_3$ 12 (?)
81.	a-gin$_7$ til-en	B$_2$ 12; B$_3$ 55[83]
82.	ér-ra u$_4$ mi-ni-in-zal	B$_2$ 21; B$_3$ 37[84]; B$_4$ i 5[84a]
83.	mà-e a-še-er-ra	B$_2$ 22; B$_3$ 57
84.	ér na-mu-un-ma-al[85]	B$_2$ 23; B$_3$ 50[86]
85.	é-mu urú-mu-šè	B$_2$ 24; B$_3$ 39 (?)
86.	buru$_5$^{mušen} líl-lá-àm buru$_5$ (?)mušen(?)buru$_x$(?) gul(?)-e(?)	B$_2$ 25

(72)cf. CBS 11393 (*BE* 30/1 no. 1) rev. iv 3–4 (last line of composition, perhaps a catchline): [. . .] ta an-ak su$_8$-ba-dè ta an-ak

(73)omits šà-kù a-se-er sù

(74)lú instead of mu-lu

(75)ám-lú-ke$_4$-ke$_4$-na (see copy) instead of ám-mu-lu-ke$_4$

(76)*MIO* 2273 (*BE* 31 no. 17)

(77)Cf. the incipit to VAT 1453 (*VAS* 2 44): ám-mi-me-en

(78)ám-mà-e instead of ám-mà

(79)Omits ám-nu-zu-a

(80)BM 23696

(81)BM 23584 (*CT* 15 pl. 23)

(82)Cf. *SBH* 5 rev. 1–2: [a-ni]m-ma-[an-na. . .] / *[me]-⌈e⌉ina la-i-ra-⌈an⌉ [AN-e . . .]*; perhaps read a é!-an-na and therefore would be same as no. 32

(83)ti-en instead of til-en

(84)mi-ni-ib-zal instead of mi-ni-in-zal

(84a)i-ni-in-zal

(85)CBS 11151 (*BE* 30/1 no. 9) obv. ii 18ff.; *PRAK* C 47

(86)Omits -un-

87.	ki-sikil a šeš-zu	B$_2$ 26; B$_3$ 42
88.	guruš-dab$_5$-ba[87]	B$_2$ 29, 66
89.	am an-eden-na	B$_2$ 30, 67
90.	ka-na-ág-šeš-a-na-šè	B$_2$ 31
91.	ki-sikil tilla$_x$(AN.AŠ.A) šeš-zu bar-ra	B$_2$ 32
92.	ú-sag-gá nu-mu-un-ti-le-en-na	B$_2$ 33
93.	am ú-sag-gá	B$_2$ 34, 68; B$_3$ 41(?)
94.	kù-šà-ga na-ám-ir-ra	B$_2$ 35, 69[88], 76(?)[89]
95.	ér-re a-še-er-re e-ne ba-an-ku$_4$-ku$_4$	B$_2$ 36
96.	tu^{mušen} a-še-er-sù[90]	B$_2$ 37, 44, 70; B$_3$ 48; B$_4$ i 2[90a]
97.	e-en gig-ga-bi[91]	B$_2$ 39
98.	tilla$_x$(AN.AŠ.A) gam-ma-ni	B$_2$ 40
99.	igi SILA mu-un-di	B$_2$ 41
100.	ur-ra lugal-bi-ir	B$_2$ 42
101.	ù-u$_8$-a šà-zu	B$_2$ 43, 85; B$_3$ 10
102.	ama-gan dumu šub-šub	B$_2$ 45
103.	ù-u$_8$ ur$_5$-re gù im-me	B$_2$ 46; B$_3$ 69
104.	gù ù-u$_8$-a bí-in-du$_{11}$ a-še-er-ra ba-daḫ	B$_2$ 47
105.	ù-u$_8$ mu-un-ak	B$_2$ 49
106.	é-gul-la ki-bé[92]	B$_2$ 50; B$_3$ 58
107.	ma-ra é-zi-mu[93]	B$_2$ 51; B$_3$ 46(?)
108.	u$_4$-gig-ga mu-un-zal	B$_2$ 53
109.	é-kur-re še àm-ša$_4$	B$_2$ 54
110.	ù-a e-ne-èm-mà-ni	B$_2$ 55
111.	u$_4$-NE-a u$_4$-NE-a	B$_2$ 56
112.	e-ne-èm-mà-ni ki mu-dúb	B$_2$ 58

(87)BM 15795 (*CT* 15 pl. 20–21)

(88)na-ám-in-ra instead of na-ám-ir-ra

(89)kù-š[à-ga na-ám]-⌜in⌝-ra

(90)L.1501 (*ISET* 1 p. 227); VAT 3606 (*VAS* 10 167)

(90a)-su$_x$(BU)

(91)VAT 617 (*VAS* 2 2) obv. to rev. iii 21; *RA* 8 161–169

(92)CBS 475 (*BE*30/1 no. 12)

(93)VAT 1548 (*VAS* 2 62)

113.	é ù-a-li-a	B_2 59; B_3 70
114.	kur-gar-ra me-ri-zu-šè	B_2 60; B_3 71
115.	a-akkil-di-mu	B_2 61; B_3 72
116.	ki-sikil gi-du-ru[94]	B_2 62
117.	šu-pe-el en	B_2 63
118.	su$_8$-ba[. . .]	B_2 72
119.	su$_8$-ba[. . .]	B_2 73
120.	su$_8$-ba[. . .]	B_2 74
121.	su$_8$-ba[. . .]	B_2 75
122.	ma-e di ⸢x⸣ na-nam	B_2 77
123.	ù-mu-un nigin-ù	B_2 79
124.	sim^{mušen}-tur-ra na-nam	B_2 80; B_4 i 3
125.	ma-gur$_4$-gu$_4$-ná[95]	B_2 81
126.	ù-u$_8$ ù-u$_8$	B_2 82
127.	ù-u$_8$ é-gi$_4$-a	B_2 83
128.	a zi-mu á-mu	B_2 84
129.	ma-a ⸢ge⸣$_{16}$?-le-⸢èm⸣?-mà	B_3 4
130.	u$_4$-zal-la me-li-e-a	B_3 5
131.	ér-gig-ga urú-na	B_3 7
132.	šu-ir-ra-mà	B_3 8
133.	a-ra-li a [x(-x)]	B_3 9
134.	ám-[. . .]	B_3 11
135.	i-lu-šà-mà	B_3 33
136.	[x] àm-ši-ma-al	B_3 34
137.	[x] urú-gin$_7$ ba-ir-ra	B_3 36
138.	[. . .] ér-ra a-še-er-ra	B_3 38
139.	[. . .] a é-mu	B_3 40
140.	[. . .]-mu	B_3 43
141.	[. . .]-te	B_3 44
142.	[. . .]-⸢x⸣-da	B_3 47
143.	[. . .]si-si-ig	B_3 49
144.	ám-ma-ma-al-la ba-e(?)-ak(?)	B_3 52
145.	ù-zu-úr-bi na-MÈN	B_3 53
146.	urú-kur-kur-zé-ba	B_3 54
147.	im-ma-al-e gù-àm	B_3 56
148.	GÌR.⸢KU⸣(?) (x)-me-en	B_3 59

(94)Perhaps gi-du-ru is a variant for hé-du$_7$-ra

(95)This is probably a variant for the incipit má-gur$_8$-kù-an-na, edited by Å. Sjöberg, *Mondgott* pp. 44f.; BM 13930 (*CT* 15 pl. 16–17); VAT 414 (*SBH* 38); VAT 3561 (*VAS* 10 109)

149. ù-u$_8$-a é-mu a urú-[mu] B$_3$ 60
150. a-še-er-gig-ga-ke$_4$ B$_3$ 61
151. egí u$_4$ a-še-er-ra B$_3$ 62
152. al-lá-e-na B$_3$ 64
153. é-ta gar-ra-me-en[96] B$_3$ 65
154. gi-ér-ra bí-in-mú B$_3$ 67
155. dè-em-mar dè-em-mar B$_3$ 68
156. Aratta^{ki}-kù-ge B$_3$ 73
157. ù-u$_8$-a bí-in-du$_{11}$ B$_3$ 74
158. [. . .][97]
159. [. . .] ⸢x⸣ é ⸢x⸣ [. . .][98]
160. mušen-dù kur-úr-ra-na gu i-ni-in-lá[99]
161. ur-sag ^{d}Ut-u$_{18}$-lu[100]
162. ù-mu-un na-ám-zu ka-na-ág-gá še-er-ma-al ní-te-na[101]
163. en-zu sá-mar-mar[102]
164. [ù lú-lirum-ma] lirum ta me-a[103]
165. šeš-e dab$_5$-a-na urú ér-ra na-nam[104]
166. urú a gi$_{16}$-sa bar-mu ba-e-ga-àm[105]
167. ŠUBUR.DU ŠUBUR.DU[106]

(96)K.2789+K.4964+K.4966 rev. 15 ff.; K.3895 (BL 167); K.13567 (BL 142)

(97)BM 15793 (*CT* 42 7 iv)

(98)BM 96940 (*CT* 36 pl. 41–42)

(99)K.2789+K.4964+K.4966 obv. 22 ff.; N 3335+N 4226

(100)Metropolitan Museum 86.11.288 rev. 19–28: ur-sag ^{d}Ut-u$_{18}$-lu NU.SAR(= la šaṭir); this is not the same composition as no. 45

(101)BM 13963 (*CT* 15 pl.10); K.9312 (*BA* 10/1 18) 6 ff.; Ni.9798 (*ISET* 1 p. 185); see M. Civil, *JCS* 28 (1976) pp. 72–81.

(102)BM 29644 (*CT* 15 pl. 11–12); CBS 15089 obv. i; K.8728 obv.; K.11174 (*BA* 5/5 6) obv. Rm. 272 (BA 10/1 19); VAT 617 (*VAS* 2 2) rev. iii 23 to iv 8

(103)BM 22741 (*CT* 15 pl. 14)

(104)BM 29628 (*CT* 15 pl. 19)

(105)BM 85005 (*CT* 15 pl. 22); VAT 617 (*VAS* 2 2) rev. iv 10 ff.

(106)Incipit cited in R. Caplice, *op. cit.*, 119 line 38 as an eršemma of dingir-maḫ

168. sig an-na gù-dé[107]
169. sipa-zi-da é-zu[108]
170. ù-ma umun-gìr-ra[109]
171. a-ra-li-me-en a-ra-li-me-en ám-mu ám-gal-la-àm[110]
172. ur-sag pa-è-a[111]
173. ama-bi aš-tar-ra-na[112]
174. [. . .][113]
175. [. . .][114]
176. [. . .][115]
177. íb-bi-zu ù na-na-na[116]
178. [. . .][117]
179. ^{d}Utu lugal-àm[118]
180. [. . .]⸢x⸣ ad-mu ^{d}Mu-u[l-líl . . .]-gul-gul — B_1 rev. 13
181. [. . .]⸢x⸣ ám ⸢x⸣[. . .]⸢x⸣a — B_1 rev. 14
182. [. . .] li ia u-ma-ni mu-un-ba(?) — B_1 rev. 19
183. ù-u_8-a ama-gan[119]
184. ù-mu-un-e du_6-du_6-dam e_4-nag im-ma-ra[119a]

(107)BM 65145 (*CT* 42 10)

(108)K.8728 rev. 11 ff.

(109)Cal K obv. 20; cf. no. 14 incipit (same composition?)

(110)BM 15793 (*CT* 42 7) i-iii; partially edited by J. Krecher, *WO* 4 252 ff.; A.6742

(111)AO.5377 (*TCL* 15 no. 11) obv. 1–20

(112)BM 29617 (*CT* 42 19)

(113)VAT 4112 (*VAS* 10 101)

(114)CBS 145+170

(115)CBS 15089 ob. ii 1–11

(116)CBS 15089 obv. ii 12 ff.; cf. the incipit íb-bi ù-na-[nam] of a kirugu in the balag-lamentation of Nabû, ukkịn-ta ès-bar til-la, (see W.G. Lambert, *Studies Albright* 344)

(117)L.1489 (*ISET* 1 p. 220)

(118)R. Acc. 34:13, 40:11

(119)VAT 5448 (*VAS* 10 198): ⸢ér⸣-[$šem_5$-ma]-dingir-maḫ-a-kam

(119a)BM 96927 rev. vi 18 ff.

185.	u$_4$ AN [. . .][119b]	
186.	an-né nam-ma-gub šud$_x$-dè nam-ma-ra-e in-gá-e-re$_7$-dè-en[119c]	
187.	[. . .]-e na-ám mu-na-⌜KU⌝(?)	B$_4$ i 4
188.	[. . . z]i-ga-na	B$_4$ i 6
189.	[. . .]-⌜x⌝-ḫul-ḫul	B$_4$ i 7
190.	si(?) [. . .]	B$_4$ ii 1
191.	me-[. . .]	B$_4$ ii 2
192.	é-[. . .]	B$_4$ ii 3
193.	el(?)/egí(?) [. . .]	B$_4$ ii 4
194.	ma-[. . .]	B$_4$ ii 5

(119b)BM 96927 rev. v 1′ ff.

(119c)BM 96927 i ff.

The Characteristics and Evolution of the Eršemma

Among the liturgy of the gala-priests were the Sumerian compositions designated as eršemmas, a term which means "wail of the šem-drum."[120] This drum, called a *ḫalḫallatu*-drum in Akkadian, was constructed with a copper base (occasionally gold is attested) and a drumskin. The term "wail" may appear somewhat misleading, since, to judge from the context of certain eršemmas, the content is not always mournful or sad. However, we are ignorant of the cadence to which the eršemma was sung. And, as is obvious, even the most joyful words can be transformed into a dirge with the proper tune and meter.

There are four properties common to all eršemmas preserved in Old Babylonian copies:

1) The text is in the Sumerian Emesal dialect.
2) The compositions concern only deities; there are no eršemmas involving kings.
3) The structure consists of one single literary unit.
4) The opening lines of the eršemma contain a list of epithets, cities or buildings.

Since other works in the gala-priest's liturgy, e.g., balag-lamentations, eršaḫungas, šuillas and širnamšub(ba)s are in the Emesal dialect, it is to be expected that the eršemma is also in this dialect of Sumerian.[121]

Each eršemma, whether from the Old Babylonian period or from the First Millennium B.C.E., concerns and is addressed to deities. The following is a list of gods whose eršemmas are preserved:

Eršemmas Preserved in Old Babylonian Copies

Baba	no. 166
Dingirmaḫ	no. 183
Dumuzi	nos. 60, 88, 97, 165, 175

(120)Cf. J. Krecher, *Kultlyrik* 21 n. 11 for the term ér-šèm-ma translated as "Weinen zur š e m -Pauke." In the colophons to the Old Babylonian eršemmas, the term is written ér-šem$_5$-ma; whereas in the First Millennium B.C.E. texts ér-šèm-ma occurs. For šem$_{3-5}$ as the *ḫalḫallatu*-drum, see H. Hartmann, *Die Musik der sumerischen Kultur* 98 ff.; CADḪ 41 and *AHw* 311. The argument advanced by F. Galpin, *Music of the Sumerians,* Strasbourg, 1955, p. 17 for šèm/*ḫalḫallatu* as "double-pipe" is not convincing.

(121)For a discussion of the Emesal dialect, see J. Krecher, "Zum Emesal-Dialekt des Sumerischen," *Falkenstein Festschrift* 87 ff.; *Kultlyrik* 12 ff.

Enki	no. 186
Enlil	nos. 1, 30, 35, 160, 162, 163, 174
Gula	nos. 159, 171, 175
Inanna	nos. 32, 34, 59, 75, 84, 96, 97, 107(?)
Iškur	nos. 23, 168, 184, 185
Martu	no. 158
Nergal	no. 164
Ningirgilu	no. 79
Ninisina	(see sub Gula)
Ninurta	nos. 163, 176, 177
Nisaba	no. 178
Suen	no. 125
Ṣirtur	no. 88
Utu	nos. 5, 22

Eršemmas Preserved in First Millennium B.C.E. Copies

Asarluḫi	nos. 2, 29, 37, 50(?), 172(?)
Enlil	nos. 4, 14, 15, 35, 53, 160, 162, 163, 169
Inanna	nos. 34, 59
Marduk	nos. 2, 13, 47
Nabû	no. 27
Nergal	no. 45(?)
Nintinugga	no. 10
Ninurta	nos. 24, 39, 45, 46
Panunanki	no. 53(?)

There is an eršemma in which the god of the composition as listed in the colophon is not the deity being addressed or about whom the composition is concerned. Although no. 163 is designated in the colophon as being an eršemma of Enlil, the text is clearly an address to Enlil's son, Ninurta, despite the fact that Ninurta's relationship with his father Enlil is stressed throughout the work.

In three instances the god of the eršemma as listed in the catalogue is not the deity of the extant eršemma. These three compositions are all listed in catalogue B_3 as eršemmas of Inanna. Yet according to content and colophon no. 1 is an eršemma of Enlil, not Inanna.[122] The colophon to no. 79 states the work to be an eršemma of Ningirgilu. In this instance such confusion is clearly understandable, due to the identification of Ningirgilu with Inanna by the Old Babylonian period. Lastly, no. 153 is an

(122)This observation was noted by S. N. Kramer, "Two British Museum iršemma "Catalogues," *A. Salonen Festschrift.*

eršemma of Panunanki according to content; however, in this case we possess only a First Millennium B.C.E. recension.

The colophons to the eršemmas state "an eršemma of DN" and in two instances "an eršemma of DN_1 and DN_2." We assume this genitive construction signifies that the particular eršemma was recited in the cult of the deity named in the colophon.

Three categories of subject matter can be discerned among the preserved eršemmas, narratives based upon mythological motifs, wails over catastrophes and, finally, hymns of praise. Of course, there is a degree of overlapping. The narrative eršemmas may describe mythological events with catastrophic implications for the nation. Or the narrative may constitute praise of a deity. And while describing catastrophic events throughout the nation, the greatness of the deity responsible, usually Enlil, may be stressed, thus a work of praise. Among the narrative eršemmas based upon mythological backgrounds, seven tales are recognizable:

1) the destruction of the Eanna-temple and Uruk during Inanna's detention by Ereškigal in the netherworld
   no. 79–Upon being informed of Uruk's destruction in her absence, Inanna receives permission to leave the netherworld in order to entreat Enlil to halt the destruction.
   no. 32–Inanna's plea to Enlil
   no. 106–Inanna's lament over the Eanna
2) the capture and death of Dumuzi
   no. 97–In the sheepfold the gala-demons surround Dumuzi who then manages to escape. Utu turns Dumuzi into a kid in order that he might outdistance his pursuers. Dumuzi is finally captured and carried by boat to the netherworld.
   no. 88–Geštinanna and Ṣirtur search for Dumuzi, who has been beaten by the gala-demons. Dumuzi asks Geštinanna to have his mother, Ṣirtur, seek the help of her personal god on his behalf.
   no. 165–Geštinanna and Inanna vie to bribe a fly in order to discover Dumuzi's hiding place.
   no. 60–Inanna searches for her dead husband, Dumuzi.
3) the capture and death of Nergal
   no. 164–The body of Nergal, mutilated by the gala-demons, is lamented over by his mother.
4) the plight of Ninisina
   no. 171–Ninisina travels to Enlil to plead that her ill-fate be changed. Upon the refusal of Enlil to remedy her misfortune, Ninisina goes to the steppe Arali, the land of the dead, and to her chagrin no one seems to care. Her mother then promises to intercede on her daughter's behalf with Enlil.
   no. 159–Ninisina resolves to return to her destroyed temple.

5) the plight of Šerida

no. 30–Enlil has destroyed the temple and city of Utu's wife, Šerida, who determines to flee from Enlil's wrath.

6) the investiture of Iškur

nos. 23.1, 168, 184, 185–Enlil (in one version An) commissions Iškur as the storm in order to avenge Enlil (or An).

7) Iškur ends a famine–

no. 23.2 (narrative unclear)

It is interesting to note that to date no post-Old Babylonian copies of these narrative eršemmas have been found. We wonder if this might indicate that in the Old Babylonian period the process in which certain eršemmas found their way into the liturgy for the cultic calendar intentionally excluded these works, perhaps due to their possible lack of relevance and adaptability in servicing a wide range of cities. A concern for the relevancy of the eršemmas for many cities manifests itself in that the eršemmas frequently mention or list several cities in the opening section, apparently a conscious attempt to make the work less parochial.

All eršemmas, whether preserved in Old Babylonian or only First Millennium B.C.E. copies, share the first two characteristics, being Sumerian Emesal compositions concerning and addressed to a deity. However, the late eršemmas differ sharply from the Old Babylonian eršemmas regarding the number of structural units constituting the entire work. Whereas all eršemmas preserved in Old Babylonian copy have but one unit, the compositions preserved in First Millennium B.C.E. copy may consist of as many as three structural units, the scribe indicating the division(s) by a heavy line drawn horizontally across the tablet. The following is a list of eršemmas preserved from the First Millennium B.C.E. with the number of units in each work:

One unit	Two units	Three units
no. 1	no. 10	no. 4
35	13	34
160	14	
	15	
	45	
	53	
	59	

Of those eršemmas divided into two or three units, the last unit either begins with or contains within it the heart-pacification unit, this unit having three basic properties:

1) the unit begins with the refrain šà-zu ḫé-en-ḫun-gá bar-zu ḫé-en-

šed$_7$-dè (or a variation thereof), "May he pacify your heart! May he calm your liver!"[123]

2) a short list of gods follows.

3) Type I: After each deity in the list the refrain šà-zu ḫé-en-ḫun-gá or an alternation with bar-zu ḫé-en-šed$_7$-dè occurs.

Type II: After each deity in the list the refrain a-ra-zu dè-ra-ab-bé, "May a prayer be uttered to you!" occurs. At the conclusion of this list of deities occurs the line na-an-šub-bé-en dè-ra-ab-bé a-ra-zu dè-ra-ab-bé me-na-šè GN na-an-šub-bé-en dè-ra-ab-bé a-ra-zu dè-ra-ab-bé, "May 'You should not desert!' be uttered to you! May a prayer be uttered to you! May 'Enough! You should never desert GN!' be uttered to you! May a prayer be uttered to you!"[124]

The sudden appearance of this new unit of the eršemma raises a question. Whence and why did the heart-pacification unit develop? Since no preserved Old Babylonian eršemma contains any passage even remotely similar to the heart-pacification unit, it can be asserted fairly confidently that this unit did not evolve from the Old Babylonian eršemma. If, indeed, there is an Old Babylonian (or older) forerunner to the heart-pacification unit, any valid identification of such a text necessitates that the text contain all three aforementioned properties of the heart-pacification unit. Moreover, should such a text be found, it will be necessary to establish a relationship between that text and the eršemma permitting such a development to occur.

Although the phrase šà ḫun, "to pacify the heart," occurs as early as Cylinder A of Gudea,[125] quite possibly the oldest song in which the phrase occurs in a refrain-like construction is the "Drinking Song" published by M. Civil.[126] Civil saw three sections within the composition. Note the second part, labeled by Civil as a "toast to an unnamed individual, apparently a woman:"

58. šà-dingir-za ḫu-mu-ra-ab-ḫun-e
59. igi-^{gi}gakkul-àm igi-me na-nam
60. šà-^{gi}gakkul-àm šà-me na-nam
61. èm šà-zu gur$_4$-gur$_4$-ru ní-bi-a

(123)Texts employing the refrain šà-zu ḫé-en-ḫun-gá are nos. 10, 45 and 53; those with the alternation with bar-zu ḫé-en-šed$_7$-dè are nos. 14, 15 and 34. Note that no. 59 is somewhat an anomaly in that the line u$_4$ šà-ab ḫun-e-ta, is repeated as the refrain. Also note that nos. 4 and 14 conclude the heart-pacification unit with me-na-šè ^{d}Mu-ul-líl šà-zu ḫé-. . .

(124)Examples of the Type II construction are nos. 2 and 13.

(125)Gudea Cyl. A xviii 2

(126)M. Civil, "A Hymn to the Beer Goddess and a Drinking Song," *Studies Oppenheim* 67 ff.

62. šà-me-a gur$_4$-gur$_4$-ru ní-bi-a
63. ur$_5$-me bí-šag$_5$ šà-me bí-ḫúl

* * *

May the heart of your god be well-disposed towards you!
Let the eye of the gakkul vat be our eye!
Let the heart of the gakkul vat be our heart!
What makes your heart feel wonderful,
Makes (also) our heart feel wonderful.
Our liver is happy, our heart is joyful

Like the last unit of the eršemma this passage opens beseeching the heart to be favorable, employing the phrase šà ḫun. Also in common with the heart-pacification unit, the ensuing lines reiterate the basic theme of the heart being well-disposed. And in the concluding line of the toast, the heart and liver occur in parallel as they do in the opening line of the heart-pacification unit. However, this toast lacks a list of gods. Moreover, there appears to be no connection between this song and the eršemma to suggest a development from the former to the latter. The phrase šà ḫun also occurs as a refrain in a hymn to Ninḫursag:[127]

i_x a-bi mu-ra-an-ba a-šà še-bi mu-ra-an-ba
šà-zu šà-diri-bi šà-zu ḫé-em-ḫun-e
i_x a-bi mu-ra-an-ba a-šà še-bi mu-ra-an-ba
šà-zu ḫé-em-ḫun-e bar-zu ḫé-em-ḫun-e
i_x a-bi mu-ra-an-ba a-šà še-bi mu-ra-an-ba
šà-zu ḫé-em-ḫun-e kèši^{ki} ḫa-pa(?)-an-e$^!$

* * *

She offered to you a river and its water; she offered to you a field and its grain.
Your heart, your surpassing heart, may she pacify your heart!
She offered to you a river and its water; she offered to you a field and its grain.
May she pacify your heart! May she pacify your liver!
She offered to you a river and its water; she offered to you a field and its grain.
May she pacify your heart! May . . . Kesh!

The recurrence of the refrain šà-zu ḫé-em-ḫun-e as well as the line šà-zu ḫé-em-ḫun-e bar-zu ḫé-em-ḫun-e is very similar to the construction of the heart-pacification unit. But, as in the "Drinking Song," the list of gods and any apparent connection with the eršemma are lacking. However, it is

(127)CT 36 49:1–6; the transliteration is according to B. Alster, *Dumuzi's Dream* 109.

apparent from these two works that by the Old Babylonian period the phrase "to pacify the heart and liver" was a fully developed poetic refrain.[128]

Other Old Babylonian sources containing the refrain "to pacify the heart, to calm the liver" are some Old Babylonian redactions of Emesal balag-lamentations to Enlil. Note the next to final kirugu, or unit, of the balag-lamentation entitled e-lum gu_4-sún, "Honored one, wild ox:"[129]

é-e $šud_x$-da $šud_x$-da [mu-un-re_7-en-dè-en]
balag é-e si-a $šud_x$-da [mu-un-re_7-en-dè-en]
balag nigin-na-e $šud_x$-da ^{d}Mu-[ul-líl-šè mu]-
balag dìm-me-er mu-lu $šud_x$-da ^{d}Mu-ul-[líl]-
dìm-me-er lú-ulù nigi-dè-en $šud_x$-da mu-un-re_7-[en-dè-en]
me-en-dè é-e-šè a-ra-zu-a mu-un-re_7-en-dè-[en]
me-en-dè ki-e-šè a-ra-zu-a mu-un-re_7-dè-en ^{d}Mu-[ul-líl]-
ù-mu-un šà-ab ḫun-e-da in-ga-re_7-dè-en ^{d}Mu-[ul-líl]-
šà-ab ḫun-gá bar ḫun-gá-da in-ga-re_7-dè-en ^{d}Mu-[ul-líl]-
me-en-dè šà-ab-ù-mu-un-na mu-un-ḫun-dè-en ^{d}Mu-[ul-líl]-
šà-ab-an-na šà-ab-^{d}Mu-ul-líl-lá mu-un-ḫun-dè-[en . . .]
^{d}Mu-ul-líl-lá dam-a-ni ^{d}Nin-líl-lá
^{d}En-ki ^{d}Nin-ki ^{d}En-mul ^{d}Nin-mul
i-lu a-di ig-ga-am-ma-ru

* * *

At the house in supplication, in supplication we go.
The balag-instrument filling the house, in supplication we go.
Toting about the balag-instrument, in supplication [we go to Enlil].
The balag-instrument, god and man, in supplication [we go to Enlil].
God and man, we go about. In supplication we go.
We go to this house in prayer.
We go to this place in prayer. [To] Enlil [we go].
We go to pacify the heart of the lord. [To] Enlil [we go].
We go to pacify the heart, to calm the liver. [To] Enlil [we go].
So that we pacify the heart of the lord, [to] Enlil [we go].
So that we pacify the heart of An, the heart of Enlil, [to Enlil we go].
Enlil, his wife Ninlil,
Enki, Ninki, Enmul, Ninmul,
(*the gods until they shall be completed*)[130]

(128)For another instance of this poetic device, cf. *TCL* 16 93 rev. 9–11 (J. vDijk, *La Sagesse Suméro-accadienne,* Leiden 1953, 82)

(129)Collated

(130)For the gods that complete this list, see S. N. Kramer, *JCS* 18 36–37 n. 8 wherein Kramer lists and discusses duplicates and variants to *CT* 42 3.

Also note the concluding kirugu of the balag-lamentation u_4-dam ki àm-ús, "It is a storm; it touches the earth:"

> an-e ki-e dè-mà-ḫun-e
> an-ki-a-bi-ta dè-mà-e-ḫun-e
> an-uraš ki-še-gu-nu
> ^{d}En-ki ^{d}Nin-ki ^{d}En-mul ^{d}Nin-mul
> (*a list of gods follows*)
>
> May heaven and earth pacify you!
> May both heaven and earth pacify you!
> (May) heaven and earth, the place of mottled barley, (pacify you)!
> (May) Enki, Ninki, Enmul, Ninmul (pacify you)![131]

In these final and next-to-final kirugus of Enlil balag-lamentations are found all three properties of the heart-pacification unit, the refrain of the heart and liver being pacified, a subsequent list of deities, and presumably the phrase "to pacify the heart" being understood after each god in the list. Thus we have found the apparent forerunner of the heart-pacification unit in the last or next-to-last kirugus of two Old Babylonian balag-lamentations to Enlil. But the question still remains as to a reason for the development of the heart-pacification unit of the eršemma from the balag-lamentation. The answer is not difficult to discern. As is known from colophons, catalogues, ritual texts and ritual calendars, by the First Millennium B.C.E. many eršemmas were recited by the gala-priests in conjunction with the balag-lamentations and in fact were considered to be the concluding

(131)Since the final section of the balag-lamentation u_4-dam ki àm-ús occupies only the final column of *VAS* 2 17, it cannot be restored by the entire standard litany as can be done for the lamentation e-lum gu_4-sún, (see n. 130 above). Quite possibly this concluding section can be restored on the basis of the Old Babylonian balag-lamentation ^{d}Utu-gin_7 è-ta (*VAS* 2 5 rev. iii 13 ff.; *VAS* 2 10 rev. 50 ff.) 109–128 and with the aid of the First Millennium B.C.E. recension of the balag-lamentation am-e amaš-a-na (*SBH* II rev. 11–63). The following is our proposed restoration of u_4-dam ki àm-ús:

> ^{d}En-ki ^{d}Nin-ki ^{d}En-mul ^{d}Nin-mul
> (list of gods follows)
> [dìm-me-er-an-na dìm-me-er-ki-a a-ra-zu dè-ra-ab-bé]
> [urú-zu na-an-šub-bé-en dè-ra-ab-bé a-ra-zu dè-ra-ab-bé]
> (list of cities and buildings with the refrain of the preceding line follows)
> [za-e ù-mu-un-bi bí-mèn dè-ra-ab-bé a-ra-zu dè-ra-ab-bé]
> [za-e sipa-bi bí-mèn dè-ra-ab-bé a-ra-zu dè-ra-ab-bé]
> [u_4 é-ba gi_4-gi_4 dè-ra-ab-bé a-ra-zu dè-ra-ab-bé]

If our proposed restoration of the text is correct, then this final kirugu of the lamentation u_4-dam ki àm-ús is the forerunner of the Type II construction of the heart-pacification unit of the eršemma.

portion of the total balag-composition.[132] Since the eršemma had become, for all practical purposes, the new conclusion to the lamentation, the eršemma adopted the form of the conclusion to some Old Babylonian lamentations to Enlil, namely the heart-pacification unit, albeit the list of gods was drastically reduced.[133] This new conclusion perfectly summed up the reason for the recitation of the work—the placating of the gods. In the lamentation u_4-dam ki àm-ús what we wish to identify as the forerunner of the heart-pacification unit is the final kirugu of the composition. However, in the lamentation e-lum gu_4-sún the forerunner is the next-to-final kirugu of the work. What is worthy of note is that the final kirugu of e-lum gu_4-sún is, in fact, the forerunner of eršemma no. 13. It seems probable that later scribes, reading this balag-lamentation, assumed the next-to-last kirugu to be the conclusion, since it contained the forerunner to the heart-pacification unit, thereupon interpreting what in reality was the concluding kirugu to be an eršemma.[134]

(132)See the fourth line of the colophon to nam-mu-un-šub-bé-en (no. 29) for the eršemma being part of the balag-lamentation in the First Millennium B.C.E. Also note BL 189 wherein the colophon indicates another tablet to the lamentation even though the closing line of the balag occurs on that tablet. This additional tablet can only contain the eršemma:

> [$šud_x$-dè še]-eb-é-an-na-ta ki ne-en-gi_4-[gi_4]
>
> ---
>
> [ki]-šú-bi-im balag-dInanna-kam
>
> ---
>
> dub-2-kam a urú-mu im-me nu-al-til (It is the second tablet; (the lamentation entitled) a urú-mu im-me is not finished).

(133)The minimum number of gods listed in the heart-pacification unit is two in nos. 14 and 15; the maximum is twelve in no. 34.

(134)There is little evidence for the assertion that the eršemma was the concluding section of the balag-lamentation in the Old Babylonian period. Firstly, in no colophon to any Old Babylonian eršemma is there any mention of the balag-lamentation at all. The only two balag-lamentations which might be construed as containing eršemmas at the conclusion are e-lum gu_4-sún (discussed above) and a-ab-ba-ḫu-luḫ-ḫa, wherein the third(?) tablet contains the catchline: x [. . .] x nigin-ù urú-zu ga-e-du_{11}, which, of course, seems to parallel the incipit of eršemma no. 1. In the lamentation e-lum gu_4-sún the standard closing line of the lamentations: "A supplication that the brickwork of the . . .-temple should return to its place" occurs after, not before, the final unit, clearly indicating this unit to be part of the lamentation, not an appended eršemma. Still persisting, one might further argue that the eršemma was originally in the main body of the lamentation. However, against this argument is the fact that over a hundred independent eršemmas existed contemporaneously, if not earlier than the balag-lamentation. Moreover, of the other seven balag-lamentations in which the final kirugu or unit before the standardized closing line is preserved (u_4-dam ki àm-ús (*VAS* 2 17); MAH 16066; *RA* 17 50; *CT* 36 pl. 35–38; urú àm-i-ra-bi (YBC 9862); *CT* 42 no. 15; urú-ḫul-a-ke_4 of Inanna (*TCL* 16 nos. 69 and 95; *TMHnF* 4 56) not one of these final kirugus also occurs or is catalogued as an eršemma. Rather, we believe that the fact that the next to last kirugu contained the heart-pacification unit forerunner caused later scribes to presume

If, as we suggest, the heart-pacification unit was appended to the eršemma when the eršemma in turn was appended to the balag-lamentation, it follows that those eršemmas preserved from First Millennium B.C.E. copies not appended to a lamentation, in other words those eršemmas listed in catalogue K_1 iii under the heading eršemma *kidudû*, should not contain the heart-pacification unit.[135] This is precisely the case with nos. 1 and 35, which are listed as an eršemma *kidudû* in catalogue K_1 iii, and with nos. 50, 160 and 172, which are extant on a tablet containing just eršemmas, not being connected in any way with balag-lamentations. This explains why these First Millennium B.C.E. texts contain but one unit.[136]

The fourth and final characteristic common to all eršemmas involves the form of the opening section. All extant eršemmas contain a list of epithets and/or cities and buildings. The following patterns occur:

Pattern A (eršemmas 10, 23, 32, 34.1, 164):
line 1: (phrase A) (phrase B)
line(s) 2-n: epithets (phrase A) (phrase B)
A_1 (eršemmas 35, 166): cities and buildings instead of epithets

---

erroneously that the last kirugu was an eršemma. Regarding the lamentation a-ab-ba-ḫu-luḫ-ḫa, first let us note that according to the spacing and traces, the restoration d[ilmun]^{ki} at the beginning is highly questionable, despite the rest of the line paralleling eršemma no. 1. Secondly, once more, the closing line "A supplication that . . ." does not occur before this catchline, which would be the case, were this catchline the eršemma. If one wishes to insist that this closing line occurred after the eršemma in the Old Babylonian period, we point out that no such line is found on any Old Babylonian eršemma tablet. In addition, were dilmun nigin-ù the closing kirugu of the lamentation and thus, the eršemma of a-ab-ba-ḫu-luḫ-ḫa, we would be hard pressed to explain why catalogue K_1 lists that lamentation eršemma as being [x]-dam kur-ra mú-a. Rather, it seems almost certain that x[. . .] x nigin-ù urú-zu ga-e-du$_{11}$ is merely the catchline for the next tablet of the lamentation and is not the end as Kutscher indicates in *YNER* 6. Even were we to restore dilmun$^{(ki)}$ at the beginning of the line, this would only be another example wherein the balag-compositions adapted eršemma material when being composed.

(135)In catalogue K_1, those eršemmas not listed beside the balag-lamentation with which they were recited are listed in col. iii under the heading er-šem̃-ma-meš *ki-du-[du]*. For *kidudû* as "ritual performance," see CAD K 347. Col. iii cannot consist of a list of all eršemmas not found to be associated with lamentations, since nos. 1, 16 and 24 occur in both sections. Rather, it is likely that col. iii consists of those eršemmas which the compiler found on tablets unconnected with balags. The fact that no. 1 is preserved in First Millennium B.C.E. copy, both on a tablet of just eršemmas (K.3506) and as part of a balag on other tablets, supports this supposition.

(136)There are First Millennium B.C.E. recensions of eršemmas that have a heart-pacification unit despite occurring independently of lamentations, nos. 45, 53 and 59. However, in these instances, the eršemmas are poorly reworked or composed, their slipshod craftsmanship being further exemplified in that the heart-pacification units have been erroneously appended, despite the fact that these works were not recited along with lamentations.

A_2 (eršemmas 88, 165): after lines 2-n, the "a guruš" refrain in which epithets of Damu are listed occurs.

Pattern B (eršemmas 1, 50, 60, 97, 160, 168):
line 1: (phrase A) (phrase B)
line(s) 2-n: epithets (phrase B)

Pattern C (eršemmas 45, 53, 59, 79, 171):
line 1: (phrase A) (phrase B)
line(s) 2-n_{-1}: epithets
line n: epithet (phrase A) and/or (phrase B)

Pattern D (eršemmas 13, 30, 106, 125, 159, 162, 163):
line 1: (phrase A)
line(s) 2-n: epithets

Note that the only eršemma seemingly not of this form is 34.2; yet we see that the Old Babylonian recension 34.1 did, indeed, contain a list of epithets, albeit very short. To our knowledge, in no other classification of compositions is this "listing" constantly present. This aforementioned pattern does frequently occur in some kirugus of balag-lamentations. This, we believe, may be due to the incorporation of eršemma contents into the balag as well as the influence of the eršemma style upon the gala-priests when composing the balag-lamentations.

Eršemma No. 29 (nam-mu-un-šub-bé-en): An Anomaly

A most singular composition whose structure is wholly dissimilar to the other eršemmas is no. 29, nam-mu-un-šub-bé-en. Not only does this text which is appended to a balag-lamentation not possess a heart-pacification unit, but its very content and structure is identical to that of the eršaḫunga, another hymnal classification in the liturgy of the gala-priest.

Text A K. 4630 (BL 192)+K. 10205 (BL 193; *BA* 10/1 4b)
B K. 5160 (*BA* 10/1 4a) reverse
C K. 13534 (BL 125)
D VAT 9440 (*KAR* 9) reverse

1.	[nam-mu]-un-šub-bé-en umun-mu nam-mu-un-šub-bé-en	
	[la ta]-nam-da-an-ni be-lum la ta-nam-da-an-ni	
2.	^{d}Am-an-ki	nam-mu-un-šub-bé-en
3.	[ur]-sag ^{d}Asar-lú-ḫi	nam-
4.	[umun] ^{d}En-bi-lu-lu	nam-
5.	[ur]-sag ^{d}Mu-zé-eb-ba-sa$_5$-a	nam-
6.	[umun] ^{d}Di-ku$_5$-maḫ-àm	nam-
7.	umun-Tin-tir^{ki}	nam-
8.	umun-é-sag-íl-la[137]	nam-
9.	umun-Barsip^{ki}	nam-
10.	umun-é-zi-da	nam-
11.	umun-é-maḫ-ti-la	nam-
12.	umun-é-te-me-an-ki	nam-[138]
13.	umun-é-dàra-an-na[139]	nam-
14.	mu-lu ér mar-ra-mèn	nam-
	šá-kin taq-rib-ti ana-ku[140]	
15.	mu-lu-sizkur-ra-mèn	nam-
	šá ik-ri-bi ana-ku	
16.	mu-lu-a-ra-zu-mèn	nam-
	šá tes-li-tim[141] *ana-ku*	

(137)C omits -la

(138)D omits entire line

(139)B:[ù-mu]-un-

(140)B: *šá tag-rig-ti šá-kin-ti ana-ku*

(141)B: *te-es-li-ti*

17. a-a-tu-ud-da-a-mèn nam-
a-bi a-li-du[142]
18. tukundi[143] ḫun-gá[144] nam-
a-di sur-ri nu-ḫi[145]
19. me-na ù-mu-un bi[146]-ge-en nam-
ia-ti : a-di ma-ti be-el ki-na-a-ti
20. íb-si me-na-šè nam-
ma-ṣi a-di ma-ti
21. nam-mu-un-šub-bé-en e-ne-ra ga-an-[na-ab-du_{11}]
la ta-na-da-an-ni ana šu[!]*-a-šu lu-[uq-bi]*
22. šìr-re nu-ti-le ba-ni-[. . .]
ṣi-ri-iḫ la qa-te-e liq-[. . .]
23. ér-re sig_{11} nu-di ba-[. . .]
bi-ki-ti la šu-us-sú-ki[147] [. . .]
(break in text of unknown number of lines)
a+24. [i]-bí-[zu bar-mu-un-ši-ib dè-ra-ab-bé]
ki-niš [. . .]
a+25. gú-zu [gi-mu-un-ši-ib dè-ra-ab-bé]
re-ši-ka [. . .]
a+26. šà-zu dè-[en-ḫun-gá dè-ra-ab-bé]
a+27. bar-zu dè-[en-$šed_7$-dè dè-ra-ab-bé]
[ka-bat-ta]-ka lip-šaḫ [. . .]
a+28. šà-zu šà-ama-ù-tu-ud-da-gin_7 [ki-bi-šè ḫa-ma-gi_4-gi_4]
ki-ma um-me a-lit-ti [. . .]
a+29. ama-tu-ud-da a-a-u-tu-ud-da-gin_7 [ki-bi-šè ḫa-ma-gi_4-gi_4]
[ki]-ma a-bì a-li-di [. . .]

ér-šèm-ma-[^{d}Asar]-lú-ḫi-ke_4
ér-šèm-ma [en-z]u sá-mar-mar

---

umun še-er-ma-al-la-an-ki-a m[u-lu] ta-zu mu-un-zu
6-šú nis-ḫu en-zu sá-mar-mar *AL.TIL*

* * *

(142)B(-di

(143)B:ÈN.TUKUN

(144)B:ḫun-e

(145)B:-*ḫa*

(146)B:bi-; perhaps this line is a corruption of umun bí-me-en, "You are the lord."

(147)Orthography for *šunsuku,* (see J. Krecher, *Kultlyrik* 105).

You should not desert me! My lord, you should not desert me!
Enki, you should not desert me!
Warrior Asarluḫi, you should not desert me!
[Lord] Enbilulu, you should not desert me!
Warrior Mudugasa, you should not desert me!
[Lord] Dikumaḫam, you should not desert me!
Lord (of) Tintir, you should not desert me!
Lord of the Esagil, you should not desert me!
Lord of Borsippa, you should not desert me!
Lord of the Ezida, you should not desert me!
Lord of the Emaḫtila, you should not desert me!
Lord of the Etemeanki, you should not desert me!
Lord of the Edaranna, you should not desert me!
I am the one who sets up a wail. You should not desert me!
I am the one of offerings. You should not desert me!
I am the one of prayer. You should not desert me!
I am a parent. You should not desert me!
Calm yourself quickly! You should not desert me!
When, lord, will you be just (with me)? You should not desert me!
Sufficient! For how long? You should not desert me!
"You should not desert me!" shall I say to him.
A wail that is unending [should be uttered for me].
Tears that do not give way [should be shed for me].

(break in text of unknown number of lines)

May ["Look at him!" be uttered to you]!
May "Face him!" [be uttered to you]!
May "Let your heart [be pacified!" be uttered to you]!
May "Let your liver [be calmed!" be uttered to you]!
Like the heart of a mother, may your heart [return to its place for me]!
Like a mother and father [may you return to me]!

---

an eršemma of Asarluḫi
the eršemma (of the lamentation entitled) en-zu sá-mar-mar

(The catchline to the next lamentation is) umun še-er-ma-al-la-an-ki-a ta-zu mu-un-zu
the sixth extract. (The lamentation entitled) en-zu sá-mar-mar is (now) completed.

The conclusion of eršemma no. 29, lines a+24 through a+29, is the standard conclusion to the eršaḫunga.[148] Moreover, other lines in this work

(148)Cf. the eršaḫungas *OECT* 6 pl. ii rev. 17–22; *SBH* 30 rev. 5–9; *SBH* 30 rev. 49–53; *OECT* 6 pl. xx 11–16; *4R*[2] 10 rev. 50–51.

are attested only in eršaḫungas.[149] Thus, in all but classification, no. 29 is identical to the eršaḫunga.

The term ér-šà-ḫun-gá means "wail which pacifies the heart."[150] In contrast to the communal hymns in the corpus of the gala-priest, the eršaḫunga, also a hymn to assuage the anger of a god, seems to have been a private prayer.[151] All texts identifying the work as being an eršaḫunga by the colophon are from the First Millennium B.C.E., the rubric not occurring any earlier. Within these texts the most notable characteristics of the eršaḫunga are:

1) the speaker petitions the deity, referring to himself as "your servant,"
2) imperative verbal formations are frequently employed,[152]
3) a refrain alternating sizkur dè-ra-ab-bé a-ra-zu dè-ra-ab-bé,[153] and
4) a standard closing section (cf. eršemma no. 29: a+24 to a+29).[154]

Since no texts with the rubric eršaḫunga can be dated before the First Millennium B.C.E., there has been speculation as to the date for the introduction of the eršaḫunga into the corpus of the gala-priest.

There is a composition perhaps dating as early as the beginning of the Kassite period (ca. 1600–1500 B.C.E.) which may be an eršaḫunga.[155] The text, addressed to the god Martu, asks that his anger be assuaged. Most significant is its formulaic ending common to the eršaḫunga:

šà-zu šà-a-ma-du-da-ki ki-bé ḫa-ma-gi-gi
ama-du-de a-ia-du-da-a-ki ki-bé ḫa-ma-gi-gi

(149)Lines 42–47 of the eršaḫunga me-e di-ku$_5$-ta (*SBH* 30 and *OECT* 6 pl. 8) are identical to no. 29:14–16. No. 29:14 also occurs in the eršaḫunga am erén-na di-di (*OECT* 6 pl. iii 25).

(150)The term also occurs as ér-šèm-šà-ḫun-gá, "wail (of) the šem-drum which pacifies the heart," in F. Thureau-Dangin, Rituels accadiens.

(151)S. Langdon, *OECT* 6 III-VIII

(152)mu-uš tuk-ma-ab (*OECT* 6 pl. iv 13,15); si-bi ba-mu-un (*OECT* 6 pl. ii 12); ak-a-ab (*OECT* 6 pl. ii 12); zalag-ga-[ab] (*OECT* 6 pl. ii 14); du$_{11}$-ga-ab (*OECT* 6 pl. xix 17 and pl. xx 7); arḫuš tuk-an-na-ab (*OECT* 6 pl. xix 21); silim-ba-ab (*SBH* 30 rev. 31); si-ig-ga-na-ab (*OECT* 6 pl. xx 7); šu gíd-ba-an-ni-ib (*4R*^{2} 10 rev. 37); du$_8$-a-ab (*4R*^{2} 10 rev. 49)

(153) *OECT* 6 pl. xx 8 ff.; *SBH* 30 rev. 1 ff.; *SBH* 30 rev. 37ff.

(154)An exception is *OECT* 6 pl. i (K.5016): ma-e e-re-zu ka-tar-zu g[a-si-il], "I, your servant, shall utter your praise!"

(155)*PBS* 10/2 no. 3 edited by E. Bergmann *ZA* 57 (1965) 33–42. For observations on this text, see also J. Krecher, *ZA* 58 (1967) 28 in which he states "den Eršaḫunga-Liedern nahestehend und also wahrscheinlich aus der frühen Kassitenzeit(?)." W. W. Hallo, *Studies Speiser* p. 80.

"Like the heart of a mother, may your heart return to its place for me!
Like a mother and father may you return to me!"

This text would appear to be an earlier exemplar of the eršaḫunga. A still earlier text, in fact Old Babylonian, has recently been published and W. W. Hallo has labeled it as a "forerunner" to the eršaḫunga.[156] This composition contains traces of the closing two lines:

šà-zu š[à(?)-. . .]
ama-[. . .]

Moreover, two other lines are identical to a passage in the aforementioned Kassite composition.[157] So too is the imperative present.[158]

Lastly there is another Old Babylonian Emesal composition that might indeed be an eršaḫunga:

VAS 2 no. 72:[159]
[(NE) ^{d}U]tu-ra ne-di ga-na-[ab-du]
[ur-sa]g su-lu ^{d}Utu NE ^{d}Utu-ra ne-di ga-na-ab-du
[am-é-bar]-ba-ra NE ^{d}Utu-ra ne-di ga-na-ab-du
[su$_6$-m]ú-^{d}Nin-gal NE ^{d}Utu-ra ne-di ga-na-ab-du
[. . .]-ne-di$_5$-ne-re-ne-me-en
[. . .-a]-nu-um-ke-ne-me-en
[n]e-di ga-na-ab-du di-bi ḫa-ma-ku-de
[di-ku] ka-aš-bar ‹ga›-na-ab-du ka-aš-bi a ma(?)-su-re
[a]-ia(?) ^{d}Utu-mu im-du-ta mi-te-iš-e ga-e
[. . .]⸢x⸣ al-gu-ba-ta me-te-iš-e ga-e
[. . .]⸢x⸣ma(?) ki al-gu-ba-ta me-te-iš-e ga-[e]
[a-ia-zu] ḫe-me-en ama-zu ḫe-me-en
[ama]-zu ḫe-me-en a-ia-zu ḫe-me-en
[x]⸢x⸣ ^{d}Utu dumu mu-zu-ne mu-ši-ma-al-le

(156)W. W. Hallo, *JCS* 24 (1971) p. 40 note on L. 1493

(157)This was noted by Hallo, *ibid.*

(158)du$_8$-mu-un-na-ab (line 2)

(159)Our tentative translation of this syllabic text is based upon the following assumed correspondencies: -ra ne-di = -ra a-ne-di; su-lu = šul (for our lines 2–4 cf. *VAS* 2 70, 71 and 73, *VAS* 10 152); di$_5$-ne-re-ne = dingir-re-e-ne; a-nu-um-ke-ne = a-nun-na-ke$_4$-ne; ku-de = ku$_5$-dè; su-re = sar-re (cf. Å. W. Sjöberg, *TCS* 3 178); mi/e-te-iš-e ga-e = me-te-eš-e ga-i-i; gu-ba = gub-ba; (could dumu-mu equal du$_{14}$ mú-mú ?); ḫu-ne = ḫun-e; i-gá-e-ri-in-di-in-nu-li-iš is sandhi for in-gá-e-re$_7$-en-dè-en ul-le-eš (see J. Krecher, *WO* 4 p. 4); a-ma-du-da = ama-tu-ud-da.

[. . .]⌜x⌝ LU ^{d}Utu dumu mu-zu-ne mu-ši-ma-al-le
[ ]-ág-gá KA nu-un-zu-ni mu-ši-ma-[al-le]
[. . .]-gá⌜x⌝ nu-un-zu-ni mu-ši-ma-al-le
[šà ḫu]-ne-da bar^{ar} ḫu-ne-da i-gá-e-ri-in-di-in-nu-li-⌜iš⌝
[. . .]-ra-ta ḫu-ne-da i-gá-e-ri-in-di-in-nu-li-[iš]

(break of approximately 14 lines)

[. . .]⌜x⌝[. . .]
[šà-zu šà-a]-ma-du-da-g[in$_7$ ki-bé ḫa-ma-gi]-gi
[ama-du-da a]-ia-du-da-gin$_7$ ki-bé ḫa-⌜ma⌝(?)-gi-gi

* * *

I shall *rejoice* . . . Utu.
I shall *rejoice* . . . the warrior, the he-man Utu, . . . Utu.
I shall *rejoice* . . . the bull of the Ebabbar, Utu.
I shall *rejoice* . . . the bearded one (of) Ningal, . . . Utu.
"You are the [. . .] of the gods!"
"You are the [. . .] of the Anunna-gods!"
I shall*rejoice* . . . *him*. May he decide that case for me!
I shall tell it to the [judge], the decision-maker . . . determine that decision for me.
When my father Utu comes, I shall give praise.
When [. . .] stands [. . .], I shall give praise.
When [. . .] stands (on) the earth, I shall give praise.
"You are my(!) father! You are my(!) mother!"
"You are my(!) mother! You are my(!) father!"
"[. . .] Utu . . . knows, . . . present before you."
"[. . .] Utu . . . knows, . . . present before you."
"[. . .] . . . does not know, . . . present before you."
"[. . .] . . . does not know, . . . present before you."
We go to calm (his) heart, to calm (his) liver! Joyfully (we go)!
We go to calm [. . .]! Joyfully (we go)!

(break of approximately 15 lines)

"Like the [heart] of a mother, may [your heart] return to its place [for me]!"
"Like [a mother] and father may you return to me!"

In this work, addressed to the sun-god in his capacity as judge, the petitioner asks Utu to judge his case. The line "we go to calm (his) heart, to calm (his) liver" seems to indicate that Utu may well be angry at the petitioner, thus a similarity with the eršaḫunga. But more significant, of course, are the two closing lines, the formulaic ending of the eršaḫunga. Thus, although lacking a rubric, this text might well be another example of an Old Babylonian eršaḫunga and thus, further indication of the existence of this classification in the liturgy of the gala-priest by the Old Babylonian period.

W. W. Hallo has suggested that the eršaḫunga may have originally evolved from the neo-Sumerian letter-prayers.[160] These latter Emegir works were pleas written in standard epistolary style to a god or deceased king. These "letters reflect a practice of leaving petitions in the temple, at the feet of the cult statue or at least in its own cella."[161] Now, however, with the likelihood of the eršaḫunga already existing by the Old Babylonian period, we face the possibilities that either the eršaḫunga had evolved from the letter-prayer already by the Old Babylonian period or else these two groups of texts existed side by side, presumably each with its own *Sitz im Leben*. An argument for the parallel development of the eršaḫunga is that these texts are Emesal, thus in the liturgy of the gala-priest; whereas the letter-prayer apparently did not involve this priest. And, as Hallo points out, "the new genre has lost all formal traces of any epistolary origins, with the one exception, namely, the use of the phrase, 'your servant' to refer to the penitent."[162] It is not inconceivable that whereas the letter-prayer was deposited by a statue of the addressee, the eršaḫunga may have had an entirely different use, namely, being chanted as part of sacrificial ceremonies conducted by the gala-priest on behalf of and in the presence of the petitioner.

What then is the relationship of eršemma no. 29 with the eršaḫunga? Although this eršemma is attested only in First Millennium B.C.E. copies, nonetheless, an Old Babylonian origin is possible. The refrain na-an-šub-bé does occur in the Old Babylonian balag-lamentation entitled ^{d}Utu-gin$_7$ è-ta.[163] Both the lament and the eršemma contain the same stereotyped list of cities and temples directly before the refrain na-an-šub-bé(-en). Thus, it is not impossible that eršemma no. 29 has Old Babylonian antecedents. Unfortunately, why and when the similarity of no. 29 with the eršaḫunga developed, we cannot say.

(160) *Studies Speiser*, 71ff.

(161) *Ibid.* 79

(162) *Ibid.* 80

(163) *VAS* 2 5 iii 13 ff.

Composing the Eršemma

Although we frequently lack the means to discern the processes involved in composing Sumerian literature, some insights are available regarding the eršemma.

In the Old Babylonian copies of eršemma compositions, there are several instances of two eršemmas sharing the same passage. Such literary sharing occurs in two eršemmas of Iškur, nos. 23 and 168. The structure and content of these two works are so similar that one must conclude that one text was based upon the other. Not only do both eršemmas employ the same exhortation, but they also contain the same two concluding lines to the introductory section. According to the chronology of the story line, no. 23 appears to be the earlier work, since the text describes Enlil's commissioning of Iškur followed by his exhorting Iškur to use his new found powers to avenge him. Eršemma no. 168 would seem to be the sequel to the tale, beginning with the expected list of Iškur's epithets, then recapitulating the story of Iškur's being granted the role of the weather-god, and finally continuing the narrative by describing Iškur's attack upon the rebellious lands.

Another example of one eršemma borrowing material from another may be seen in the eršemmas of Enlil nos. 162 and 174. No. 162 is structured as follows:

1) lines 1–9: introduction consisting of epithets and praise of Enlil
2) lines 10–14: description of Enlil as merchant
3) lines 15–22: praise of Enlil
4) lines 23–25: description of Enlil as merchant

Section three, praise envisioning Enlil as the master of the universe, appears to be an interruption of the theme of Enlil as merchant. Note that these lines of praise also occur in no. 174:11–18. However, in this work, this passage appears to be an integral part of the structure, which may be outlined as follows:

1) lines 1–8: the standard list of attributes of Enlil
2) lines 9–18: Enlil as supreme lord of the universe
3) lines 19–27: the uniqueness of Enlil

Complicating any attempt to reconstruct the formative procedure in composing eršemmas nos. 162 and 174 is the fact that the passage common to both also occurs in the Old Babylonian balag-lamentation a-ab-ba-ḫu-luḫ-ḫa.[164] A guess might be ventured that no. 162 incorporated material

(164)See R. Kutscher, *YNER* 6 for this lamentation.

from no. 174. But whether the lamentation took material from one of these eršemmas or even from another source we cannot say.

There are two other instances of two eršemmas containing the same passage.[165] In the case of the Old Babylonian eršemmas nos. 60 and 175 it is impossible to reach any conclusion as to primacy. The other example of sharing is the Old Babylonian eršemma no. 171 and 173, the former an eršemma of Ninisina/Gula, the latter of Inanna.[166]

As already noted, a factor to be considered in an investigation into the formation of the eršemma is the relationship between the material of the balag-lamentation and that of the eršemmas, since occasionally a passage is shared by both.[167] In fact, in some cases entire eršemmas appear as kirugus, or units, in Old Babylonian and First Millennium B.C.E. recensions of lamentations.[168] Unfortunately, there is no way to discern conclusively whether in the Old Babylonian period the eršemma borrowed from the lamentation or vice versa, or, in fact, whether the borrowing of material occurred in both directions. The balag-lamentation was composed no earlier than the Old Babylonian period and subjectively we believe the eršemma to be the older genre; therefore, the greater likelihood that the balag-lamentation appropriated material from the eršemma. Such speculation is supported by the literary quality of the two genres. The eršemma is a compact, well-structured composition, centering upon one theme. The balag-lamentation, on the other hand, is a very lengthy, rambling work, sometimes having no basic story line. Many of the kirugus of the balag-lamentation appear to be independent entities loosely tied together, thus giving the impression that the material of the lament was gleaned from many sources and then sewn together. The authoring of many new, very long lamentations in the Old Babylonian period must have been taxing on the gala-priests and the temptation to appropriate already existing material

(165)No. 60:32–41 and no. 175:a+1 to a+9.

(166)For the duplication of lines, see A. Falkenstein, *OLZ* (1961) 7/8 368; S. N. Kramer, *JCS* 18 40 n. 35.

(167)Some examples of Old Babylonian eršemmas and Old Babylonian balags sharing the same passage are no. 30:7–31 and é-e še àm-ša$_4$ viii 29–53 (J. Krecher, *Kultlyrik* 211 ff.); no. 162:15–21 and a-ab-ba-ḫu-luḫ-ḫa (R. Kutscher, *YNER* 6) *218–*223; no. 174 and a-ab-ba-ḫu-luḫ-ḫa *217–*223; no. 125:23–29 and a-gal-gal buru$_x$ su-su 27–31, 34–35 (ZA 10 277 K. 69 obv. 30–34, 39–40), this latter balag is from First Millennium B.C.E. copy.

(168)eršemma no. 1 occurs in the Old Babylonian recension of a-ab-ba-ḫu-luḫ-ḫa (*CT* 42 26 rev. 11), in the late recensions of mu-tin nu-nuz$_x$ dím-ma (*4R*^{2} 28* 4), in am-e bára-an-na-ra; no. 35 occurs in the late recension of urú a-še-er-ra 1–39 (*LKU* 10 obv. i). Non-preserved eršemmas which on the basis of the incipit were probably used as the first kirugu of a balag-lamentation are nos. 39, 50, 163.2 (in this case the eršemma is preserved, but not the lamentation), nos. 3 and 179.

must have been very real. If such is the case with the balag-lamentation, then the eršemmas, compositions of the gala-priest frequently mournful in tone, would provide a rich and available source of material.

A clear example of a First Millennium B.C.E. recension of an Old Babylonian eršemma is no. 1, an eršemma of Enlil. The two recensions are similar with but two major exceptions.[169] In the Old Babylonian redaction the southern cities Nippur, Larsa and Ur are mentioned, as well as buildings associated with them and with Isin. However, in the late redaction, although the cult center Nippur is retained, Larsa and Ur have been replaced by the northern centers Sippar, Babylon and Barsippa, a literary development reflecting the political shift in power south to north, occurring from the reign of Hammurapi onward. In like manner, the buildings of the southern cities are replaced by those from the north. The second major difference in the two recensions is that the late texts expand the Old Babylonian redaction by the simple, unimaginative insertion of city lists.

In the First Millennium B.C.E. recension of no. 35, the city and temple list of the Old Babylonian redaction is also expanded. This literary development demonstrates firstly, how a particularistic hymn, in this instance, an eršemma intended for recitation in Nippur, was adapted for recitation throughout a wider area. The Old Babylonian redaction cites only Nippur, the Ekur of Enlil and the kiur of Ninlil. However, in the First Millennium B.C.E. text, the cities Sippar, Babylon and Borsippa as well as their respective shrines have been appended. Moreover, the addition of only northerly centers indicates, as with no. 1, that the eršemma was probably reworked any time from the reign of Hammurapi onward. Note that this eršemma also occurs as the opening kirugu of the lamentation urú a-še-er-ra, which is preserved only in First Millennium B.C.E. copies.

Another instance in which an eršemma is preserved in both Old Babylonian and First Millennium B.C.E. copies is no. 163. There does not appear to be any marked difference between the two recensions. On the other hand, a great deal of difference can be noted between the Old Babylonian and First Millennium B.C.E. recensions of eršemma no. 34. The late text has dropped the opening list of epithets, as well as omitting many lines preserved in the older text. And although only the beginning of the Old Babylonian text is preserved, we would not be surprised if lines 17–27 of the First Millennium B.C.E. text were added quite late, perhaps even being an incorporation of a second Inanna eršemma.

(169)There are two additional differences. The verbal form bí-du$_{11}$ in the Old Babylonian recension is replaced by ga-e-du$_{11}$ (or a variant) in the late redaction. The second difference is the addition of line 51 in the late recension. Perhaps another as yet uncovered Old Babylonian text will include line 51.

There is one eršemma in late copy which has been clearly composed from balag-lamentations. No. 13 was composed on the basis of the final kirugu of the balag-lamentation e-lum gu_4-sún. We have already stated that the scribe may have mistakenly interpreted this final kirugu of the lament as being an eršemma. Thereupon he reworked what he believed to be an Old Babylonian eršemma into an eršemma for Marduk. There are three main differences between this Old Babylonian kirugu and the later eršemma. The list of epithets at the beginning has been lengthened, the names of the deities have been changed, and thirdly, the heart-pacification unit has been appended. In both the Old Babylonian forerunner and the eršemma, there is a confusion of epithets between father and son. In the Old Babylonian kirugu the epithets of Ninurta, ù-mu-un-guruš-a and ur-sag, occur, and in line 22a the god is the avenger of Enlil, once again Ninurta. Yet curiously it is Enlil, the father, who is invoked in the closing line. This same confusion abounds in no. 13. The eršemma begins by invoking Asarluḫi/Marduk and suddenly epithets of his son, Nabû, occur. And as in line 22a of the forerunner, line 19 of the eršemma refers to the avenger of Asarluḫi. Yet in line 21 it is Asarluḫi who is invoked. Clearly then no. 13 is an expansion of the kirugu. The names of the gods were merely changed in order that this section of a Nippurian lament would be appropriate for Babylon.

Lastly, there are three eršemmas, all preserved on one tablet, whose structure and content strongly suggest a late reworking. We have previously noted the unimaginative expansion of eršemma no. 1 in the late recensions. This same lack of creativity manifests itself in eršemmas nos. 45 and 53, both works skeletal in content, consisting of a list of epithets immediately followed by the heart-pacification unit. On this same tablet is found the late recension of i-lu-ke_4 i-lu-ke_4(no. 59), an eršemma of Inanna known from the Old Babylonian catalogue B_3. This late recension of no. 59 also consists of just standardized epithets and the heart-pacification unit. It is likely that the Old Babylonian redaction differed greatly from this late copy, for if we remove the late addition of the heart-pacification unit, all that remains is but a few epithets usually reserved for the introduction of an Inanna eršemma. Thus, no. 59 appears to have been subjected to this almost formulaic structure in which composing an eršemma seems to have consisted of merely plugging in the appropriate epithets. Whether the poor quality of these three works can be attributed to an individual, to a certain 'school' of tradition, or as being symptomatic of a certain period, these texts represent the nadir of the literary creativity and achievement of the gala-priests.

The Cultic Setting of the Eršemma

In the Old Babylonian period the gala-priest chanted the eršemma to the accompaniment of the *ḫalḫallatu*-drum. However, aside from this rather obvious fact, very little information concerning the cultic setting of the eršemma in the Old Babylonian period may be available to us. The Old Babylonian Mari ritual of the gala-priest refers to a composition which has been identified with the term eršemma. Note the following transliteration of the pertinent portion of the Mari ritual according to G. Dossin:[170]

iii 8. AN.NU.WA.ŠE *še-ra-am ša ma-*[. . .]
9. *i-za-am-mu-ru*
10. *re-eš* AN.NU.WA.ŠE *za-ma-r*[*i-im*]
11. *šarrum i-te-ib-bi-ma iz-za-az*
12. *iš-te-en i-na ka-li-e iz-za-az-ma*
13. [*i*]*-na ḫa-al-ḫa-la-tim*
14. ER.S[E.M]A.ŠE *a-na* ^{d}*En-lil i-za-mu-ur*
15. *re-eš* [ER.SE.MA.ŠE] *a-ki-lum uš-ša-am-ma*
16. *i-ka-al. . .*

We disagree with Dossin's transcription of this passage, which is so crucial for our understanding of the eršemma in the Old Babylonian period. A check of the copy reveals that the break in line 15 is far too small to enable a restoration [ER.SE.MA.ŠE] as Dossin has suggested, which he apparently did on the basis of what he assumed to be a parallel construction with line 10. In fact, part of the sign is preserved, the traces indicating LUGAL, thus, "Before(?)[171] the king the *ākilu* sits down and performs." As for line 14, although the ER and SI signs are clear, the sign Dossin has chosen to read as MA is only partially preserved. Note that the traces of the last sign do not indicate ŠE as Dossin has read, but rather MU. Throughout the column the ŠE sign is repeatedly composed of three over three Winkelhakens, not two on the top row as in our sign.

A second reason not to identify this term with the rubric eršemma is that throughout this ritual compostions are cited by their incipits. Therefore, the term in line iii 14 is assuredly an incipit, not the generic term eršemma. Nevertheless, in light of this work being recited to the accompaniment of the *ḫalḫallatu*-drum in a ritual of the gala-priest, it is quite possible that this incipit, for which we offer a reading er.si.si.mu, is indeed

(170)*RA* 35 1 ff.

(171)We expect *ina rēš šarrim.*

the incipit of an eršemma.[172] If so, then this Mari ritual is the only extant Old Babylonian text detailing the cultic implementation of the eršemma. We suggest the following translation of the passage:

> "They (the gala-priests) will chant AN.NU.WA.ŠE, a *song?* of the ba[lag-instrument].[173] At the beginning of the singing of AN.NU.WA.ŠE, the king will rise and remain standing. Together with the gala-priests he will stand and he (the king?) will chant ER.SI.SI.MU to Enlil to the accompaniment of the *ḫalḫallatu*-drum.[174] (Then) before(?) the king the *ākilu* sits down and performs."

Unfortunately, due to the many lacunae throughout the text, the occasion necessitating the recitation of this eršemma is not preserved. However, from the entire ritual it can be observed that the eršemma could be recited in the same ritual as was the balag-lamentation, that the eršemma was recited while standing, and that perhaps, even the king himself might chant the eršemma.

In the First Millennium B.C.E., the ritual use of the eršemma is better documented. Eršemmas were preserved either as appendages to balag-lamentations or on tablets consisting of several eršemmas. This twofold occurrence of the eršemma is reflected in catalogue K_1, in which column ii contains the incipits of eršemmas which the compiler of the catalogue found appended to balag-lamentations. He listed the incipit directly opposite the appropriate lament. Column iii contains the incipits of eršemmas occurring on tablets unrelated to balag-lamentations, these eršemmas being labeled *kidudû* by the scribe. Note that several works occur in both columns ii and iii. Eršemmas copied onto tablets containing just eršemmas occasionally included their own instructions concerning ritual recitation. Note CT 42 12 28 (no. 45): *ina* ITU UD.3.KAM *la-am* KIN.SIG *i-na* É *pa-pa-hi* ᵈ*Taš-me-tum iz-za-[mur]*, "on the 3rd day of the month, before the late afternoon meal, in the chapel of Tašmetum, it is to be sung;" the neo-Babylonian text MLC 382 reverse (incipit of the eršemma is not preserved): ITI-*us-su* UD.3.KAM *x x x x ti ina* É *pa-pa-ḫa* ᵈ*Na-na-a ana* IGI ᵈ*Na-na-a iz-za-mu-ur*, "Every month, on the 3rd day . . . in the chapel of Nanâ, before Nanâ, it is to be sung." Thus, it is clear that eršemmas

(172)We suggest that ér-si-si-mu is for ér(-ra) si-si-mu, "my being filled with tears" (for ér si, see B. Alster, *Dumuzi's Dream* line 1).

(173)We suggest interpreting *še-ra-am* in this peripheral text as being a cognate of Hebrew *šîr*, "song." And rather than reading *ma-[. . .]* as has Dossin, we suggest *ba-[lag-gi]*.

(174)For the king reciting a prayer or hymn during a ritual cf. R. Caplice, "Ritual for the Royal Army," *OrNS* 39 119.

were part of a fixed liturgy, being recited on the same date each month.

The eršemma *kidudû,* in other words, the eršemma functioning independently from the lamentation, was also recited on certain ceremonial occasions. In Uruk the eršemma was recited during the covering of a sacred kettle-drum.[175] According to the ritual, after purifying a bull, a ring of flour is drawn about the animal. The gala-priest, standing by the bull's head, sings the eršemma dilmun nigin.na to the accompaniment of the *ḫalḫallatu*-drum. Interestingly, another copy of this ritual omits the recitation of the eršemma as part of the process.[176] The eršemma was also recited during the repair of a temple wall.[177] Elaborate procedures were undertaken by the gala-priest during the process of razing the old edifice to ensure that the gods would not be angry. An altar was erected and part of the concomitant ritual included the recitation of three eršemmas, dilmun nigin.na, ^{d}Utu lugal.àm, and é.šà.ab.ḫun.gá.ta to Ea, Šamaš and Marduk respectively. Unfortunately, we possess just these two passages which detail the recitation of the eršemma apart from the balag-lamentation. Therefore, we are unable to determine the exact purpose and function of the independent eršemma in First Millennium B.C.E. ritual.

As previously stated, by the First Millennium B.C.E., many eršemmas had been appended to lamentations, serving as their new concluding sections. The following is a transliteration of columns i and ii of catalogue K_1, wherein the scribe has listed the balag-lamentation incipit in col. i and in col. ii the incipit of the eršemma which he found appended to the last tablet of the series constituting the lament:

i	1. [balag].meš [dingir.re.e.ne]		
	2. abzu pe.el.lá.àm	ii	[é-a x . . .-x-NE . . . *ù ki-i* dilmun nig]in-na[178]
	3. urú a.še.er.[ra]		[. . .].zu
	4. é tùr.gin$_7$ nigin.na.àm		[ušum gù]d nú.a
	5. ^{d}Utu.gin$_7$ è.ta		[ù.li.li] en.zu sá.mar.mar

(175)*ANET* 334 ff.

(176)*ANET* 335

(177)*ANET* 339 ff.

(178)dilmun nigin-na has been restored on the basis of Cal K obv. 27. However, the remaining portion of the eršemma which is appended in the First Millennium B.C., after the lamentation abzu pe-el-lá-àm (*SBH* 35 rev. & *CT* 51 189), is not dilmun nigin-na. M. Civil has suggested that this incipit may be partially preserved in *SBH* 35 rev. 18: [. . . MU.MEŠ].BÚR.MEŠ *šá* é a⌈x⌉[. . .]⌈x⌉ NE (for the expression MU.MEŠ.BÚR.MEŠ cf. *SBH* 35 obv. 19 wherein this phrase seems to refer to missing or destroyed lines).

6.	u$_4$.dam ki àm.ús	[umun].bára.kù.ga
7.	am.e amaš.an.na	[ur.sag] abzu.ta
8.	e.lum di.da.ra	⌜x⌝[. . .] ér i.si.iš
9.	e.ne.èm.mà.ni i.lu i.lu	a [še.eb].é.kur.ra
10.	an.na e.lum.e	ù.[u$_8$] a.ba mu.un.ḫul
11.	mu.tin nu.nuz$_x$ dím.ma	me.er.[ra].mu.dè
12.	urú.ḫul.a.ke$_4$ ^{d}Gu-la	é.zi ⌜x⌝(x)⌜x⌝ *ù ki-i* a mu.un.ga.mu
13.	e.lum gu$_4$.sún.e	umun.mu za.e
14.	am.e bára.an.na.ra	alim.ma umun.gìr.[ra] / e.lum gu$_4$.sún
15.	zi.bu.um zi.bu.um	gakkul.àm.ma al.šú
16.		balag.^{d}[A].usar.ke$_4$
17.	[zi.bu.ù.um] zi.bu.ù.um	[MIN?] balag.^{d}En.líl.lá.ke$_4$
18.	[a.ab.ba.ḫu].luḫ.ḫa *šá*^{d}En-líl	[x].dam kur.ra mú.a
19.	[. . .] : nu.pà.da	[x] ⌜x⌝ e!.ne.èm.mà.ni gakkul.àm.ma al.šú
20.	[a.ab.ba.ḫu.luḫ.ḫa *ša*^{d}] Marduk[179]	[šà.b]a.ni ga.an.ḫun
21a.	[. . .]	[a].ab.ba.ḫu.luḫ.ḫa še.ša$_4$
21b.		*ù ki-i* ušum gùd nú.a
22.	[en.zu sá.mar.mar][180]	nam.mu.un.šub.bé.en
23.	[umun ṣe.er.ma.al.la.an.ki].a[181]	dilmun^{ki} nigin.na.àm
24.	[. . .].UD	dilmun^{ki} nigin.na imin.àm
25.	[. . .] é.kur.ra	umun.aga.kù.ga
26.	[^{d}Utu] lugal.àm[182]	^{d}Utu è.ma.ra
27.	[u$_4$.dam] gù.dé.dé.aš	gu$_4$.maḫ pa.è.a
28.	[gu$_4$].ud.nim.é.kur.ra	ù.ma gul.gul.e
29.	ušum.gin$_7$ ní.si.a *šá* ^{d}MAŠ	ur.sag zag.zu.ta

(179)Restored on the basis of Cal K obv. 22

(180)Although Cal K obv. 16 lists the eršemma nam-mu-un-šub-bé-en with the lament e-lum bar-ra me-a, note our edition of nam-mu-un-šub-bé-en (no. 29) wherein the colophon lists nam-mu-un-šub-bé-en as being recited with en-zu sá-mar-mar; also K.3653 obv. 3 lists nam-mu-un-šub-bé-en as being recited in conjunction with en-zu sá-mar-mar. We have restored the latter, since the colophon just referred to states that the next work in order is umun-še-er-ma-al-la-an-ki-a as in our catalogue line 23. That the order of the catalogue K$_1$ was a standardized order has been further demonstrated to us by M. Civil, who informed us that the order of the lamentation excerpts in *UET* 6/2 200–207 is the same order as catalogue K$_1$.

(181)restored on the basis of Cal K obv. 8 and 31; *R. Acc.* 0.174 (*ANET* 341) 9; K.3653 obv. 14

(182)restored on the basis of *R. Acc.* 34 ff. (*TCL* 6 46:11=/*ANET* 341 9)

30.	nir.gál lú.è.dè	umun urú.mu in.di.bi maḫ.a[182a]
31.	ukkin.ta eš.bar til.la	ur.sag a.ma.ru$_x$.ḫu.luḫ.ḫa
32.	ušum gùd nú.a	NU.IGI
33.	a.gal.gal buru$_x$ su.su	ur.sag a.ma.ru$_x$.gal
34.	é.tùr.gin$_7$ nigin.na.àm BAR-*ú*	
35.	^{d}Utu.gin$_7$ è.ta BAR-*ú*	nam.mu.un.šub.bé.en
36.	u$_4$.dam ki àm.mu.ús BAR-*ú*	TUM$_{10}$ kur.ra šèg.gá
37.	am.e amaš.a.na BAR-*ú*	šà.ba.ni ga.an.ḫun
38.	umun še.er.ma.al.la.an.ki.a BAR-*ú*	dilmun^{ki} nigin.na
39.	[g]u$_4$.ud.nim.é.kur.ra BAR-*ú*	
40.	é tùr.gin$_7$ ḫul.àm	
41.	dingir pa.è.a	umun.ra a.ra.zu.a

42. šu.nigin 39 balag.^{d}En.líl.lá.ke$_4$

43.	áb.gin$_7$ gù.dé.dé	a é.an.na a gi$_6$.pàr.kù
44.	é.gi$_4$.a é.ta nam.ta.è	
45.	urú.àm.me ir.ra.bi	
46.	im.ma.al gù.dé.dé	me.e gašan.mu
47.	⌈x⌉ é.mu	
48.	[a] urú.mu im.me	
49.	[sag].kul ma.ra.ta	
50.	[. . .].re a.še.er.ra	
51.	[urú.ḫul].e.ke$_4$ *šá* ^{d}INANNA	an.sù.ud.ág izi.gin$_7$
52.	eden.na ú.sag.gá.ke$_4$	
53.	[a.še.er] gi$_6$.ta	gakkul.àm.ma al.šú
54.	[guruš] mu.lu ér.ra	
55.	[. . . ama].gan.kur.kur.ra	
56.	[. . .] ga.sig	
57.	[. . .] gakkul àm.šú.šú	
58.	[ḫul.gál.la][183] mu.un.du	
59.	[. . .] gá.a	
60.	[é.e še à]m.ša$_4$	

61. [ŠU+NIGIN 18] balag.^{d}Inanna.ke$_4$

(182a)the pairing of the eršemma and this balag is further attested in K. 11979 obv. 6

(183)restored according to the H. Clark Cylinder, *AJSL* 26 28; *Atiqot* 4 99:9

The following is our interpretation of this catalogue:

1. (The following are the incipits of) the lamentations of the gods:

2. (The lamentation) abzu pe.el.la.am (of the god Enki is recited with the eršemma) [. . .] or (the eršemma) dilmun.nigin.na.
3. (The lamentation) uru a.še.er.ra (of the god Enki is recited with the eršemma) [. . .].zu.
4. (The lamentation) e tur.gin nigin.na.am (of the god Enki is recited with the eršemma) ušum gud nu.a.
5. (The lamentation) Utu.gin e.ta (of the god Enlil is recited with the eršemma) u.li.li en.zu sa.mar.mar.
6. (The lamentation) u.dam ki am.us (of the god Enlil is recited with the eršemma) umun.bara.ku.ga.
7. (The lamentation) am.e amaš.an.na (of the god Enlil is recited with the eršemma) ur.sag abzu.ta.
8. (The lamentation) e.lum di.da.ra (of the god Enlil is recited with the eršemma) [. . .] er i.si.iš.
9. (The lamentation) e.ne.em.ma.ni i.lu i.lu (of the god Enlil is recited with the eršemma) a še.eb.e.kur.ra.
10. (The lamentation) an.na e.lum.e (of the god Enlil is recited with the eršemma) u.u.a.ba mu.un.ḫul.
11. (The lamentation) mu.tin nu.nuz dim.ma (of the goddess Nintinugga is recited with the eršemma) me.er.ra.mu.de.
12. (The lamentation) uru.ḫul.a.ke (of) the goddess Gula (is recited with either the eršemma) e.zi [. . .] or (the eršemma) a mu.un.ga.mu.
13. (The lamentation) e.lum gu.sun.e (of the god Enlil is recited with the eršemma) umun.mu za.e.
14. (The lamentation) am.e bara.an.na.ra (of the god Enlil is recited with either the eršemma) alim.ma umun.gir.ra (or the eršemma) e.lum gu.sun.
15. (The lamentation) zi.bu.um zi.bu.um (is recited with the eršemma) gakkul.am.ma al.šu; (this is) the lamentation (with the incipit zi.bu.um zi.bu.um) of Aššur.
17. (The lamentation) zi.bu.u.um zi.bu.u.um (is recited with) the same (eršemma as above, i.e. gakkul.am.ma al.šu); (this is) the lamentation (with the incipit zi.bu.u.um zi.bu.u.um) of Enlil.
18. (The lamentation) a.ab.ba.ḫu.luḫ.ḫa (of the god Enlil is recited with the eršemma) [x].dam kur.ra mu.a.
19. (The incipit of this lamentation) has not been recovered[184] (for the

(184)For a similar usage of pà, "to recover," see W. W. Hallo, *JAOS* 83 170 line 44.

beginning of the tablet is destroyed, but it is recited with the eršemma) [x] x e.ne.em.ma.ni gakkul.am.ma al.šu.

20. (The lamentation) a.ab.ba.ḫu.luḫ.ḫa (of the god Marduk is recited with the eršemma) ša.ba.ni ga.an.ḫun.
21. (The lamentation) [. . .] (is recited with either the eršemma) a.ab.ba.ḫu.luḫ.ḫa še.ša or ušum gud nu.a.
22. (The lamentation) en.zu sa.mar.mar (of the god Asarluḫi is recited with the eršemma) nam.mu.un.šub.be.en.
23. (The lamentation) umun še.er.ma.al.la.an.ki.a (of the god Asarluḫi is recited with the eršemma) dilmun nigin.na.am.
24. (The lamentation) [. . .].UD (of the god Utu(?) is recited with the eršemma) dilmun nigin.na imin.am.
25. (The lamentation) [. . .] e.kur.ra (of the god Utu is recited with the eršemma) umun.aga.ku.ga.
26. (The lamentation) Utu lugal.am (of the god Utu is recited with the eršemma) Utu e.ma.ra.
27. (The lamentation) u.dam gu.de.de.aš (of the god Iškur is recited with the eršemma) gu.maḫ pa.e.a.
28. (The lamentation) gu.ud.nim.e.kur.ra (of the god Ninurta is recited with the eršemma) u.ma gul.gul.e.
29. (The lamentation) ušum.gin ni.si.a (of the god Ninurta is recited with the eršemma) ur.sag zag.zu.ta.
30. (The lamentation) nir.gal lu.e.de (of the god Ninurta is recited with the eršemma) umun uru.mu in.di.bi maḫ.a.
31. (The lamentation) ukkin.ta eš.bar til.la (of the god Nabû is recited with the eršemma) ur.sag a.ma.ru.ḫu.luḫ.ḫa.
32. (The lamentation) ušum gud nu.a (of the god Nergal(?));no (eršemma) seen (appended to it).
33. (The lamentation) a.gal.gal buru su.su (of the god Nergal is recited with the eršemma) ur.sag a.ma.ru.gal.
34. The non-standardized version (of the lamentation) e. tur.gin nigin.na.am; (no eršemma seen appended to it).
35. The non-standardized version (of the lamentation) Utu.gin e.ta (is recited with the eršemma) nam.mu.un.šub.be.en.
36. The non-standardized version (of the lamentation) u.dam ki am.mu.us (is recited with the eršemma) TUM kur.ra šeg.ga.
37. The non-standardized version (of the lamentation) am.e amaš.a.na (is recited with the eršemma) ša.ba.ni ga.an.ḫun.
38. The non-standardized version (of the lamentation) umun še.er.ma.al.la.an.ki.a (is recited with the eršemma) dilmun nigin.na.
39. The non-standardized version (of the lamentation) gu.ud.nim.e.kur.ra; (no eršemma seen appended to it).

40. (The lamentation) e tur.gin ḫul.am (of the god . . .); (no eršemma seen appended to it).
41. (The lamentation) dingir pa.e.a (of the god Nanna is recited with the eršemma) umun.ra a.ra.zu.a.

---

42. A total of 39 lamentations of male deities

(Hereafter is the list of lamentations summed up as "a total of 18 lamentations of female deities.")

In addition to these pairings of lamentations and eršemmas, several ritual and calendar texts cite other pairings of eršemmas and lamentations:

lamentation	eršemma
a) ^{d}Utu.gin$_7$ è.ta	ù.u$_8$ a.ba mu.un.ḫul[185]
b) ur.sag.gal me.ni še.er. ma.al.la íl.la	an.na za.e maḫ.me.en[186]
c) [. . .]⸢x⸣te na⸢x⸣	ù.ma umun.gìr.ra[187]
d) nir.gál lú.è.dè	ur.sag ^{d}Ud.u$_x$.lu[188]
e) ^{d}Utu.gin$_7$ è.ta	šà.ba.ni ga.an.ḫun[189]
f) (. . .) ì.bu ì.bu	šà.ba.ni ga.an.ḫun[190]
g) e.lum bar.ra me.a	nam.mu.un.šub.bé.en[191]
h) [. . .] egí.re	šaḫ.du šaḫ.du[192]

The source material for our knowledge of the recitation of the eršemma in conjunction with the balag-lamentation consists of rituals of the gala-priests,[193] calendar texts and even a namburbi[194] (a "[ritual for] undoing [of a portended evil]").[195] In the rituals proscribed for the gala-priest, the

(185)AO.6472 obv. 6, (see *R. Acc.*)

(186)Cal K obv. 12–13

(187)Cal K obv. 20

(188)Cal K obv. 23

(189)Cal K obv. 33

(190)Cal K rev. 1

(191)Cal K obv. 16

(192)R. Caplice, *OrNS* 39 119

(193)For translations of the most pertinent texts, see A. Sachs, *ANET* 334–345.

(194)R. Caplice, "Namburbi Texts in the British Museum," *OrNS* 188 ff.

(195)The translation of the term namburbi is according to R. Caplice, "The Akkadian

chanting of a balag was but one element in a highly intricate ceremony, as observed in the following ritual for the laying of a temple foundation:[196] "A tablet of that which is required of the gala-priest:

When laying the foundation of a temple, in an auspicious month, on a favorable day, you shall open the (old) foundation of the temple. When you lay the foundation of the temple, during the night, you shall set up five offering tables, (one each for the gods) Sîn, Marduk, Ninmaḫ, Kulla and Ninšubur. You shall make offerings, scatter seed all about, kindle a fire and libate beer, wine and milk. You shall chant the lamentation u.dam ki am.us and the eršemma umun.bara.ku.ga. Afterwards, you shall set up three offering tables, (one each) for the god of the temple, the goddess of the temple and the genie of the temple. You shall kindle a fire and set up water. You shall draw the curtains shut. You shall chant (the work) e.ša.ab.hun.ga.e.ta to the accompaniment of the *ḫalḫallatu*-drum in the direction of the temple. After this, in the morning you shall set up three offering tables, (one each) for An, Enlil and Ea. You shall chant the lamentation umun še.er.ma.al.la.še an.ki.a and the eršemma dilmun nigin.na. You shall chant (the work) u An En.lil.la mu.un.dim.dim.e.ne. You shall dismantle the offering tables and lay the foundation. Then the (foundation ceremony) of the temple will be finished. You shall not interrupt the offerings and the lamentations. Once the foundation is laid, you shall (perform) the purification ritual and consecrate the site."

In a ritual for the demolition of a buckling temple wall, procedures similar to those proscribed above are observed.[197] At night offering tables are erected, sacrifices and libations performed, while the gala-priest "shall chant the lamentation Utu.gin e.ta and the eršemma u.u a.ba mu.un.ḫul."

Two significant aspects of the ritual function of the lamentation with its appended eršemma may be discerned. Firstly, the lament was recited to the gods while the offerings and libations were being performed. And secondly, the laments were chanted during the demolition of the old edifice, not during ceremonies commemorating the erection of the new structure. Thus, the lamentation served the same function as the offerings, to appease the divine anger the city might incur while the workmen were tearing down sacred structures, albeit to erect new ones. It is interesting that a lamentation was recited on the fifteenth day of a ceremony for the covering of a sacred kettledrum.[198] It is unusual that the lament was recited after the recovering

namburbi Texts: an Introduction," *Sources from the Ancient Near East* vol. I, Urdena Press, Malibu 1974.

(196)Cf. *R. Acc.* 42–44

(197)A. Sachs, *op. cit.,* 339–340

(198)A. Sachs, *op. cit.,* 334 ff.

process had been completed, rather than while the drum lay uncovered, in the process of repair, as with the temple wall and foundation. Moreover, in this ritual, sacrifices and libations did not accompany the recitation of the lament. We believe that, in this instance, the lamentation was chanted to the accompaniment of the kettledrum as a means of testing the new drum.

The actual content of the lamentation, i.e., the continual references to the destruction of temples, is obviously appropriate for the aforementioned rituals involving the razing of dilapidated or partially destroyed temple structures. Since the function of the lament is to assuage divine anger, a seemingly secondary use of the lament developed for other occasions when the priest or king needed to placate the passions of the gods, lest misfortune befall the nation. Such usage is attested in a text expressly labeled namburbi, a ritual to avert portended evil,[199] and in a series of rituals, though not designated as being numburbis, nonetheless, functioning as such.[200] It was the function of the lamentation recited as part of the namburbi to soothe the anger of the gods and thus, avert the impending evil. The laments were recited as part of rituals to avert evils portended by earth tremors, the entrance of a dog or wild beast into a temple, and the breakage of a statue of a past or present king of the country. The namburbi employing the lamentation is for the purpose of insuring "that headaches, plague (and) pestilence may not approach the king's ho[rses and] troops." Thereafter followed an elaborate ritual which involved the erecting of:

> " . . . four reed altars to Lugalgirra, Meslamtaea, Ninkilim . . . You offer four sacrificial sheep. Firewood . . . You strike the bronze *lilissu*-drum. You have the king sit upon a reed seat. He wears a crown upon his head. You grasp his hands in (the folds of) a turban. You sing the lament 'Great waters drowning the crops,' the eršemma 'Warrior, great flood.' You take the king's hands, and he rises and stands before the cultic installation. You have the king recite 'Lord, the strong one of all the great gods.' "[201]

Serving not only to placate divine anger over specific activities, the balag-lamentation was one vehicle by which the priests maintained an ever-constant vigil against the capriciousness of the gods. The regular recitation of lamentations on fixed days of each month and on festivals hopefully ensured tranquility for a nation ever afraid it might unknowlingly commit an offense against the divine powers. In each month, certain days were

(199)See n. 194 above.

(200)A. Sachs, *op. cit.,* 339–340

(201)Translation according to R. Caplice, "namburbi Texts in the British Museum," *OrNS* 39 121.

designated for the chanting of one or more laments with their eršemmas, the days being determined perhaps on the basis of numerical superstitions. The Uruk calendar, listing lamentations to be recited on the same date every month, designated lamentations for the first, second, seventh, fourteenth, fifteenth and twentieth of every month, with special recitations during the months of *Nisannu* and *Araḫšamnu*.[202] Although the calendar only cites the lamentation, not the accompanying eršemma, most probably it was understood that the appropriate eršemma was also recited in conjunction with the lament.

The calendar from Aššur, partially preserved, describes the liturgy in Aššur for the months *Šabaṭu, Adaru* and *Nisannu.* The following is an excerpt of the Aššur calendar:[203]

> On the 23rd (of *Šabaṭu*), the lamentation ur.sag.gal me.ni še.er.ma.al.la an.ki.a and the eršemma an.na za.e maḫ.me.en for Aššur in the temple of Dagan. After the sacrifices, the lamentation u.dam ki am.us and the eršemma umun.bara.ku.ga for Aššur in the house of Dagan, (the ceremony) "arousing the temple."
>
> On the 24th (of *Šabaṭu*), the lamentation e.lum bar.ra me.a and the eršemma nam.mu.un.šub.be.en for Aššur in the house of Dagan. After the sacrifices, the lament am.e amaš.a.na and the eršemma ur.sag abzu.ta for Aššur in the house of Dagan, (the ceremony) "arousing the temple."

The lamentation was also recited in Uruk on the tenth and eleventh days of the important *akitu*-festival in the month of *Tashritu.* Since this was the occasion when the great gods assembled to determine the fates for the coming year, the chanting of lamentations to soothe the anger of the gods was most vital.

In summary then, the eršemma *kidudû,* those eršemmas ritually employed independently of the balag-lamentation, were part of a fixed liturgy for certain days of each month, every month. So, too, were they recited as part of ceremonies centered about certain cultic activities. The lamentation, which included the eršemma as its conclusion, also served as part of a fixed liturgy. In addition, the lamentation was recited for any occasion when the priests wished to soothe the anger of the gods, the heart-pacification unit of the eršemma being expertly fashioned for just such a role.

(202)S. Langdon, "Calendars of Liturgies and Prayers," *AJSL* 42 110 ff.

(203)S. Langdon, *ibid.,* 115

PART II

(Selected Texts, Transliteration and Translation)

A. Eršemmas Preserved Only in Old Babylonian Copies

We are fortunate that there are preserved five eršemmas of the storm-god Iškur (who was identified with the Semitic weather god Adad). Three of these compositions are found on the remains of a large tablet (originally 7 by 10 inches) which contained twelve eršemmas. The first line on the obverse states "eršemmas of the gods" and at the conclusion on the reverse is inscribed:

3 eršemmas of Iškur;
2 eršemmas of Suen;
4 eršemmas of Ninurta;
3 eršemmas of Enki;

12 eršemmas of the gods

Four of the eršemmas of Iškur are based upon the tale of Iškur's assuming the role of storm-god. In two texts it is Enlil who bestows this power, while in another it is An. Although there are differences in content among these four works, i.e., expansion of the theme at different points, nonetheless, lines and whole sections are mutually shared to such a degree as to suggest that either they were composed by the same individual(s) or that one of these eršemmas (or perhaps another as yet uncovered one) served as a model from which the others were developed.

The fifth work (which shares the same incipit with one of the previous four eršemmas) is based upon a different motif. Unfortunately, since portions of the text are destroyed, it is difficult to reconstruct the narrative. However, the following four sections can be discerned:

1) There is a plea, most likely to Iškur, involving the grain goddess, Ašnan.
2) Iškur calls forth to his vizier.

3) Iškur enters his house unto the goddess Medimša (whom tradition identified as being Iškur's wife).
4) Iškur's actions have caused the livestock to survive.

It is the relationship of these four episodes that is unclear. The work apparently refers to a famine which has caused much of the livestock to perish. Iškur, as the god of storms, would have the power to bring rain and thus, allow the grain to be abundant, thereby ending the famine. Nowhere in the literary tradition is there any reference to Ašnan serving as Iškur's vizier, thus, we doubt if Iškur's call to his vizier is a call to Ašnan. Perhaps Iškur is commanding his vizier to make preparations for a visit to Medimša and, in turn, it is the union of Iškur and Medimša which brings fertility, causing the famine to end.

Eršemma no. 23.1

Text: BM 29631 (*CT* 15 pl.15–16). Collated: S. N. Kramer, *RA* 65 25. Previous translations: A. Falkenstein, *SAHG* 81–83;[204] S. N. Kramer, *ANET* 3rd edition 577–578

1.	[gu$_4$-maḫ pa]-è-a	mu-zu ⌜an-z⌝[à-šè (. . .)]
2.	[alim(?)-ma(?)] ^{d}Iškur gu$_4$-maḫ pa-è-a	mu-zu ⌜an⌝-[zà-šè]
3.	[d]Iškur dumu-an-na gu$_4$-maḫ pa-è-a	mu-zu an-z[à-šè]
4.	⌜ù⌝-mu-un-Karkara(IM)^{ki}-ke$_4$ gu$_4$-maḫ pa-è-a	mu-zu an-z[à-šè]
5.	^{d}Iškur ù-mu-un-ḫé-gál-la gu$_4$-maḫ pa-è-a	mu-zu ⌜an⌝-[zà-šè]
6.	maš-tab-ba-ù-mu-un-^{d}Am-an-ki-ga gu$_4$-maḫ pa-è-⌜a⌝	(mu-zu an-zà-šè)
7.	a-a ^{d}Iškur ù-mu-un u$_4$-da u$_5$-a	mu-zu an-zà-šè
8.	a-a ^{d}Iškur u$_4$-gal-la u$_5$-a	mu-zu an-zà-šè
9.	a-a ^{d}Iškur úg-gal-la u$_5$-a	mu-zu an-zà-šè
10.	^{d}Iškur úg-an-na gu$_4$-maḫ pa-è-a	mu-zu an-zà-šè
11.	mu-zu kalam-ma mu-un-du$_7$-du$_7$-du$_7$	
12.	me-lám-zu kalam-ma túg!-gin$_7$ im-mi-in-dul	
13.	za-pa-ág-zu-šè kur-gal a-a ^{d}Mu-ul-líl sag im-da-sìg-ge	
14.	ur$_5$-ša$_4$-zu ama-gal ^{d}Nin-líl ba-e-de-ḫu-luḫ-e	
15.	^{d}En-líl-le dumu-ni ^{d}Iškur-ra á mu-un-da-an-ág	
16.	lú-BÀNDA-mu u$_4$ um-me-ši-si-si u$_4$ um-me-ši-lá-lá	
17.	^{d}Iškur-re u$_4$ um-me-ši-si-si u$_4$ um-me-ši-lá-lá	
18.	u$_4$-imin ḫaš$_x$(TUMxEŠ)-gin$_7$ ḫé-ri-lá u$_4$ um-me-ši-lá-lá	
19.	u$_4$-gù-di-zu ka-bi ḫa-ra-ab-ba u$_4$ um-me-ši-lá-lá	

(204)See the review by S. N. Kramer, *BiOr* 11 (1954) 173.

nim-gír sukkal-zu igi-šè mu-ra-du u_4 (um-me-ši-lá-lá)
lú-BÀNDA-mu ul gin-na gin-na a-ba zi-ge-en te-ba
ki-bal ḫul-gig a-a-ugu-zu-šè a-ba za-e-gin$_7$ te-ba
na$_4$-IM-tur-tur-e šu um-me-ti a-ba za-e-gin$_7$ te-ba
na$_4$-gal-gal-e šu um-me-ti a-ba za-e-gin$_7$ te-ba
na$_4$-tur-tur-zu na$_4$-gal-gal-zu ugu-ba ù-me-àm
ki-bal-a zi-da-zu ù-mu-e-gul gáb-bu-zu ù-mu-e-sì
^{d}Iškur-re inim-du$_{11}$-ga-a-a-ugu-na-šè giz-zal ba-ši-in-ak
a-a ^{d}Iškur é-ta è-a-ni u_4-gù-di na-nam
é-ta urú-⸢ta⸣⸢è-a⸣-ni úg-bàn-da na-nam
urú-ta ⸢an-šè⸣ ⸢gù⸣-gar-ra-ni u_4-GÙ-mur-ra na-nam

⸢30⸣ ⸢ér⸣-šem$_5$-ma-^{d}Iškur

* * *

[Great ox who is radiant], your name [is to the limits] of heaven.
[Honored one], Iškur, great ox who is radiant, your name [is to the limits] of heaven.
Iškur, son of An, great ox who is radiant, your name [is to the limits] of heaven.
Lord of Karkar, great ox who is radiant, your name [is to the limits] of heaven.
Iškur, lord of abundance, great ox who is radiant, your name [is to the limits] of heaven.
Twin to the lord Enki, great ox who is radiant, [your name is to the limits of heaven].
Father Iškur, lord who mounts the storm, your name (is) to the limits of heaven.
Father Iškur, who mounts the great storm, your name (is) to the limits of heaven.
Father Iškur, who mounts a great lion, your name (is) to the limits of heaven.
Iškur, lion of heaven, great ox who is radiant, your name (is) to the limits of heaven.
Your name continually gores the nation.
Your splendor covers the nation like a garment.
At your cry the great mountain, father Enlil, lowers his head.
Your thundering causes the great mother, Ninlil, to tremble before you.
Enlil commissioned his son, Iškur:
"My young man, . . . the storms for yourself! Harness the storms for yourself!
Iškur, . . . the storms for yourself! Harness the storms for yourself!

Let the seven storms be harnessed for you like a team (of draft
animals)! Harness the storms for yourself!

Let your howling storm roar for you! Harness the storms for yourself!

20. Lightning, your messenger, will precede you. Harness the storms for
yourself!

My young man, joyfully go forth! Go forth! Who is like you when
approaching?

(To) the rebellious land hated by your father, your begettor! Who is like
you when approaching?

Take small . . .-stones! Who is like you when approaching?

Take large (hail?)-stones! Who is like you when approaching?

25. Rain down your small (hail?)-stones and your large (hail?)-stones upon
it!

In the rebellious land destroy at your right! Overthrow at your left!"

Iškur gave heed to the spoken words of his father begettor.

When father Iškur goes forth from the house, indeed he is a howling
storm.

When he goes out from house (and) from city, indeed he is a fierce lion.

30. When from the city he raises his voice heavenward, indeed he is a
roaring storm.

---

30 (lines) an eršemma (of) Iškur

Eršemma no. 23.2

Text: BM 96927 rev. v 38'-vi 16

1. gu₄-maḫ pa-è-a [. . .]
2. alim-ma ᵈIškur [. . .]
3. ur-sag-gal en DUMU [. . .]
4. alim-ma ù-mu-un-[. . .]
5. ur-sag-gal⌈x x⌉ᵈIšk[ur . . .]
6. maš-tab-ba-ᵈ[. . .]
7. a-a ᵈIškur ù-[. . .]
8. a-a ᵈIškur [. . .]
9. a-a ᵈIškur [. . .]
10. ᵈIškur u₄-g[ù-. . .]
11. mu-zu kalam-m[a. . .]
12. me-lám-zu kalam-m[a. . .]
13. ur₅-ša₄-ni-ta k[ur(?). . .]
14. u₄-gal-an-na [. . .]
15. a-a ᵈIš[kur. . .]
16. [. . .]⌈x⌉ NE(?) DU.DU ḫé-⌈x⌉-[. . .]

17. [. . .]-maḫ u$_5$-a ù-mu-[. . .]
18. [. . .]⸢x⸣-da-ka še-gu-n[u. . .]
19. [. . .]⸢x⸣-gur-gur-e za-⸢e⸣(?) [. . .]
20. [. . .]⸢x⸣ še al-ù-tu [. . .]
21. [(. . .) ^{d}Aš]nan še ka-na-ág-gá al-⸢x⸣-[x (x)] ù-mu-un-⸢dé⸣(?)-[e(?)]
22. [. . .]-⸢x⸣-la-^{d}Mu-ul-líl-[lá(-ke$_4$)]
23. [. . .]-a(?)-bi kiri$_4$-zal-la GÙ mu-da-an-zi
24. [. . .]^{d}Iškur nu-sík íl-íl-mu nu-mu-un-su ri-ri-e-mu
25. [ù-m]u-un sukkal-a-né gù mu-un-na-dé-e
26. [ù]-mu-un a-a ^{d}Iškur sukkal-a-né gù mu-na-dé-e
27. [ga-š]a-an-maḫ ki-sì-ga tuš-a-ra é-a-na àm-ku$_4$-ku$_4$
28. [^{d}]Me-dím-ša$_4$ ki-sì-ga tuš-a-ra é-a-na àm-ku$_4$-ku$_4$
29. [ur]-sag gu$_4$ mu-gi e-zé mu-gi ga-ḫúl-ḫúl-le-dè-en
30. [gu$_4$]-bi mu-un-gi e-zé-bi mu-un-gi ga-ḫúl-ḫúl-le-dè-en
31. [x]-e ka-tar-ra-ni mu-un-gul-gul ga-ḫúl-ḫúl-le-dè-en

ér-šem$_5$-ma

Great ox who is radiant, [. . .]
Honored one, Iškur, [great ox who is radiant, . . .]
Great warrior, (. . .) lord (. . .), [great ox who is radiant, . . .]
Honored one, lord [. . . , great ox who is radiant, . . .]
Great warrior, . . . Iškur, [great ox who is radiant, . . .]
Twin [to Enki, great ox who is radiant, . . .]
Father Iškur, [lord who mounts the storm, . . .]
Father Iškur, [who mounts the great storm, . . .]
Father Iškur, [who mounts a great lion, . . .]
Iškur, [your] howling storm [. . .]
Your name [continually gores] the nation.
Your splendor [covers] the nation [like a garment].
At your thundering [the great] mountain, [father Enlil, . . .]
Great-storm-of-heaven [. . .]
Father Iškur [. . .]
[. . .]. . .go(?). . .[. . .]
[. . .] who mounts an exalted [. . .]. Lord(?) [. . .]
[. . .] late barley [. . .]
[. . .]. . .[. . .]
[. . .] produces grain [. . .]
Call(?) forth [to] Ašnan, [who produces(?)] grain in the land!
"[. . . of] Enlil!
[. . .] raises the voice(?) in joy.
[. . .] Iškur, my orphaned girl who carries! My widow who gleans!"

The lord calls out to his vizier.
The lord, father Iškur, calls out to his vizier.
He enters his house unto the lofty lady who is sitting . . .
He enters his house unto Medimša, who is sitting . . .
The warrior has restored the oxen! He has restored the sheep! Let us rejoice!
30. He has restored those [oxen]! He has restored those sheep! Let us rejoice!
[. . .], his praise is great(?). Let us rejoice!

---

an eršemma

Eršemma no. 168

Text: BM 65145 (CT 42 10)

1. sig an-na gù-d[é . . .]
2. ^{d}Iškur dumu-an-na gù-dé
3. dumu-sag-an-kù-ga gù-dé
4. maš-tab-ba-ù-mu-un-^{d}Am-an-ki-ke$_4$ gù-dé
5. ^{d}Iškur úg-an-na gù-dé
6. za-pa-ág-zu kur-gal a-a ^{d}Mu-ul-líl ⌜sag⌝ im-da-sìg-ge
7. ur$_5$-ša$_4$-zu ama-gal ama ^{d}⌜Nin-líl⌝ ḫu-«luḫ»-luḫ-ḫe
8. ^{d}Iškur-e a-a-ni an-gal(-e) ⌜á⌝ ⌜mu-da-ág⌝-e
9. [. . .]-bi ul$_4$ gin ul$_4$ ⌜gin-a⌝ a-ba zi-gi-in te-ba
10. [. . . a-a-u]gu-zu ul$_4$ DU.DU a-ba zi-gi-in te-ba
11. [. . .]-⌜DIRI⌝ a-ba zi-gi-in te-ba
12. [. . .]⌜x⌝ ⌜a-ba⌝ ⌜zi⌝-[gi]-in te-ba

(19 lines destroyed)

32. [. . .]⌜x x⌝ (x) mu-un-ti
33. ⌜u$_4$-ba⌝ ⌜idim⌝-an-eden-na ugu-bal-la um-me-šú
34. ki-sikil abgal nu-me-a síg-bar-ra bí-in-du$_8$
35. guruš-bi ^{dug}šakan-šub-ba ^{dug}šakan-na mu-lá!
36. di$_4$-di$_4$-lá-bi še-mu-ra-gin$_7$ ur$_5$-re ba-ab-laḫ$_4$
37. ki-bal-a zi-da-bé mu-un-gul gáb-bu TÚG mu-un-sì
38. ur-sag-gá ní-te-a-ni silim-me-eš erén-ga-me
39. ^{d}Iškur-e ní-te-a-ni silim-me-eš erén-ga-me
40. IM.MA.A.A-gin$_7$ ra-ra-mu-ni e$_4$ mu-da-gá-gá
41. [e$_4$]-ma-ru-gin$_7$ zi-ga-mu-ni a-ba sag ba-ab-sum-mu

---

41 mu-bi-im ér-šem$_5$-‹ma›-^{d}Iškur-kam

1. Calling forth below and above [. . .]
Iškur, child of An, calling forth,
First-born of holy An, calling forth,
Twin to the lord Enki, calling forth,
Iškur, lion of heaven, calling forth,
Your cry causes the great mountain, father Enlil, to lower (his) head.
Your thundering causes the great mother, Ninlil, to quake.
"Oh Iškur," commands his father, great An,
"[. . .] Hurry! Go forth! Hurry! Who is like you when approaching?
[. . .] your [father] begettor, hurry! Go forth! Who is like you when approaching?
[. . .] Who is like you when approaching?
[. . .] Who is like you when approaching?"

(*19 lines destroyed*)

[. . .] resides.
On that day pour out the subterranean waters of the high steppe upon the rebellious!
The young girl, though she is not an *apkallu*-priest, lets her hair hang loosely down her back.
Its man lies prone, an overturned vessel among vessels.
The daylight(?) dries(?) out its children like threshed grain.
In the rebellious land he destroyed at its right; he overthrew at the left.
The warrior praises himself.
Iškur praises himself:
40. "When I beat down like the rain(?), I cause flooding!
When I rise up like a flood, who can oppose (me)?"

It is 41 lines. It is an eršemma of Iškur.

Eršemma no. 184

Text: BM 96927 rev. vi 17–67

1. ù-mu-un-e du$_6$-du$_6$-dam e$_4$-nag im-ma-ra
2. ù-mu-un a-a ^{d}Iškur du$_6$-du$_6$-dam e$_4$-nag im-ma-ra
3. ^{d}Iškur dumu-aṇ-na du$_6$-du$_6$-dam
4. [dum]u-^{d}En-líl-lá-ka du$_6$-du$_6$-dam
5. [an]-úr an-pa-šè du$_6$-du$_6$-dam
6. [tum$_{10}$]-mi-ir-ta tum$_{10}$-mu-šè du$_6$-du$_6$-dam
7. [ki ^{giš}]ḫa-lu-úb diri-dè ^{giš}mes mú-mú-dè
8. [ki ^{d}Ut]u è-dè ^{d}Utu ku$_4$-ku$_4$-dè

9. [(x) x I]M ^{d}Iškur e lú-ḫi lú-ḫi
10. [x x (x)] ⌜a⌝(?) DU$_7$ u$_6$-da e$_4$-silim-da giš-e sù-sù
11. [. . .]⌜x⌝-ra pa$_5$-da dù-dù
12. [x x]⌜sila⌝-dagal-la a-gi$_6$-a du$_7$-du$_7$
13. [^{d}Iškur]-e a-a-ni ^{d}En-líl-lá á mu-un-da-ág-e
14. [lú-bànda]-mu um-me-en-šè-si-sá um-me-en-šè-lá-lá
15. [u$_4$-imin] ḫaš$_x$(TUMxEŠ)-bi ḫe-ri-lá u$_4$ um-me-en-šè-lá-lá
16. [u$_4$-gù]-dé-dé-da-zu ḫe-ri-lá u$_4$ um-me-en-šè-lá-lá
17. [. . .]⌜x⌝-bi an-úr-an-pa-šè muru$_x$ ḫu-mu-ra-sír-⌜ra⌝
18. [. . .]-mu u$_4$ me-en-šè-zi-ge u$_4$ me-en-šè-DU.DU
19. [. . . ^{d}]En-líl-šè nu-še-ge-da u$_4$ me-en-šè-DU.DU
20. [. . .-m]u(?) ^{d}En-líl-šè gú nu-gar-ra-šè u$_4$ me-en-šè-DU.DU
21. [na$_4$-d]i$_4$-di$_4$-lá šu um-mi-ta na$_4$-di$_4$-di$_4$-lá
22. [na$_4$]-gal-gal-e šu um-mi-tag na$_4$-gal-gal-lá
23. ki-bal á-zi-da-mu mu-un-gul gáb-bu-bi mu-un-sì
24. ur-sag-e inim-a-a-ugu-na-šè gis-sa-al ba-ši-in-ak
25. ur-sag-gal é-ta è-a-ni ug-bàn-da na-na
26. a-a ^{d}Iškur ki-e di-da-ni ki ur$_5$-ša$_4$ na-na
27. ù-mu-un-mu ambar-ra di-da-ni u$_4$-GÙ-mu-ra na-na
28. ^{giš}gigir-ra me-ri-ni nam-mi-gub ul mu-un-gùr-ru-a
29. ur-sag-gá IŠ NÍ-ta-na KA KA mi-ni-sù-NI-eš
30. mar-uru$_5$ an-ta zi-zi DI-DI sag an-šè mi-ni-in-íl
31. lirum-maḫ-mu u$_4$-da DILI -bé sag mu-ni-ib-gi-e-NI
32. nimgir ^{giš}tukul IM-gin$_7$ ši-DU.DU suḫuš-bé ba-ši-in-gi
33. ki-bal-da IM-gin$_7$ ba-da-gul ^{giš}Ú.GÍR-gin$_7$ ba-da-sù
34. ki-bal-da ur im-ta-an-è-a KA mi-ni-in-sù-NI-eš
35. ki-bal-da me-er im-ta-an-è-a dar^{mušen}-ra mi-ni-sù-NI-eš
36. kur KA kur-ra-na tu^{mušen} mi-ni-ib-dal-dal-e
37. kur-kur-bi gú-nu-gar-ra-ba ka-me-a-ka
38. nì-ki-luḫ-bi-ne nam-in-lá ù-mu-un nam-tar-re-da
39. ab-ba gù-sa-ra nu-me-a gú ki ba-ni-ma-al
40. di$_4$-di$_4$-lá še-ga-ra-di nu-me-a u$_4$-dè ba-ab-la-ḫe
41. um-ma-bi kaš ì-nun-na ZÚ i-im-ku-ku-uš-ša
42. ki-sikil-bi abgal nu-me-a síg-bar-ra bí-in-du$_8$
43. guruš-bi ^{dug}sa-ma-an-šub-ba ^{dug}sa-ma-na mu-un-lá
44. lugal-mu níg-e-rib-ba-za nu-uš-in-ga-zu-a
45. a-a dingir-maḫ nì-maḫ-a-za nu-uš-in-ga-zu-a
46. ur-gu-la-gin$_7$ á-tuk-gin$_7$ nu-uš-in-ga-zu-a
47. ur-maḫ-gin$_7$ kun ur$_4$-ur$_4$-ra-za nu-uš-in-ga-zu-a
48. ušumgal-gin$_7$ sag-giš-ra-ra-za nu-uš-in-ga-zu-a
49. nam-maḫ-zu kalam-ma ba-ši-è ka-tar-zu si-il-dè

za-e maḫ-me-en za-e maḫ-me-en za-e a-ba è-da-sa
ù-mu-un a-a ^{d}Iškur za-e <maḫ>-me-en za-e a-ba e-da-sa

ér-šem$_5$-ma

The lord has watered the hills with soaking water.
The lord, father Iškur, has watered the hills with soaking water.
Iškur, the son of An, has watered the hills with soaking water.
The son of Enlil has watered the hills with soaking water.
To the horizon and to the very depths of the sky has he watered the hills with soaking water.
From north to south has he watered the hills with soaking water.
Where the ḫaluppu-trees abound and the mesu-trees sprout forth,
[where] the sun rises and (where) the sun sets
(has) . . . Iškur, oh Luḫi! Luḫi!
. . . who sprinkles the trees with health-giving waters,
. . . who plants . . . at the side of a canal,
. . . a torrent goring the wide streets, (he has watered the hills with soaking water).

"Oh Iškur!" commands his father, Enlil:
"My [young man], . . ., harness (the storms)!
Let [the seven storms], that team (of draft animals), be harnessed for you! Harness the storms!
Let your howling [storms] be harnessed for you! Harness the storms!
. . . may the clouds be thick for you to the horizon and to the very depths of the sky!
My . . ., raise up a storm against him! Bring a storm against him!
Bring a storm against him who does not obey Enlil!
M[y(?) . . .], bring a storm against him who is not submissive to Enlil!
Lay hold of small stones! (Lay hold of) small stones!
Lay hold of large stones! (Lay hold of) large stones!
My right hand has destroyed the rebellious; this left has overthrown it."

The warrior gave heed to the words of his father begettor.
When the great warrior goes out from (his) house, indeed he is a fierce lion.
When father Iškur walks upon the earth, indeed the earth rumbles.
When my lord walks in the marshes, indeed he is a roaring(?) storm.

He steps into the chariot, glory enveloping him.
. . . warrior . . .

proceeding(?), a devastating flood, rising high, he is majestic.
My most mighty one rushes forward with the . . . of a storm.
The lightning bolt, (his) weapon, proceeds like the wind; *he holds firmly onto its base.*

He destroys the rebellious land like the wind. He makes it barren like the *ašagu*-plant.
He who chases out the . . . from the rebellious land . . .
He who chases out the . . . from the rebellious land . . . *dar*-bird . . .
He makes the doves fly . . .
When those lands did not submit, in the mouth of battle
has he . . ., the lord who decides the fates.

Though the elder . . ., he bows low.
Though the children are not piles of grain, the daylight dries them out.
Its old woman . . . beer and butter.
Though its young girl is not an *apkallu*-priest, she lets her hair hang loosely.
Its young man lies prone, an overturned vessel among vessels.

My king, if only your titanic strength were known!
Father, exalted god, if only your exaltedness were known!
Like the lion, like the muscle man were you but known!
Were your *stalking* known like that of the lion!
Were your deadliness known like that of a dragon!
Your greatness goes out to the nation, your praise being uttered.
You are exalted! You are exalted! Who can compare to you?
Lord, father Iškur, you are exalted! Who can compare to you?

---

an eršemma

Eršemma no. 185

Text: BM 96927 rev. v 1′–37′

1. u_4 AN [. . .]
2. ^{d}Iškur [. . .]
3. dumu-^{d}En-[líl-lá. . .]
4. dumu-an-uraš-[a. . .]
5. a-a ^{d}Iškur [. . .]
6. za-pa-ág-zu-šè [. . .]
7. ur_5-$ša_4$-zu-šè ama[. . .]
8. ^{d}Iškur-e a-a-ni [. . .]
9. lú-BÀNDA-mu [. . .]

10. ki-bal ḫul-gig [. . .]
11. urú EN-šè nu-še-[ga. . .]
12. u$_4$-imin ḫaš$_x$-bi ḫe-[. . .]
13. muru$_x$(IM.DUGUD)-diri-ga bar-ús u[m-. . .]
14. u$_4$-gù-dé-dé ka-ba ḫe-[. . .]
15. nim-gír sukkal-zu i-bí-šè [. . .]
16. IM-di$_4$-di$_4$-lá šu um-[. . .]
17. IM-gal-gal-e šu [. . .]
18. na$_4$-tur-tur-zu n[a$_4$-. . .]
19. ù-mu-un-e i[nim(?)-. . .]
20. ^{d}Iškur ki-bal [. . .]
21. a-a ^{d}Iškur ⌜x⌝[. . .]
22. ur-sag-e ⌜x⌝[. . .]
23. KA⌜x⌝[. . .]
24. ur-sag⌜x⌝[. . .]
25. ^{d}Iškur-e ⌜x⌝[. . .]
26. za-pa-ág-gá-ni [. . .]
27. za-pa-ág-gá-ni-⌜ta⌝(?) [. . .]
28. nam-lú-u$_x$-lu u$_4$-da [. . .]
29. um-ma-bi kaš ì-nun-[na. . .]
30. ki-sikil-e abgal nu-me-a [. . .]
31. guruš-bi ^{dug}sa-ma-an [. . .]
32. di$_4$-di$_4$-lá še-garadin-da-nu-[me-a. . .]
33. ur-sag ní-ta-na ⌜ár⌝(?) ⌜x⌝ [. . .]
34. ^{d}Iškur ní-ta-na silim-[. . .]
35. gá-e an-gin$_7$ E rib-ba$^{!}$ (DA)-mu-dè [. . .]
36. mar-uru$_5$-gin$_7$ zi-ga-mu-dè [. . .]

ér-[šem$_5$-ma]

. . .[. . .]
Iškur, [the son of An, . . .]
The son of Enlil [. . .]
The son of heaven and earth [. . .]
Father Iškur [. . .]
At your cry [the great mountain, father Enlil, bows his head].
At your thundering the [great] mother, [Ninlil, trembles before you].

"Oh Iškur," [commands] his father [Enlil]:
"My young man, [joyfully go forth! Go forth! Who is like you when approaching?]
(To) the rebellious land hated [by your father, your begettor! Who is like you when approaching?]

[To] the city which doesn't obey. . .! [Who is like you when approaching?]
Let the seven storms, that team (of draft animals), [be harnessed for you! Harness the storms!]
[Drive] the floating clouds (with) a goad! [Harness the storms!]
Let the howling storm roar [for you]! [Harness the storms!]
Lightning, your messenger, [will precede you]! [Harness the storms!]
Take the small. . .[. . .]
Take the large. . .[. . .]
[Rain down] your small (hail)-stones and [your large] (hail)-stones [upon it]!"

The lord [gave heed to the words of his father begettor].
Iškur [destroys] the rebellious land [at its right; he overthrows it at the left].
[When] father Iškur [goes forth from the house, indeed he is a howling storm].
[When] the warrior [goes out from house and from city, indeed he is a fierce lion].
. . .[. . .]
The warrior [. . .]
Iškur [. . .]
(. . .) his cry [. . .]
From his cry [. . .]
(. . .) mankind in the storm [. . .]

Its old woman [. . .] beer and butter.
Though its young girl is not an apkallu-priest, [she lets her hair hang loosely].
Its young man [lies prone, an overturned] vessel [among vessels].
Though the children are not piles of grain, [the daylight dries them out].

The warrior praises himself.
Iškur praises himself.
"When I am surpassing like the heavens, [. . .]"
"When I rise up like a flood, [who can oppose me?]"

---

an eršemma

In this work a wail over the disappearance of the goddess Ningirgilu is uttered. Since tradition identified Ningirgilu with Inanna, this eršemma may be based upon the tale of Inanna's detention in the netherworld by Ereshkigal as narrated in the composition "Inanna's Descent." The opening soliloquy utilizes an elsewhere attested literary device, directing the monologue to an imaginary passerby, rather than to the audience or to the gods. In this speech there is reference to Ningirgilu as "my mother" and to Nanna as "my father." Inanna was Nanna's daughter, Nanna's wife being Ningal. Thus, these epithets would seem to be ones of respect, rather than referring to actual parentage. Ningirgilu is asked when she will return, for during her absence the city has been plundered. Nanna is then beseeched to intercede in releasing his daughter, Ningirgilu. Ningirgilu, wandering about the steppe—the steppe was a place of deprivation and thus became identified with the land of the dead, the netherworld—hears of the plight of her city and determines to obtain Ereshkigal's permission to leave in order to see Enlil, who as leader of the gods, has it within his power to end the destruction of Ningirgilu's city. Ningirgilu goes into mourning for her city, at which point her sister, the queen of the netherworld, Ereshkigal, lets her go. The use of the verb "to move about" rather than "to release" perhaps implies that Ereshkigal gives permission only to see Enlil and that having done this Ningirgilu is obligated to return.[205] See eršemma no. 32 for a work based upon Inanna's speech before Enlil.

Eršemma no. 79

Text: BM 23584 (*CT* 15 pl. 23)

1. ul-e pa-pa-al-ta ér àm-da-n[i-še$_8$-še$_8$]
2. kù-zu-mu egí ga-ša-an-gir-gi$_4$-lu
3. kur-gul-gul mu-gi$_{17}$-ib ga-ša-an-an-na
4. egí-zi-mu ga-ša-an-é-mùš-a-ra
5. ^{d}Unú-mà-i-bí-ma-al ama-uburú-bi-ur-zi-da
6. la-bar-é-e ga-ša-an munus-sa$_6$-<ga>
7. ul-e pa-pa-al-ta tuš-a-ta
8. ul-e pa-pa-al-an-kù-ga-ta
9. ul-e pa-pa-al-uraš-a-ta
10. ki ám-me-e-gá-ar ba-an-a$_5$-an-na
11. lú-di ama-mu-ra du$_{11}$-ga-na-ab me-na mu-un-du$_8$-e

(205)S. N. Kramer's interpretation of this text differs (*RA* 65 [1971] 26 n. 2): "The goddess, held captive in the Netherworld, is eager to be freed and to leave it for the world above (lines 1–9). With tears in her eyes she sends a messenger to plead with her mother (presumably Ningal) and her father Nanna (lines 10–23). The poet then continues to depict the goddess weeping for her city and temple that lay in ruins, presumably as a result of her disappearance into the Netherworld (lines 24–35), but ends on a note of comfort: her prayer is heard and she leaves the world below (lines 36–38)."

12. ga-ša-an-gir-gi$_4$-lu-ke$_4$ du$_{11}$-ga-na-ab me-na mu-un-du$_8$-e
13. la-bar-é-e ga-ša-an munus-sa$_6$-ga <du$_{11}$-ga-na-ab> me-na mu-un-du$_8$-e
14. ^{d}Nanna-ra giš-gi$_4$-ta du$_{11}$-ga-na-ab me-na mu-un-du$_8$-e
15. giš-gi$_4$-dagal-an$^{!}$-kù-ga-ta a-a-mu-ra du$_{11}$-ga-na-ab
16. me-na kù mu-un-tu$_9$tu mu-un-du$_8$-e me-na mu-un-du$_8$-e
17. me-na za mu-un-tu$_9$tu mu-un-du$_8$-e me-na mu-un-du$_8$-e
18. kù ì-tuk-a kù-mu ba-ti
19. za-gìn ì-tuk-a za-mu ba-ti
20. é-èš-da-mu igi-ni-šè ba-gul
21. urú-[è]š-da-mu igi-ni-šè ba-gul
22. [kù] ⸢a⸣-a-mu igi-ni-šè ba-pe-⸢el⸣
23. [za] ⸢a⸣-a-mu igi-ni-šè ⸢ba⸣-⸢i⸣-[ra]
24. [. . .] i-lu-nu-a-še ér àm-da-n[i-še$_8$-še$_8$]
25. [ga-ša-an]-⸢gir⸣-gi$_4$-lu-ke$_4$ i-lu-nu-a-še ér àm-d[a-ni-še$_8$-še$_8$]
26. [. . .] i-lu é-me-a [. . .]
27. [. . .]⸢x⸣[. . .]
28. eden-na a-še-er-ér-ra-ta e[den(?) . . .]
29. ama-ugu-mu ér-hul-aka-na me-⸢e⸣ [. . .]
30. me-e ^{d}En-líl-šè ga-àm-ši-gin a mu-⸢lu⸣-[mu ga-àm-du$_{11}^{?}$]
31. a urú-gul-a-mu ga-àm-ši-gin a mu-lu-[mu ga-àm-du$_{11}^{?}$]
32. é-gul-la urú-gul-la-mu zi-dè-e[š. . .]
33. šu-ni EL-ta im-ta-zur-zur$_{zu-ur-zu-ur}$ ér-gig ⸢ì⸣-[še$_8$-še$_8$]
34. gaba-ni ^{kuš}ub-kù-ga al-gul-e ér-gig ì-š[e$_8$-še$_8$]
35. ⸢síg⸣-ni ^{ú}numun-sar-ra ì-dúb-e ér-gig ì-⸢še$_8$⸣-[še$_8$]
36. u$_4$-bi-a e-⸢ne-èm⸣-bi giš ba-an-tuk-a-ta
37. EN-bànda ^{d}Ereš-ki-gal-la⸢ke⸣$_4$ nin$_9$-a-ni ⸢šu⸣ mu-un-na-ni-me-en
38. kù-zu-mu egí ga-ša-an-gir-gi$_4$-lu kur-ta nam-ta-è

ér-šem$_5$-ma-^{d}Nin-gir-gi$_4$-lu

. . .among the shoots I shed tears.
My clever one, the princess Ningirgilu!
The devastatrix of the mountain, the hierodule, Inanna!
My faithful princess, the lady of the Emuš!
Unmaibimal, the mother of the right breast!
The messenger of the house, the lady, the beautiful woman!
While(?) sitting . . . among the shoots,
. . .among the shoots in the clear sky,
. . .among the shoots on the earth,
upon the place where I stay silent, (I shed tears).

Passerby, speak to my mother! When will she release her?

Speak to Ningirgilu! When will she release her?
Speak to the messenger of the house, the lady, the beautiful woman! When will she release her?
From the marshlands speak to Nanna! "When will she release her?"
From the wide marshlands of holy An speak to my father!
"When will she release her, (my) silver (which) she heaped up? When will she release her?
When will she release her, (my) precious stones (which) she heaped up? When will she release her?
I who had silver, my silver has been . . .!
I who had lapis-lazuli, my precious stones have been. . .!
Before her(?) very eyes, my house of the ešda-barrel has been destroyed!
Before her(?) very eyes, my city of the ešda-barrel has been destroyed!
Before her(?) very eyes, (oh) my father, (my) [silver] has been debased!
Before her(?) very eyes, (oh) my father, (my) [precious stones] have been plundered!"

At the lament of the reposing one [. . .] sheds tears.
At the lament of the reposing one Ningirgilu sheds tears.
[. . .] a lament over our house [. . .].
[. . .]
In the steppe in sighs and tears [. . .].
My mother, while shedding sorrowful tears, (says), "I [shall. . .]!"
I shall go to Enlil! "Oh [my] men!" [shall I say].
"Oh my destroyed city!" I shall go to him! "Oh [my] men!" [shall I say].
"My destroyed house and city!" faithfu[lly. . .]

Her hands *have become heavy* . . . She cries bitter tears.
She destroys her breasts (as if beating) a drum. She cries bitter tears.
She pulls out her hair (like) reeds. She cries bitter tears.
On the very day when that word was heard
The. . .Ereškigal, caused her sister to go about (freely).
My clever one, the princess Ningirgilu, came out from the netherworld.

An eršemma of Ningirgilu

In the following eršemma, Inanna, lamenting the destruction of the Eanna-temple complex (Inanna's residence in Uruk) and of the gipar, (that part of this complex which was the residence of the en-priest and the entu-priestess), goes to plea for her city before Enlil. The fact that Inanna is referred to as "she who roams the netherworld" is a clue that the Eanna's ruination is an indirect result of Inanna's disappearance, her captivity by her sister, Ereškigal, in the netherworld. This is exactly the scenario in eršemma no. 79 in which Ningirgilu/Inanna is trapped in the netherworld, while her city is being ravaged in her absence. In that eršemma, Inanna finally receives Eršekigal's permission to go to Enlil in order that she ask him to end Uruk's misfortune. Our work, then, seems to be a continuation of the tale, for after Inanna's lament over Uruk (lines 1–35), she sorrowfully goes to Enlil (lines 36–38), pleading her case (lines 39 to 48). Enlil, apparently concerned for Inanna's welfare, asks what will happen to her (lines 49–54). But Inanna continues her account of the misery Enlil's terror has engendered.

Eršemma no. 32

Text: L. 1492 (ISET 1 pp. 221–222)

1. [a é-an-na a gi$_6$-par$_4$-kù]
2. [ga-ša-an-an-na-mèn   a é-an-na a gi$_6$-par$_4$-kù]
3. [ga-ša-an-é-an-na-mèn   a é-an-na a gi$_6$-par$_4$-kù]
4. [ga-ša-an-k]i-Zaba[lam^{ki}-mèn]   [a] é-an-˹na˺[a gi$_6$-par$_4$-kù]
5. [ga-ša-a]n-ki-sìg-mèn   a é-an-na a[gi$_6$-par$_4$-kù]
6. [ga]-ša-an-gi$_6$-par$_4$!-ra-mèn   a é-an-na a gi$_6$-p[ar$_4$!-kù]
7. ˹^{d}˺˹Da˺-da nu-nuz$_x$-sa$_6$-mèn   a é-an-na a gi$_6$-par$_4$!-kù
8. ^{d}Na-na-a dumu-˹šag$_5$˺-é-e-mèn   a é-an-na a gi$_6$-par$_4$!-kù
9. ga-ša-an-uru$_x$(EN)-gal-DU.DU-mèn   a é-an-na a gi$_6$-par$_4$!-kù
10. ù!-tuk-é-mu é an-ta ki-a gub-ba-mu
11. ma-˹x˺-mu še-eb an-úr-ta ki gi$_4$-ra-mu
12. é-mu é gál-lu-e na ma-rú-rú-a-mu
13. mu-gig-an-na-mèn ama$_5$-mu é-dur-an-ki-mu
14. ga-ša-an-é-an-na-mèn erim$_3$-mu gi$_6$-par$_4$!-imin-mu
15. mu-gig-an-na-mèn ma-é-mu èš é-an-na-mu
16. ga-ša-an-é-an-na-mèn ˹še˺-eb-Unu^{ki}-ga še-eb-Kul-aba(AB)^{ki}-mu
17. mu-gig-an-na-mèn ˹unú-šuba˺ ˹an-ta-sur˺-ra-mu
18. ga-ša-an-é-an-na-mèn é-bappir-e laḫtan $^{dug(?)}$˹x˺-[mu]
19. mu-gig-an-na-mèn ká-maḫ-é-na-ám-tar-ra-m[u]
20. ga-ša-an-é-an-na-mèn sig$_7$-i-bí-kù é-ta íl-l[a(?)-mu]
21. mu-gig-an-na-mèn dúr an-ta dúr ki-ta-mu
22. ga-ša-‹an›-é-an-na-mèn uš-ù-mu-un-di-ka-na-ág-˹x˺-[mu]
23. mu-gig-an-na-mèn kun-sag-˹maḫ˺(?) šà e$_4$ ku$_4$-ku$_4$-m[u]
24. ˹é˺(?) KA˹x x˺[. . .]˹x˺˹sù˺-ga-mu
25. ga-ša-an-[é-an-na-mèn . . .]˹x˺˹ub˺(?)-e-mu
26. mu-gig-a[n-na-mèn . . .]-˹e˺-mu

27. ⌜x⌝ an ⌜x⌝[. . .]⌜x⌝[. . .]
28. [x x] an⌜x⌝[. . .]
29. [. . .]⌜èš⌝(?) [. . .]
30. [. . .] TAR(?)⌜x⌝[. . .]
31. ga-ša-an-⌜é⌝-[an-na-mèn . . .]
32. mu-gig-an-⌜na-mèn⌝ ⌜x⌝[. . .]
33. ga-ša-an-é-an-na-mèn [. . .]
34. mu-gig-an-na-mèn ub-a ⌜x⌝[. . .]
35. ga-ša-an-é-an-na-mèn é-gal⌜x⌝[. . .]
36. uru$_x$(EN)-gal-DU.DU! ⌜x⌝[. . .]
37. uru$_x$(EN)-gal-DU.DU gi$_4$-ge ér-ra [. . .]
38. [ki(?)]-Zabalam^{ki} ⌜urú⌝(?) ^{d}[Mu-u]l-líl ba-⌜x⌝-an-[. . .]
39. [é(?)]-ib-gal é ⌜šu⌝[. . .]⌜šu⌝(?) ba-ab-du$_{11}$
40. [mu]-gig-an-na-mèn é-[la]-⌜ga⌝-me nu-me-a[-(mu)]
41. [ga-š]a-an-é-an-na-mèn urú-[la]-ga-me nu-me-a[-(mu)]
42. [mu]-gig-an-na-mèn é la!-la!-bi nu-mu-ni-gi$_4$-[a-(mu)]
43. [ga-š]a-an-é-an-na-mèn ama$_5$ ḫi-li-bi nu-mu-e-til-l[a-(mu)]
44. [é]-an-na-ta ur ⌜im⌝!-[ta]-è ur nu-zu-à[m]
45. [é]-an-na-ta mi-ir! im-ta-⌜è⌝ ⌜mi⌝!-⌜ir⌝ nu-⌜zu⌝-à[m]
46. ⌜é⌝-an-na-ta mu-lu im-ta-⌜è⌝[mu-l]u nu-z[u-àm]
47. é-an-na saḫar ba-da-dub-dub [saḫar ba-da]-šú-šú
48. é-an-na saḫar-gar-i$_7$-da-ke$_4$ [šu àm-ši]-⌜nigin⌝
49. u$_4$ é-za gù ba-ab-ra-a-ba za-[e me-a ì-tuš]-en
50. ama$_5$-za gù ba-ab-du$_{11}$-ga-ba za-⌜e⌝ [me-a ì-tuš-e]n
51. gù gi$_6$-ù-na ba-ab-ra-a-ba za-e me-a ì-[tuš-e]n
52. gù an-bir$_x$(NE) ma-ra-ni-ib-gi$_4$-a-ba za-e me-a ì-tuš!-e[n]
53. u$_4$ urú-za šu-ir-ra-a-ba za-e me-a ì-[tu]š-en
54. ⌜é⌝-za šu ba-e-lá-ba za-e me-a ì-tuš-en
55. ⌜un⌝(?) ní ba-da-te sim^{mušen}-gin$_7$ ba-dal-e
56. [mu(?)]-⌜lu⌝(?) dili-ba-an še-gur ri-ri ur$_5$-⌜gin$_7$⌝ mu-e-ak-e
57. [ì]-gul-gul a-gin$_7$ ì-gul-gul ní-zu a-gin$_7$! ì-⌜x⌝-[(x)]
58. [x]⌜x⌝ a-gin$_7$ ì-gul-gul ní-zu a-gin$_7$ ì-⌜x⌝-[(x)]
59. [. . .]-ra a-gin$_7$ mu-un-na-zé-èm ní-zu a-[gin$_7$ ì-x-(x)]
60. [. . . a-gi]n$_7$ mu-un-na-zé-èm [ní-zu a-gin$_7$ ì-x-(x)]
61. [. . .]⌜x⌝[. . .]

(break of a few lines)

a+62. [. . .](x)⌜x⌝mu-un-TÁL me[r](?)-⌜sig⌝(?)
a+63. [. . .](x)⌜x⌝mu-un-TÁL ⌜mer⌝(?)-[sig(?)]

ér-šem$_5$-ma-^{d}Inanna-kam!

* * *

[Oh Eanna! Oh holy gipar!
I am Inanna. Oh Eanna! Oh holy gipar!
I am the lady of the Eanna. Oh Eanna! Oh holy gipar!
I am the lady] of "the place"-Zabalam. Oh Eanna! [Oh holy gipar]!
I am the lady (who) shakes the earth. Oh Eanna! Oh [holy gipar]!
I am the lady of the gipar. Oh Eanna! Oh holy gipar!
I am Dada, the beautiful woman. Oh Eanna! Oh holy gipar!
I am Nanâ, the beautiful child of the house. Oh Eanna! Oh holy gipar!
I am the lady who roams the netherworld. Oh Eanna! Oh holy gipar!
The *genie(?)* (of) my house! My house which stands from the very heavens upon the earth!
. . . my . . .! My brickwork which *sinks* below the earth at the horizon!
My house! My house at whose opening stelae were erected for me!
I am the hierodule of heaven. My cella! My Eduranki!
I am the lady of the Eanna. My treasure-house! My Giparimin!
I am the hierodule of heaven. . . . my house! My shrine, Eanna!
I am the lady of the Eanna. My brickwork of Uruk and of Kulaba!
I am the hierodule of heaven. My ornaments of šuba- and antasurra-stones!
I am the lady of the Eanna. Oh the brewery! The beer-vat (and) the [. . .]-vessel (?)!
I am the hierodule of heaven. [My] great gate of the Enamtar!
I am the lady of the Eanna. [My] holy "eyebrow" which is raised above the house!
I am the hierodule of heaven. My seat in heaven and (my) seat upon earth!
I am the lady of the Eanna. My . . . the nation!
I am the hierodule of heaven. My great (?) reservoir into which water (continually) enters!
[. . .] house [. . .] my . . .
[I am] the lady [of the Eanna. . . .] my . . .
[I am] the hierodule [of heaven. . . .] my [. . .]
. . . [. . .]
[. . .]. .[. . .]
[. . .]. .[. . .]
[. . .]. .[. . .]
[I am] the lady of the Eanna. [. . .]
I am the hierodule of heaven. [. . .]
I am the lady of the Eanna. [. . .]
I am the hierodule of heaven. In the corner [. . .]
I am the lady of the Eanna. [. . .] the palace [. . .]

"She who roams the netherworld" [. . .]
"She who roams the netherworld," sick, in tears [. . .]
["The place"] Zabalam, the city (?) Enlil does not [. . .]
"Eibgal, the house [. . .] has been . . .

I am the hierodule of heaven. Our(?) *treacherous* house is no more!
I am the lady of the Eanna. Our(?) *treacherous* city is no more!
I am the hierodule of heaven. The house which is not sated with its joy (is no more)!
I am the lady of the Eanna. The cella, whose luxuriance is unending, (is no more)!
The . . . has gone out from the Eanna. He is no longer known (there).
The . . . has gone out from the Eanna. He is no longer known (there).
The . . . has gone out from the Eanna. He is no longer known (there).
Dust has been heaped on the Eanna; it is covered with dust.
Silt has accumulated at the Eanna."

"While the storm howls in your house, where are you going to stay?
While it roars in your cella, where are you going to stay?
While it howls (at) night, where are you going to stay?
While it screeches against you (at) noon, where are you going to stay?
While the storm is *attacking*(?) in your city, where are you going to stay?
While it is defiling your house, where are you going to stay?"

"The people(?) are afraid; they fly away like swallows.
(As) one who is (forced) to glean for (his) one measure of grain, thus, have you made me!
It destroys. Thus, does it destroy. Thus, does your *terror* . . .
[. . .] Thus, does it destroy. Thus, does your *terror* . . .
Thus [. . .] give to [. . .]. Thus, does your *terror* . . .
Thus, [. . .] give to [. . .]. [Thus, does your *terror* . . .]
[. . .]

(break of a few lines)

a+62. [. . .]. . . *storm(?).*
[. . .]. . . *storm(?).*"

It is an eršemma of Inanna.

Continuing the theme of Inanna's concern for her devastated Uruk is the following brief eršemma. The text consists solely of Inanna's lament, there being no narrative tale.

Eršemma no. 106

Text: CBS 475 (*BE* 30/1 no. 12 = *PBS* 10/2 15) 2–23

é-gul-la ki-bi me-na gi$_4$-gi$_4$-mu
nu-gig-an-na ^{d}Ga-ša-an-an-na-mèn
kur-gul-gul ga-ša-an-é-an-na-mèn
é ma-mú-da ma-dù-a-mu
urú ma-mú-da ma-dù-a-mu
é tùr amaš-gin$_7$ lu-lu-a-mu
e-zé-gin$_7$ amaš-gin$_7$ lu-lu-a-mu
bur-gul-e bur ba-an-gul-la-mu
za-gìn-dím-e za-gìn ba-an-dím-ma-mu
ká-bi-ta ki-u$_6$-di-mu
ki-šu-me-ša$_4$-na-ám-lú-ulù-mu
ma-ám-ma-ra-kur-kur-ra-mu
ì-dù-àm kur in-ga-dù-àm
ba-gul-gul kur ba-da-gul-gul
dam-ša$_6$-ga kur-re ba-da-ab-ga
dumu-ša$_6$-ga kur-re ba-da-ab-ga
ezen-gal-bi šu nu-du$_7$-du$_7$
me-gal-gal-bi é àm-gi$_4$
me-bi al-ur$_4$-ur$_4$ ub ba-ra-an-gub
billudu-bi ám ba-da-an-kúr bala-bi ba-kúr-kúr
é-zi-da bala$^{!}$-bi bala$^{!}$-kúr-ra šu-bal-ak-a-bi
é-zi a mu-gi-ga nam-me-a líl-àm ba-ni-in-ku$_4$

* * *

My destroyed house which, (who knows) when, will be restored!
I am the hierodule of heaven, Inanna!
I am the devastatrix of the mountain, the lady of the Eanna!
My house which was built for me in a dream!
My city which was built for me in a dream!
My house which had been abundant like the cattle pen and the sheepfold!
My (house) which had been abundant like the sheep, like the sheepfold!
My (house whose) stonecutter used to carve bowls!
My (house whose) lapidary used to make jewelry!
My (house) from(?) its gate was a place of marvel!
My (house), the cult center of mankind!
My (house), the storehouse of all the lands!

(When) it was built, the land was also built up.
(But when) it was destroyed, so, too, was the land destroyed.

The enemy has carried off the good spouse.

The enemy has carried off the good child.
Its great feast is no longer carried out.
Its great "me's" have been locked up in the house.
Its "me's" (which) had been gathered unto it, do not stand in the corner.
Its rites have become unfamiliar; its terms of duty have been altered.
The terms of duty of the faithful house have been changed into altered terms.
The faithful house which no longer *says(?) "Oh hierodule!"* It has become haunted.

The tale of Inanna's ill-fated descent to the netherworld, resulting in the demons seizing her husband, the shepherd Dumuzi, as her substitute, was a fertile source for the authoring of new works which retold, elaborated upon, or alluded to this story. The most complete and informative version of this adventure was edited by S. N. Kramer, who titled the composition "Inanna's Descent to the Netherworld." This work told of Inanna's entrapment in the netherworld, her release, the demons' pursuit of Dumuzi and finally Dumuzi's faithful sister, Geštinanna's, volunteering to serve as Dumuzi's substitute. A recently edited composition, "Dumuzi's Dream" (the modern title stems from a dream in which Dumuzi is forewarned of his impending peril), also recounts the demons' pursuit of Dumuzi. The following four eršemmas also are based upon this pursuit of Dumuzi, with the same cast: the loving mother, the faithful sister, the revengeful wife and, of course, the demons.

Eršemma no. 97[206]

The work begins by describing Inanna's sorrow over Dumuzi, followed by her lament for Dumuzi. Although according to other works, Inanna was responsible for her husband's death, nonetheless, she is portrayed here, as being overcome by grief once he has died. With the conclusion to the lament, the poet recapitulates the events leading up to Dumuzi's death. This eršemma parallels those portions of "Dumuzi's Dream" which relate of the

(206)Sections of this text were translated by S. N. Kramer, *Sacred Marriage Rite,* 127 ff. and more recently by Th. Jacobsen, *The Treasures of Darkness* pp. 49 ff. Both of these translations contain ideas and insights into the work. Unfortunately, lacking their text editions and commentary, it is very difficult to compare our translation to theirs, since their translations may be based upon other texts or interpretations of words unfamiliar to us. We find ourselves in the predicament of wanting to alert the reader to the great variances in the three interpretations, yet not being in a position to offer the scholarly reasoning behind each interpretation. Therefore, we can only alert the reader that two other varying interpretations of this work exist and that they should be read in conjunction with ours.

demons pursuing Dumuzi, who then prays to Utu, his brother-in-law, to change him into a four-legged animal that he might escape his pursuers. A notable difference between the two versions is the order of events. In our eršemma the demons surround the sheepfold, each one entering and creating havoc. Dumuzi escapes and prays to Utu. According to "Dumuzi's Dream," however, the order is reversed. The section in which Dumuzi asks for Utu's help occurs first. Later the demons enter the sheepfold, destroy it and successfully capture Dumuzi. Our work also concludes with the death of Dumuzi. Although the final events are not spelled out, it is suggested that when Dumuzi fled for protection from the demons, he foolishly went to his wife, Inanna, rather than to his mother or sister. Inanna, apparently, turned him over to the demons. At the conclusion, Dumuzi is taken by boat to the netherworld.

There are two aspects of this eršemma which we wish to note in particular. The first concerns the burial of Dumuzi. We read that he was buried at the Emuš in Badtibira, Badtibira being the original center of the Dumuzi cult in Sumer. In the "Myth of Inanna and Bilulu," which also discusses the death of Dumuzi (though the circumstances are entirely different), Dumuzi is killed in the steppe, yet his body is returned to his birthplace (=Badtibira?) by a bird for burial. Thus, both works inform us that Dumuzi was killed away from his native city, Badtibira, and that his body was returned for burial.[207]

The second aspect involves the betrayal of Dumuzi by his friends. In our eršemma the demons claim that his friends (Dumuzi is a shepherd and his

(207)There are many texts based upon the death of Dumuzi by the galla-demons. Yet one text, "The myth of Inanna and Bilulu," (Th. Jacobsen, *Image of Tammuz* 52 ff.) differs entirely from these, in that Dumuzi's death was caused by the old woman Bilulu, her son Girgire and SIR.RU of the haunted steppe. We suggest the possibility that this latter work, so different from all other Dumuzi texts, is a mythological account of the death of Ur-Nammu, king of Ur. We believe there is a general similarity in tone and terms between this work and the composition "The death of Ur-Nammu" (S. N. Kramer, *JCS* 21 [1967] 104 ff.). More significantly, note "The death of Ur-Nammu" 59–61:

> [ki]-lul-la Ur-^{d}Nammu dug-gaz-gin$_7$ e$_4$ ba-ni-in-tag$_4$-aš
> [. . .]-a-ni tum$_{11}$-u$_4$-sù-da-gin$_7$ gal-bi im-ši-gub
> [. . .]nu-gá-gá e$_4$ nì-šà-ge šu nu-gíd-i im-me
> "When(?) in a treacherous(?) place Ur-Nammu ran out of water like a broken jug,
> his [. . .] stood up solidly against him(?) like an ancient wind.
> [. . .] was not there. He could not reach the water, that which he craved. . . ."

(For e$_4$ tag$_4$, "to run out of water," see S. Cohen *ELA* commentary to 262. For e$_4$ šu gíd cf. Suruppak line 56.) If our interpretation of this difficult passage is correct, then Ur-Nammu died of thirst on his campaign. This would then explain the puzzling punishment inflicted by Inannna upon Bilulu, namely, that she be turned into a waterskin to provide water for him who is in the steppe.

friends obviously are involved with shepherding), the lead-sheep, the ram, and the shepherd, all will betray Dumuzi. So, too, is Dumuzi's betrayal by a friend prominent in "Dumuzi's Dream." Although Geštinanna refuses to divulge her brother's hiding place, Dumuzi's friend (unnamed) succumbs to a bribe and reveals it to the demons. And, of course, pervading the entire tale is the theme of betrayal of Dumuzi by his own wife, Inanna.

Text A: VAT 617 (*VAS* 2 no. 2 obv.-rev. iii 21)
B: *RA* 8 161–169 (photo in *RA* 8 and H. Hartmann, *Die Musik der sumerischen Kultur,* Frankfurt am Main 1960 p. 342)
C: AO 7697 (*TCL* 16 pl. 144)

1.	A	i	1)	en gig-ga-bi na-ám-dam-ma-na
	B	i	1)	[e]-en gig-ga-bi na-ám-dam-a-na
	C		1)	[. . .]-ám-da-ma-na
2.	A	i	2)	ga-ša-an-an-na-ra na-ám-dam-ma-⌈na⌉
	B	i	2)	ga-ša-an-an-na-ke$_4$ na-ám-dam-a-na
	C		2)	[. . .]-ám-da-ma-na
3.	A	i	3)	ga-ša-an-é-an-na-ra na-ám-dam-ma-⌈na⌉
	B	i	3)	ga-ša-an-é-an-na-ke$_4$ na-ám-dam-a-na
	C		3)	[. . .]-⌈na⌉-ra na-ám-da-<ma>-na
4.	B	i	4)	ga-ša-an-ki-Unu^{ki}-ga-ke$_4$ na-ám-dam-a-na
5.	B	i	5)	ga-ša-an-ki-Zabalam^{ki}-ke$_4$ na-ám-dam-a-na
6.	A	i	4)	ú na-ám-dam-ma-na ú na-ám-dunu-[na]
	B	i	6)	ù na-ám-dam-a-na ù na-ám-dumu-na
	C		4)	[. . .]-ma-na ù nu-ù-dumu-na
7.	A	i	5)	ú na-ám-é-a-na ú na-ám-urú-[na]
	B	i	7)	ù na-ám-é-a-na ù na-ám-urú-na
	C		5)	[. . .]-mi-ia ù na-ám-uri$_3$-na
8.	A	i	6)	dam-dab$_5$-ba-na dumu-dab$_5$-ba-[na]
	B	i	8)	dam-dab$_5$-ba-a-na dumu-dab$_5$-ba-a-na
	C		6)	dam-da-pa-na du$_{13}$(DUMU)-mu-da-pa-na
9.	A	i	7)	dam-ug$_5$-ga-na dumu-ug$_5$-ga-na
	B	i	9)	dam-ug$_5$-ga-a-na dumu-ug$_5$-ga-na
	C		7)	dam-mu-ga-na du$_{13}$(DUMU)-mu-ù-ga-na
10.	A	i	8)	dam Unu^{ki}-šè ba-šè-dab$_5$-ba-na
	B	i	10)	dam Unu^{ki}-šè ba-šè-dab$_5$-ba-na
	C		8)	dam ù-[nu]$^{ki(?)}$-ši ba-ši-da-pa-na

11.	A	i	9)	Unu^{ki}-šè! Kul-aba$_4$^{ki}-šè! ba-šè!-ug$_5$-ga-na
	B	i	11)	Unu^{ki}-šè Kul-aba$_4$^{ki}-šè ba-šè-ug$_5$-ga-na
	C		9)	ù-nu⸢x⸣ [. . .] x-ab-ši ba-ši-ù-ga-na
12.	A	i	10)	é-urú-zé-ba^{ki} nu-tu-a-na
	B	i	12)	e$_4$-urú-zé-ba^{ki} nu-tu$_5$-a-na
	C		10)	é-⸢urú-zé-ba⸣ nu-tu-a-na
13.	A	i	11)	na-ám-É.NUN-na-na nu-su-ub-a-na
	B	i	13)	na-ma-É.NUN-na nu-su-ub-ba-a-na
	C		11)	[. . .]-⸢x⸣-pa-na
14.	A	i	12)	amalu ama-ni-gin$_7$ nu-gin-na-a-na
	B	i	14)	amalu ama-ni-gin$_7$ nu-um-gin-na-a-na
	C		12)	[. . .]-na
15.	A	i	13)	ki-sikil uru^{ki}-ni-gin$_7$ síg nu-zu-a-na
	B	i	15)	ki-sikil-urú-na-ka síg nu-zé-ba-a-na
	C		13)	[. . .]-na
16.	A	i	14)	guruš uru^{ki}-ni-gin$_7$ sa nu-<x>-a-na
	B	i	16)	guruš-urú-na-ka gaba nu-sìg-ga-a-na
17.	A	i	15)	kur-gar-ra urú^{ki}-ni-gin$_7$ gìri nu-ak-a-na
	B	i	17)	kur-gar-ra-urú-na-ka gíri nu-ak-a-na
18.	A	i	16)	ì-lum-sag-gá-a ⸢nu⸣-kal-a-na
	B	i	18)	ì-lum-sag-gá nu-kal-la-a-na
19.	B	i	19)	ga-ša-an-an-na mu-ud-na-tur-ra-na ér-gig ì-še$_8$-e
20.	A	i	17)	x dam-zé-ba da[m]-mu ba-gin
	B	i	20)	u$_4$ dam-zé-ba dam-mu ba-gin
21.	A	i	18)	x dumu-zé-ba ⸢dumu⸣-mu ba-gin
	B	i	21)	u$_4$ dumu-zé-ba dumu-mu ba-gin
22.	A	i	19)	[dam]-⸢mu⸣ u$_4$-sag-⸢gá⸣ ba-e-gin
	B	i	22)	dam-mu ú-sag-gá <ba>-e-gin
23.	A	i	20)	[dumu]-⸢mu⸣ u$_4$-eger-ra ba-e-gin
	B	i	23)	dumu-mu ú-eger-ra <ba>-e-gin
24.	A	i	21)	[x] u$_4$ ke-en-ke-ne gin-na-mu u$_5$-a ba-e-gin
	B	i	24)	dam-mu ú kin-kin-da gin-na-a-ni ú-e ba-ni-ib-gi$_4$
25.	A	i	22)	[dumu-mu é ke]-⸢en⸣-[ke]-⸢ne⸣ [. . .]-⸢ne⸣ gin-na-mu gin-na-mu é-bé ḫa-ba-da-ab-z[é-èm]

	B	i	25)	dumu-mu e$_4$ kin-kin-da gin-na-a-ni e$_4$-e ba-an-zé-èm-mà
26.	A	i	23)	[. . .]⸢x⸣dul-dul-la-gin$_7$ urú-ta ba-ra-è-a
	B	i	26)	mu-ud-na-mu-šè(?) nim-dul$^{!?}$-dul-la-gin$_7$ urú-ta ba-ra-è
27.	A	i	24)	[. . .]⸢x⸣dul-dul-la-gin$_7$ urú-ta ba-ra-è-a
	B	i	27)	nim ú-sag-gá nim-dul-la-gin$_7$ urú-ta ba-ra-è
28.	A	i	25)	[. . .]⸢x⸣la e-ne ba-an-su-ru-ne-eš-a
29.	A	i	26)	[. . .]⸢x⸣ ka e-ne ba-an-. . .
30.	A	i	27)	[. . .]⸢x⸣ ba-an-su-ru-ne-⸢eš$^{!}$-a⸣$^{!}$
31.	A	i	28)	[. . .e]-ne <ba-an>-su-⸢ru⸣(?)-⸢ne⸣(?)-eš-a
32.	A	i	29)	[. . .]⸢e⸣-ne ⸢ba⸣-an-. . .
33.	A	i	30)	[. . .] ba-. . .
	B	ii	1)	u$_4$-bi-a [. . .]
34.	A	i	31)	[. . .] ⸢ba⸣-an-. . .
	B	ii	2)	amaš-kù [. . .]
35.	A	i	32)	[. . . ba]-⸢an⸣-. . .
	B	ii	3)	ma-aš-kù [. . .]
36.	A	i	33)	[. . .] ⸢x⸣
	B	ii	4)	du$_8$-du$_8$-kù ⸢a⸣? [. . .]
37.	A	i	34)	[. . .]-du$_8$
	B	ii	5)	gal$_5$-lá-tur-tur gal$_5$-l[á-. . .]
38.	A	i	35)	[. . .]-e
	B	ii	6)	gal$_5$-lá guruš-e imin-bi [. . .]
39.	A	i	36)	[. . .]-bal-e
	B	ii	7)	gal$_5$-lá ^{d}Dumu-zi-dè imin-b[i. . .]
40.	A	i	37)	[. . .]-⸢ra⸣?-e
41.	A	i	38)	[. . . amaš líl-lá] al-dù
42.	A	i	39)	[. . .]⸢x⸣ e
43.	A	i	40)	[. . .]⸢x⸣e
44.	A	i	41)	[. . .]⸢e⸣
45.	A	i	42)	[. . .]⸢e⸣
45a.	A	i	43)	[. . .]⸢e⸣
45b.	A	i	44)	[. . . amaš líl-lá al]-dù
45c.	A	i	45)	[. . .]⸢e⸣
45d.	A	i	46)	[. . .]
45e.	A	i	47)	[. . .]

40′.	B	ii	8)	gal$_5$-lá dub-sag amaš-e ku$_4$-r[a-e . . .]
41′.	B	ii	9)	gal$_5$-lá min-kam-ma amaš-e ku$_4$-r[a-e . . .] ga-sikil [. . .]
42′.	B	ii	10)	gal$_5$-lá eš$_5$-kam-ma amaš-e ku$_4$-ra-e [. . .] e$_4$-sikil ⸢x⸣[. . .]
43′.	B	ii	11)	gal$_5$-lá limmu-kam-ma amaš-e ku$_4$-ra-e ⸢x⸣-e (. . .) amaš líl-e ba-an-gar
44′.	B	ii	12)	gal$_5$-lá iá-kam-ma amaš-e ku$_4$-ra-e uš-gíd-da saḫar mu-un-si-si-ga
45′.	B	ii	13)	gal$_5$-lá àš-kam-ma amaš-e ku$_4$-ra-e ám-GAR⸢x⸣[. . .]amaš líl-«líl»-e ba-an-gar
46.	A	ii	1)	imin-kam-ma amaš mu-un-ku$_4$-re-en-na
	B	ii	14)	gal$_5$-lá imin-kam-ma amaš-e ku$_4$-ra-e
47.	A	ii	2)	[ì]-lum mu-lu nú-a ù-àm-mi-ni-in-zi-zi
	B	ii	14)	ì-lum mu-lu nú-a ù-a mi-[ni-in-zi-zi]
48.	B	ii	15)	^{d}Dumu-zi mu-lu nú-a ù-a mi-ni-[in-zi-zi]
49.	A	ii	3)	⸢dam⸣-ga-ša-an-an-ka mu-lu nú-a ù-àm-mi-ni-in-zi-zi
	B	ii	16)	dam-kù-ga-ša-an-an-ka mu-lu nú-a ù-a m[i-ni-in-zi-zi]
50.	A	ii	4)	⸢lugal⸣-mu me-e-ši-re-re-en-dè-en zi-ga im-me-e-zu
	B	ii	17)	lugal-mu mu-e-šè-re$_7$-en-dè-en zi-ga gin-[mu-e-da]
51.	A	ii	5)	^{d}Dumu-zi-dè me-e-ši-re-re-en-dè-en zi-ga
	B	ii	18)	^{d}Dumu-zi-da mu-e-šè-re$_7$-en-dè-en zi-ga gi[n-mu-e-da]
52.	A	ii	6)	dam-ga-ša-an-an-ka dumu$^{!}$-$^{d!}$Zé-er-tur-ra zi-ga im-me-e-zu
	B	ii	19)	dam-^{d}Inanna-ka dumu-^{d}Zé-er-tur-r[a-ke$_4$] zi-ga gin-mu-e-da
53.	A	ii	7)	u$_8$ lu-lu šeš-ama-^{d}Mu-tin-na zi-ga im-me-e-zu
	B	ii	20)	ú lu-lu šeš-ama-^{d}Mu-tin-na zi-ga gin-[mu-e-da]
54.	A	ii	8)	u$_8$-zu al-dib sila$_4$-zu al-rig$_7$ zi-ga
	B	ii	21)	u$_8$-zu al-dib sila$_4$-zu al-rig$_7$ zi-ga [gin-mu-e-da]
55.	A	ii	9)	ùz-zu al-dib máš-zu al-rig$_7$ zi-ga
	B	ii	22)	ùz-zu al-dib máš-zu al-rig$_7$ zi-[ga gin-mu-e-da]

56. A ii 10) men-kù sag-zu um-te-gál sag-su-zu gin-na
B ii 23) men-kù sag-za um-te-gál [. . .]

57. A ii 11) ^{túg}ba-kù bar-zu um-te-gál bar-su-zu gin-na
B ii 24) ^{túg}ma$_6$-ku bar-za um-te-[gál . . .]

58. A ii 12) [gidri]-kù šu-zu um-te-gál šu-su-zu gin-na
B ii 25) ^{giš}gidri-kù šu-za um-te-[gál . . .]

59. A ii 13) kuš-e-sír-kù giri$_3$-zu um-te-gál giri$_3$-su-zu gin-na
B iii 1) kuš-e-sír-kù me-ra-za um-te-gál [. . .]

60. A ii 14) ù-mu-un íb-ta-è-a amaš-a-na šu nu-TU-TU-dè
B iii 2) ù-mu-un ib-ta-è [. . .]

61. A ii 15) [^{d}]Dumu-zi íb-ta-è-a amaš-a-na šu nu-TU-TU-dè
62. A ii 16) ⌈sipa⌉? ⌈nam⌉-mu-dib-dib-dè-en da-e
gi$_4$-in-BI-gub
63. A ii 17) ⌈^{d}⌉?[Dumu]?-⌈zi⌉? nam-mu-dib-dib-dè-en da-e
gi$_4$-in-BI-gub
64. A ii 18) ⌈x-x⌉-kù-mu šu-si-ga-mu da-e gi$_4$-in-BI-gub
65. A ii 19) [^{d}Utu(?)]-an-na ka pa BU ra-mu da-e gi$_4$-in-BI-gub
66. A ii 20) ⌈x⌉(x)⌈x⌉-kù-^{d}Inanna šu-gar-gar-ra-mu da-e
67. A ii 21) ⌈ga⌉-mu-un-na-an-gub-bé
ga-mu-un-na-an-gub-bé
68. A ii 22) ⌈^{d}Utu⌉(?)-an-na-ra šu-n[i mu]-da-an-zi
69. A ii 23) [x]-mu-me-en ^{d}⌈Utu⌉? [. . .]⌈x x⌉-ga-mu-me-en
70. A ii 24) [šu-m]u šu-[maš-dà na-me-e]-⌈gi$_4$⌉
70a. A ii 25) «šu-[mu šu-maš-dà na-me-e-g]i$_4$»
71. A ii 26) [me-re-mu me-r]e-⌈maš-dà⌉ ⌈na-x-me-e⌉-g[i$_4$]
72. A ii 27) ⌈gal$_5$⌉-⌈lá⌉-e-na gi$_4$-ba-e-dè-kar
nam-m[a-ni-i]b-dab$_5$-ne
73. A ii 28) [ka]r?-⌈kar⌉?-a-ni-šè šà-ne-ša$_4$ ḫu-mu-un-⌈bal⌉

74. A ii 29) šu-mu šu-maš-dà na-me-e-gi$_4$
B iii 17) [. . .]-⌈gi$_4$⌉?

75. A ii 30) me-re-mu me-re-maš-dà na-me-e-gi$_4$
B iii 18) [. . .]-⌈gi$_4$⌉?

76. A ii 31) gal$_5$-lá-e-na gi$_4$-ba-e-dè-kar numun-na-ḫa-ze
B iii 19) [. . .]-è-dè

77. A ii 32) ^{d}Utu<A>.IGI-ni-šè šu ba-ši-in-ti
B iii 20) [. . .]-ma-ḫa-zu-ù (x)

78. A ii 33) igi-a šu bi-il$_5$-lá šeg$_9$-bar-ra ba-a[b]-gi$_4$
B iii 21) [. . .] a ba-an-gi$_4$

79.	A	ii	34)	máš-mi-mi-gi máš a-ba gin-na-an-ni
	B	iii	22)	[. . .] ma-a a-ba gin-na-an-[ni]
80.	A	ii	35)	máš-gin$_7$ šu mu-un-na-ak-e máš a-ba šu mu-a-BI
	B	iii	23)	[. . .] ma-a a-ba ⸢x⸣⸢a⸣? [. . .]
81.	A	ii	36)	tu^{mušen} ne-te-a ù-še-eg-e bíl-lá
	B	iii	24)	túg ní-te-ni ^{giš}ú-GÍR bí-in-[lá]
82.	A	ii	37)	íb-lá ne-te-a pár-ím-e bíl-lá
	B	iii	25)	^{túg}íb-lá ní-te-ni pár-ím-ma bí-in-[lá]
83.	A	ii	38)	gal$_5$-lá gal$_5$-lá-ra igi ḫé-em-ma-da-an-zi
	B	iii	26)	gal$_5$-lá gal$_5$-lá-ra igi ḫé-em-ma-d[a-an-zi]
84.	A	ii	39)	gal$_5$-lá-tur-ra gal$_5$-lá-gal-la gù mu-un-na-dé-e
	B	iii	27)	gal$_5$-lá-tur-e gal$_5$-lá-gal-e gù mu-un-[. . .]
85.	A	ii	40)	gal$_5$-lá-e gal$_5$-lá-tab-ba-na gù mu-un-na-dé-e
	B	iii	28)	gal$_5$-lá-e gal$_5$-lá-dab$_5$^{tab}-ba-né gù mu-u[n-. . .]
86.	A	ii	41)	guruš lú me-e-dè-⸢kar⸣-ra-na sa ab-ra-mu-ni-du$_{11}$
	B	iii	29)	guruš mu-lu mu-e-dè-kar-ra sá ba-[. . .]
87.	A	ii	42)	^{d}Dumu-zi lú me-e-dè-kar-ra-na sa ab-ra-mu-ni-du$_{11}$
	B	iii	30)	^{d}Dumu-zi mu-lu mu-e-dè-kar-[. . .]
88.	A	ii	43)	e-ri-a ka-mu-ni-in-di-be$_8$-en-de-en
	B	iii	31)	e-ri-a ga-mu-ni-[. . .]
89.	A	ii	44)	mu-lu-e-ri-a-ke$_4$ me-e-de-⸢en⸣-ḫa-ze
	B	iii	32)	lú-e-ri-a-ke$_4$ m[u-. . .]
90.	A	ii	45)	pár-ím-ri-a ka-mu-ni-in-di-be$_8$-en-de-en
	B	iii	33)	pa$_4$-e-ri-a ga-mu-[. . .]
91.	A	ii	46)	mu-lu-pár-ím-ri-a-ke$_4$ me-e-de-en-ḫa-ze
	B	iii	34)	lú-pa$_4$-e-ri-a-ke$_4$ [. . .]
92.	A	iii	1)	[udu-s]ag-gá ka-mu-ni-in-di-be$_8$-en-de-en
	B	iii	35)	udu-sag-gá [. . .]
93.	A	iii	2)	[máš-s]ag ku-li-na gi$_4$-me-e-da-LI-na
	B	iii	36)	máš-sag [. . .]
94.	A	iii	3)	[udu-]eger-ra ka-mu-ni-in-di-be$_8$-en-de-en
	B	iv	1)	udu-eger-ra ga-mu-ni-in-dab$_5$-bé-en-dè-en
95.	A	iii	4)	udu-u$_5$-a ku-li-na gi$_4$-me-e-da-LI-na
	B	iii	37)	udu-ua$_4$(AMAŠ) ku-li-[. . .]

96. A iii 5) udu-dul$_4$-a ka-mu-ni-in-di-be$_8$-en-de-en
B iii 38) udu-súb-a [. . .]

97. A iii 6) ka-ab-ús ku-li-na gi$_4$-me-e-da-LI-na
B iv 2) ga-ab-ús ku-li-ni ga-mu-un-da-[. . .]

98. B iv 3) ⸢ug⸣-gu$_7$-e ga-[. . .]

99. B iv 4) ⸢ug⸣⸢x⸣e [. . .]

100. A iii 7) ga-DU-dè-en ga-àm-ši-re$_7$-en-dè-en

101. A iii 8) am ú-lu-lu a-aš-ši e-ne-DU
B iv 5) am IŠI RA [. . .]

102. A iii 9) úr-ama-ugu-na tur-tur-ra-ka šu
gú-mu-un-DI-en-na
B iv 6) úr-ama-[. . .]

103. A iii 10) tur-tur-ama-ugu-na ama-arḫuš-a-ke$_4$ arḫuš
mu-un-na-ab-bé
B iv 7) ama-[. . .]

104. A iii 11) úr-nin$_9$-a-ni nin$_9$-arḫuš-a-ke$_4$ arḫuš
mu-un-na-ab-bé
B iv 8) ama [. . .]

105. A iii 12) úr-MUNUS.ÚS.DAM-a-ni ^{d}Inanna-ke$_4$ šu
gú-mu-un-de-en-na
B iv 9) ú[r-. . .]

106. A iii 13) ^{d}Inanna u$_4$ gù-dúb-dúb-bé gù mu-un-ši-ib-ra-ra
B iv 10) ⸢x⸣[. . .]

107. A iii 14) an u$_4$-ta-àm ki u$_4$-ta-àm
B iv 11) ⸢x⸣[. . .]

108. B iv 12) ⸢x⸣[. . .]

109. B iv 13) ⸢x⸣[. . .]

110. B iv 14) ⸢x⸣[. . .]

111. B iv 15) ⸢x⸣[. . .]

112. A iii 15) Unu^{ki}-ga sig$_4$-bi ba-sì? Unu^{ki}-ra igi-ni-šè
B iv 16) Unu^{ki}-ga [. . .]

113. A iii 16) ^{giš}ḫašḫur-e-gu-la banšur$_2$ -é-mùš-a-ka
B iv 17) ^{giš}ḫašḫur-e-gu-[la. . .]

114. A iii 17) ki-bi-a guruš ^{giš}má-gul-gul e$_4$-kur-ra ì-dé
B iv 19) ki-bi-a [. . .]

115. A iii 18) dam-ga-ša-an-an-ka ^{giš}má-gul-gul e$_4$-kur-ra ì-dé
B iv 19) dam-kù-ga-ša-an-an-k[a. . .]-dé

116. A iii 19) u$_5$ nu-me-en-na u$_5$ ba-an-da-bal-a
B iv 20) ú nu-me-a [. . .]-gu$_7$

117. A iii 20) ga nu-me-en-⸢na⸣ dug![photo ga(?)] ba-an-da-gaz
B iv 21) e$_4$ nu-me-a [. . .]-da-nag

118. B iv 22) é tùr nu-me-a ⸢líl⸣(?)-[lá(?)] ba-an-dù

119. B iv 23) ùr-e-zé nu-me-a sa ba-an-lá

120. A iii 21) gal$_5$-lá ^{gi}[. . .]x nu-me-a zà-ga-ne$^{(?)}$nam(?)-di(?)-be$_8$(?)-ne
B iv 24) gal$_5$-lá ^{giš}ukur nu-me-a zà-ga-a-na ba-an-dab$_5$-bé-eš

A: ⸢113⸣ mu-bi-im
B: [mu-bi 10]7 ér-šem$_5$-ma-^{d}Inanna ù ^{d}Dumu-zi

How horrible! The fate of her spouse!
(How horrible) for Inanna! The fate of her spouse!
For the lady of the Eanna the fate of her spouse!
For the lady of "the place"-Uruk the fate of her spouse!
For the lady of "the place"-Zabalam the fate of her spouse!
Not only the fate of her spouse, but also the fate of her child!
Not only the fate of her house, but also the fate of her city!
(The fate) of her captured spouse, of her captured child,
of her dead spouse, of her dead child,
of her spouse who was taken from Uruk,
of him who was (taken) from Uruk and Kulaba by death,
of him whom the waters of Eridu did not bathe,
of him whom the alkali of the *agrun* did not scrub,
of him to whom his personal goddess, (who was) like his own mother, did not come,
of him for whom hair was not pulled out among the maidens of his city,
of him for whom the young man of his city did not beat (his) chest,
of him for whom the *kurgarru*-(dancer) of his city. . .,
of him. . .!

Over her young husband Inanna sheds bitter tears.

"*When* the sweet spouse, my spouse, went away,
when the sweet child, my child, went away,
my spouse went among the early pastures,
my child went among the later pastures.
My spouse, seeking pasture, was killed in the pastures.
My child, seeking water, was delivered up at the waters.
(They) who like a cover of flies came out from the city against my spouse,
who came out from the city like the flies which cover the early pasture
they who went [. . .],
they who went [. . .],
they who went [. . .],
they who went [. . .],
they who went [. . .]."
On that day they who went [. . .],
they who went [to] the holy sheepfold,
they who went [to] the holy . . .
[. . .] holy . . .

The younger demons [looked(?) at the older] demons.
All seven demons *called out* "Lad!"
All seven demons [*called out*] "Dumuzi!"

The first demon to enter the sheepfold [. . .].
The second demon to enter the sheepfold [. . .] the pure milk.
The third demon to enter the sheepfold [. . .] the pure water.
The fourth demon to enter the sheepfold [. . .] and made the sheepfold haunted.
The fifth demon to enter the sheepfold filled the storehouse with dust.
The sixth demon to enter the sheepfold [. . .] . . . and made the sheepfold haunted.
The seventh demon to enter the sheepfold
wakes the honored one from (his) sleep.
He wakes Dumuzi, who is sleeping, from (his) sleep.
He wakes the spouse of holy Inanna, who is sleeping, from (his) sleep.

"My king, we have come for you! Get up and come with us!
Dumuzi, we have come for you! Get up and come with us!
Spouse of Inanna, son of Sirtur, get up and come with us!
Tender of sheep, brother of Amageštinanna, get up and come with us!
Your ewes are seized! Your lambs are ravaged! Get up and come with us!
Your goats are seized! Your kids are ravaged! Get up and come with us!
Remove the holy crown from your head! Go (away) bareheaded!
Remove the holy raiment from your body! Go (away) naked!
Remove the holy scepter from your hand! Go (away) empty-handed!
Remove the holy sandals from your feet! Go (away) barefooted!"

The lord, who has escaped, is not *apprehended* in his sheepfold.
Dumuzi, who has escaped, is not *apprehended* in his sheepfold.
"*So that I, the shepherd,* should not be captured, let him stand at (my) side!
So that I, Dumuzi, should not be captured, let him stand at (my) side!
Let my holy . . ., my . . . stand at (my) side!
Let [Utu(?)]-of-heaven, my . . ., stand at (my) side!
Let [. . .] (of) holy Inanna, my one who is kind, stand at (my) side!
I shall stand before him! I shall stand before him!"

He raised his hands to Utu-of-heaven:
"You are my [. . .]. Utu, you are my [. . .].

You should turn my hands into the 'hands' of a gazelle!
You should turn my feet into the 'feet' of a gazelle!
Let me escape the demons! They should not catch me!"
. . . he uttered his petition (again):
"You should turn my hands into the 'hands' of a gazelle!
You should turn my feet into the 'feet' of a gazelle!
Let me escape the demons! They should not seize me!"

Utu accepted his tears.
He stretched (his) hand over (his) eyes and was transformed into a boar.
. . . A kid! Who has ever gone (so)?
He causes him to *act* like a kid! A kid! Who has ever *acted* (so)?
He himself stretched his garment over a thornbush.
He stretched his belt over the ground.

One demon looked at the other demon.
The small demon speaks to the big demon.
The demon speaks to his companion:
"The lad who has escaped us has not *succeeded*!
Dumuzi, who has escaped us, has not *succeeded*!
Let us grab him in the desert!
The-man-of-the-desert will seize him with us.
Let us grab him (among) the ditches of the desert!
The-man-of-the-ditches-of-the-steppe will seize him with us.
Let us grab him among the front sheep!
The lead-kid of his friend will . . . with us.
Let us grab him among the rear sheep!
The ram of his friend will . . . with us.
Let us grab him among the shepherds!
The sheep-herder, his friend, will . . . with us.
Let us [grab him] among the *feeding(?) lions(?)*!
The . . . *lion(?)* will [. . . with us].

Let's go! Let's go get him!"

The bull. . .
Indeed he. . .in the lap of his mother, Ṣirtur.
Ṣirtur, his mother, the merciful mother, pleads mercy for him.
(In) the lap (of) his sister, the merciful sister pleads mercy for him.
Indeed he. . .(in) the lap (of) his wife, Inanna.
(But) Inanna, the bellowing storm, roars at him.

Heaven is a storm. The earth is a storm.
[. . .]
[. . .]
[. . .]
[. . .]
The brickwork of Uruk has been *levelled(?)*; [. . .] Uruk . . .

By(?) the appletree of the large dike, . . . of the Emuš,
in that place. . .the lad. . .smashed boats. . .the waters of the netherworld pour out.
The spouse of Inanna. . .smashed boats. . .the waters of the netherworld pour out.

There is no fat; the fat has been spilled out.
(Variant: There is no food; [the food has been] consumed.)
There is no milk; the jug(?) has been broken.
(Variant: There is no water; [the. . .has been] soaked up.)
There is no cattle pen; it has become haunted(?).
There is no roof for the sheep; it has been stretched out (like) a net.
Without as much as a spear the demons seized him by the shoulders.

An eršemma of Inanna and Dumuzi
(version A:) 113 lines (version B:) 107 lines

This eršemma of Dumuzi and Ṣirtur is an expansion of the theme (as presented in the compositions "Inanna's Descent to the Netherworld" and "Dumuzi's Dream") of the demons' attempt forcibly to bring Dumuzi to the netherworld as a substitute for his wife, Inanna. Our work opens with a thirteen line wail by the poet over the captured Dumuzi. Ṣirtur, Dumuzi's mother, is then portrayed as searching everywhere for her child. Then occurs a four line speech (lines 16–19); however, it is unclear whether this speech is uttered by Ṣirtur or by the poet himself. Attention is now focused upon Geštinanna, Dumuzi's faithful sister, who, when leaving her sheepfold, is informed that her brother was seen running down the road with the galla-demons in pursuit. It is further related that the demons managed to overwhelm Dumuzi, hurling him down, stripping him and binding him. There is a break in our text of six lines in which we assume that Dumuzi manages to escape and is found by his sister, Geštinanna. Seeing her beaten brother, Geštinanna begins to cry, offering to bring a new cloak to cover Dumuzi's wounds and his nakedness. Dumuzi, desperate to evade the demons, has no time to listen to his sister's cries, nor can he wait for her to fetch him clothes. Rather he instructs her immediately to go to his mother, Ṣirtur, whom he envisions as calling for the five breads and the ten breads, perhaps symbols of the sustenance the dutiful son, Dumuzi, regularly provided. He instructs Geštinanna to have his mother intercede on his behalf with her personal god.

Eršemma no. 88

Text: BM 15795 (*CT* 15 pl. 20–21)
Collated: S. N. Kramer, *RA* 65 (1971) 25

1. [guruš dab$_5$-ba] e-en [gig-ga-bi]
2. [^{d}Dumu-z]i ⸢dab$_5$⸣-ba e-en ⸢gig-ga⸣-[bi]
3. ^{d}⸢Ama⸣-ušumgal-an-na dab$_5$-ba e-en gig-ga-[bi]
4. a guruš   guruš ^{d}Da-mu-[mu]
5. a guruš   dumu ù-mu-un-mu-zi-[da]
6. a guruš ^{d}Ištaran-i-bí-š[uba]
7. a guruš ^{d}Alla ù-mu-un-s[a-pàr]
8. a guruš   li-bi-ir ù-mu-un-[šud$_x$-dè]
9. a guruš   mu-lu-šír-an-na-m[u]
10. tum$_{10}$-íb-bi nam-da-an-si-ig kur dib-bé ⸢gar-ra⸣
11. gi-gin$_7$ ì-sìg-ge sag-šè im-mi-íb-d[u$_7$-du$_7$]
12. guruš-e a šà-ba-ni a bar-ra-ni
13. su$_8$-ba ^{d}Dumu-zi-dè a su-mu-ug-ga-ni
14. ama-ni ér-re e-ne-er šár mu-un-na -te/ka[r(-x)]
15. ér-re a-še-re e-ne-er šár mu-un-na-te/ka[r(-x)]
16. ì-du-du   ér-gig ì-šeš$_4$-šeš$_4$
17. ì-tuš-en   šu šà-ga-eš im-lá
18. ér im-me   ér-bi gig-ga-kam
19. šìr im-me   šìr-bi gig-ga-kam
20. nin$_9$-a-ni amaš-ta è-da-ni
21. ^{d}Mu-tin-an-na nin$_9$-ù-mu-un-na-ke$_4$ amaš-ta è-da-ni
22. igi-du$_8$-lú-gal$_5$-lá gaba-ri gíd-da
23. ama-^{d}Mu-tin-ra gù mu-un-na-dé-e
24. ne-éš šeš-zu lú-ér-re ba-an-ku$_4$-ku$_4$
25. ne-éš ^{d}Dumu-zi lú-a-nir ba-an-ku$_4$-ku$_4$

26. gal$_5$-lá-da kaskal im-ši-gin
27. ka-ab-gaz-e ḫar-ra-an-na im-da-an-⸢zu⸣
28. ⸢lú⸣-šu-da-a e-ne-ra mu-un-da-ul$_4$-e
29. ⸢lú⸣-á-lá-a e-ne-ra mu-un-da-ul$_4$-e
30. ⸢im⸣-da-šub^{ub}-ba-aš im-da-zi-ga-aš
31. [. . .]⸢x⸣túg$^{!?}$-ga im-ši-sù-ge-eš
32. [. . .]⸢x⸣[. . .] im-ge-em-ge-⸢me⸣-eš
33. [. . .]⸢x⸣ ⸢im-di-di⸣-[. . .]
34. [. . .]
35. [. . .]
36. [. . .]
37. [. . .]
38. [. . .]
39. [. . .]⸢ma⸣[. . .]-⸢sìg-ge-eš⸣[. . .]
40. [x (x)]-⸢da⸣-zu ⸢x⸣[x (x)]-⸢dab$_5$⸣(?)-bé-eš   me-e gù ba-⸢ab-ra-ra⸣
41. [x (x)]⸢x⸣ zu ⸢ma-ni-ib⸣-sìg-ge-eš   me-e gù ba-⸢ab⸣-ra-ra
42. ⸢x⸣[x]⸢x⸣zu im-mi-in-sìg-ge-ne   me-e gù ba-⸢ab⸣-ra-ra
43. ⸢x⸣[x]⸢x⸣zu im-mi-in-sìg-ge-ne   me-e gù ba-⸢ab-ra⸣-ra
44. ⸢x⸣[x]⸢x⸣-^{d}Dumu-zi-da e-ne-èm nin$_9$-a-né mu-ni-in-du$_{11}$-⸢ga⸣ ⸢šà-šè⸣ ba-ra-an-gí[d]
45. [gù ba-a]b-ra-ra gù mu-un-na-dé-e
46. [x]⸢x⸣[x]⸢da⸣(?) gaba-ra-è me-e TÚG? ga-ba-e-da-DU
47. ⸢x x x x⸣ mu da [gaba-r]a-è me-e TÚG? ga-ba-e-da-DU
48. ⸢x⸣[x] ⸢ama(?)-mu-šè⸣ um-mi-gi$_4$-gi$_4$ ama-mu-ra ḫu-mu-ni-in-zal-eš
49. ⸢ama⸣-[mu] ⸢ninda⸣-iá-mu gù ḫé-em-me
50. [ama-mu] ⸢ninda⸣-u-gá gù ḫé-em-me
51. ⸢x⸣[x]⸢x⸣ḫé$^{!?}$-em-DU šà-tur gù ḫé-em-me
52. [x (x)]⸢x kin⸣(?)-mu me-e kin-kin
53. [i-b]í ḫa-ma-da-ḪAR kiri$_4$ ḫa-ma-da-ḪAR
54. [geš]túg ki-u$_6$-da ḫa-[ma]-da-ḪAR
55. [ki]-lú-da nu-⸢u$_6$⸣-[di] ⸢x⸣-TA(?) ḫ[a-ma-d]a-ḪAR
56. ⸢é⸣-dingir-ra-né [(. . .)] ḫa-ma-da-[. . .]-e
57. guruš-me-en gal$_5$-lá-ta mu-zal ḫa-ma-da-[. . .]-e

ér-šem$_5$-ma-^{d}Dumu-z[i-da] ù ^{d}Zí-iš-t[ur]

* * *

1. The captured young man! How horrible!
The captured Dumuzi! How horrible!
The captured Amaušumgalanna! How horrible!
Oh the young man! The young man, my Damu!
5. Oh the young man! The child, Umunmuzida!

Oh the young man! Ištaranibišuba!
Oh the young man! Alla! Umunsapar!
Oh the young man! The herald, Umunšudde!
Oh the young man! My singer of heaven!
He could not still the angry wind; beset . . . it smites the land
as if it were a reed. It gores the very head (of the land).
The young man! Oh his heart! Oh his liver!
The shepherd Dumuzi! Oh his unhappiness!
In tears his mother . . . for him.
In tears and sighs she . . . for him.
I walk—I shed bitter tears.
I sit down—*I stretch(?) (my) hand to(?) (my) heart.*
I cry—those tears are bitter.
I sing—that song is bitter.

When his sister went out from the sheepfold,
when Geštinanna, the sister of the lord, went out from the sheepfold,
an observer of the galla-demons who confronts her
calls out to Amageštinanna:
"Now your brother has been turned into a tearful man.
Now Dumuzi has been turned into a man of sighing."
He, along with the galla-demons, went down the road.
The 'murderer' knew the road.
The 'binder-of-hands' *causes him to be afraid.*
The 'binder-of-arms' *causes him to be afraid.*

. . . fall down . . . stand up.
They stripped him naked (. . .) of clothing.
They . . . him; [. . .]
[. . .] go [. . .]
[. . .]

[. . .]
[. . .]
[. . .]
[. . .]
[. . .] they beat [. . .]
"[. . .] they *seize(?)* your [. . .]!" I scream out.
"[. . .] they beat your [. . .]!" I scream out.
"[. . .] they beat your [. . .]!" I scream out.
"[. . .] they beat your [. . .]!" I scream out.

The [. . .] of Dumuzi does not consider the words his sister had spoken.

(Still) she screams out; (still) she calls out to him.

"I shall go out with [. . .]! I shall *bring a garment* for you!
I shall go out with my [. . .]! I shall *bring a garment* for you!"

"[. . .] return to my mother! Let them . . . for my mother.
My mother will call out 'My five breads!'
[My mother] will call out 'My ten breads!'
[. . .] . . . will call out.
[. . .] my [. . .]; I am being sought.
May she scratch her eyes for me! May she scratch her nose for me!
May she scratch her ears, the 'public place,' for me!
May she scratch her *buttocks(?)*, the 'secret place,' for me!
May she [go] to the house (of) her personal god for me!
May she [go] for me, (that) I, the young man, can stay away from the galla-demon!"

An eršemma of Dumuzi and Ṣirtur

Drawing upon the Inanna-Dumuzi theme this next eršemma describes the situation after the demons, here enumerated as "the-one-of-the-steppe," "the-one-with-the-gaping-mouth," "the-overpowering-one" and "the-evil-one," have abducted Dumuzi. Dumuzi has apparently escaped from his captors, but neither Inanna nor Geštinanna knows where he is hiding. To add to our interest the poet provides us with an etiological explanation for the fly frequenting the alehouses, fruit bins and around the bovines. This, the poet relates, was the fly's reward for revealing to Geštinanna the hiding place of her brother. Both Inanna and Geštinanna had attempted to bribe the fly, but Geštinanna's bribe proved more enticing. The fact that the two women are competing for the information, rather than cooperating, indicates that their motives were different. Since Geštinanna clearly sought to help her brother, it seems that Inanna's intention was to reveal Dumuzi's hiding place to the demons. Geštinanna now runs throughout the steppe, presumably the place revealed by the fly, bringing food to help her brother recover from the torturous treatment by the demons. Her bringing *maštakal* and *ardadillu*-plants might refer to her preparing some type of magical potion to help him revive. The threads of linen might be part of this elixir or might refer to clothing.

Eršemma no. 165

Text: BM 29628 (*CT* 15 pl. 19)
Collated: S. N. Kramer, *RA* 65 25

1. šeš-e dab_5-a-na urú ér-ra na-nam

2. a guruš šeš-e tab-an-na
3. a guruš su$_8$-ba en ^{d}Dumu-zi
4. dumu é-gal-a-né nu-mu-un-sù-ga-mu
5. kù ^{d}Inanna-ke$_4$ é-an-na gù im-me
6. lú-eden-na-ke$_4$ nu-mu-un-su-ga-mu
7. kù ^{d}Inanna-ke$_4$ Zabalam^{ki} gù im-me
8. lú-ka-ba-ra-ke$_4$ nu-mu-un-sù-ga-mu
9. bára KA kù ^{d}Inanna-ke$_4$ ŠITA$_x^{ki}$ gù im-me
10. lú-ka-aš-ka-sa-ke$_4$ nu-mu-un-sù-ga-mu
11. kù ^{d}Inanna-ke$_4$ šà-mu eden mu-un-si-ig
12. lú-ḫul-gál nu-mu-un-su-ga-mu
13. ^{d}Geštin-an-na-ke$_4$ ⌜dug⌝šakir$_3$ mu-un-šub
14. lú-eden-na-ke$_4$ a-na-àm šu ba-ab-du$_7$
15. lú-ka-ba-ra-ke$_4$
16. lú-ka-aš-ka-sa-ke$_4$
17. lú-ḫul-gál a-na-àm šu ba-ab-du
18. ^{d}Geštin-an-na-ke$_4$ sila$_4$ amar-ra mu-un-šub-bé
19. nim-me kù ^{d}Inanna-ra gù mu-un-na-⌜dé⌝-e
20. nim-me ki-mu-lu-ni ma-ra-an-pà-dè a-na mu-un-ba-e-e
21. é-kaš-a-ka é-girin-na-ka
22. dumu-mu-lu-kù-zu-ke$_4$-ne dè-mu-un-ti-le
23. nim-me kù ^{d}Geštin-an-na-ke$_4$ gù mu-un-⌜na⌝-dé-[e]
24. nim-me ki-šeš ma-ra-an-pà-⌜dè⌝ a-na-àm mu-un-ba-al
25. é-kaš-a-ka é-girin-na-ka dumu-lú-kù-zu-ke$_4$-<ne> amar-sag-tuk-a-na
26. ur-sag ^{giš}tukul-a sag-gá-gá-ke$_4$
27. ^{d}Geštin-an-na-ke$_4$ eden-na sag-gá-gá-ke$_4$
28. eden NIGIN.NIGIN eden NIGIN.NIGIN šeš-mu eden NIGIN.NIGIN
29. eden a-ra-li eden NIGIN.NIGIN šeš-mu eden NIGIN.NIGIN
30. in-nu-uš gada gu-bi ú!aš-ta-al-ta-al mu-<ni>-ib-DU.DU
31. i-zi-ga-na gar$_{10}$ šà-zi-zi mu-<ni>-ib-túm

---

31 ér-šem$_5$-ma-^{d}Dumu-zi-da-kam

* * *

1. Oh the brother! Indeed the city is in tears over his capture.
Oh the young man! Oh the brother! [Indeed the city is in tears] over his capture.
Oh the young man! The shepherd! The 'en' Dumuzi!
My youth who no longer rejoices at his palace!
5. Oh holy Inanna, the Eanna cries out!
Oh "the-one-of-the-steppe," my one who no longer rejoices!

Oh holy Inanna, Zabalam cries out!
Oh . . ., my one who no longer rejoices!
Oh . . ., holy Inanna, . . . cries out!
Oh "the-over-powering-one," my one who no longer rejoices!
Oh holy Inanna, my heart silenced the steppe!
Oh "the-evil-one," my one who no longer rejoices!

Geštinanna has deserted the churn.
"What has "the-one-of-the-steppe" accomplished?
(What has) "the-one-with-the-gaping-mouth" (accomplished)?
(What has) "the-over-powering-one" (accomplished)?
What has "the-evil-one" accomplished?"
Geštinanna deserts the lamb (and) the calf.

A fly speaks to holy Inanna.
The fly (says concerning) the place (of) her man, "If I reveal it to you,
what will you offer?"
"Let the young of the wise one live
in the alehouse and in the house of fruit!"
The fly speaks to holy Geštinanna.
The fly (says concerning) the place (of her) brother, "If I reveal it to
you,
what will you *offer(?)*?"
"In the alehouse, in the house of fruit, and among his(?) superb calves
(may) the young of the wise one (live)!"

She who is a hero rushing headlong into battle,
Geštinanna, who is rushing headlong in the steppe,
going about the steppe, going about the steppe, (shouting), "My
brother!," going about the steppe,
the steppe Arali, going about the steppe, (shouting), "My brother!,"
going about the steppe,
she *brings(?) maštakal*-plants, *threads(?) of linen*, and *ardadillu*-plants.
She has brought a flood of her milk and cream to revive the heart.

---

31 (lines) It is an eršemma of Dumuzi.

Eršemma no. 60

Text: BM 15821 (*CT* 15 pl. 18)
Collated: S. N. Kramer, *RA* 65 25
Recent translation: Th. Jacobsen, *Most Ancient Verse*, 21–23; *Image of Tammuz*, 102–103

Inanna searches for her dead husband, the shepherd Dumuzi, who is likened to a beaten bull. This analogy may be based upon the strength and grandeur of the bull, qualities Inanna ascribes to her spouse. In lines 4–15 the metaphor of the bull is temporarily abandoned; common epithets of Dumuzi are cited in Inanna's wail. With the death of the bull Dumuzi, the sheep and goats have died, euphemistically "they are sleeping." Inanna asks the hills of the bison what has happened to her husband, the hills replying that the bison has taken Dumuzi away to the mountain. Explaining the imagery of the bison, Jacobsen states: ". . . in the mountains was according to Sumerian belief, the realm of the dead: the powers of death itself reach out for him [Dumuzi]. In the present poem these powers are symbolized by the bison—bisons roamed the foothills bordering the Mesopotamian plain in prehistoric and early historic times—and his followers." Inanna then addresses herself to the bison of the mountain, informing him that ever since Dumuzi departed, his hut has become desolate, the forces of nature having taken possession.

Kramer and Jacobsen have suggested that the references to the young man and young woman in lines 23–24 and 32–33 may indicate that other individuals, possibly the inhabitants of Dumuzi's city, disappeared with him. We offer another possible interpretation; the hendiadys young man and young woman may refer to Dumuzi, Inanna describing her lover as being the entirety of love-making. Lastly, interpreting the verb ḫa-lam as "to destroy," Kramer suggests that lines 34 and 35 might refer to inhabitants who perished with Dumuzi; whereas, Jacobsen sees in these two lines a reference to the henchmen of death who have killed Dumuzi. We offer another possibility. By translating ḫa-lam as "to forget," we suggest that these lines state that Dumuzi's acquaintances have forgotten him. It is, therefore, only Inanna who is concerned enough to go seek the shepherd.

1.	[am mu-ra nu-un-ti]	⌈am⌉ mu-ra nu-un-ti
2.	[^{d}Dumu-zi am mu-ra] nu-⌈un-ti⌉	⌈am⌉ mu-ra nu-un-ti
3.	(x) ⌈x⌉ mu-lu-⌈sún⌉? nu-un-ti	am mu-ra nu-un-ti
4.	[x] DU mu-ud-na-mu	nu-un-ti
5.	[am]a-ušum-mu	nu-un-ti
6.	[am]a-^{d}ušumgal-an-na	nu-un-ti
7.	⌈ù⌉-mu-un-e-a-ra-li	nu-un-ti
8.	ù-mu-un-e-Bàd-tibira^{ki}	nu-un-ti
9.	sú$_{8}$-ba en ^{d}Dumu-zi	nu-un-ti
10.	ù-mu-un-e-⌈du$_{6}$-su$_{8}$⌉-ba	nu-un-ti
11.	mu-ud-na-ga-ša-⌈an-na⌉?-ka	nu-un-ti
12.	ù-mu-un-e-é-⌈mùš⌉-a	nu-un-ti
13.	⌈šeš⌉-⌈ama⌉-mu-tin-na	nu-un-ti
14.	⌈i-bí⌉-LUM.LUM-ka-na-ág-gá	nu-un-ti
15.	⌈ù-mu⌉-un-⌈gìr⌉-ka-na-ág-gá	nu-un-ti

16. ⌜am⌝-e a-gin$_7$ nú-dè-en u$_8$ silá-bi ù-bi a-gin$_7$ bí-ku
17. am-e a-gin$_7$ nú-dè-en ùz máš-bi ù-bi a-gin$_7$ bí-ku
18. me-e du$_6$-da   èn ga-àm-ma-tar
19. du$_6$-alim-ma   èn ga-àm-ma-tar
20. ⌜guruš⌝ mu-lu-mu me-a   ga-àm-ma-ab-du$_{11}$
21. [ú] nu-gu$_7$-a-mu   ga-àm-ma-ab-du$_{11}$
22. [e$_4$] nu-nag-a-mu   ga-àm-ma-ab-du$_{11}$
23. ⌜ki⌝-sikil-sa$_6$-ga-mu   ga-àm-ma-ab-du$_{11}$
24. [guruš]-sa$_6$-ga-mu   ga-àm-ma-ab-du$_{11}$
25. [mu-l]u-zu alim-e   kur-ÁŠ ba-u$_5$
26. [guruš?-z]u alim-e   kur-ÁŠ ba-u$_5$
27. [ali]m-kur-ra   i-bí-gùn-nu-gùn-nu-e
28. [ali]m-kur-ra   KA-ḫu-tu-ul-ḫu-tu-ul
29. alim ù-mu-un-da   ù-mu-un-da
30. ⌜ú⌝ nu-gu$_7$-a-mu   ù-mu-un-da
31. e$_4$ nu-nag-a-mu   ù-mu-un-da
32. ki-sikil-ša$_6$-ga-mu   ù-mu-un-da
33. guruš-ša$_6$-ga-mu   ù-mu-un-da
34. guruš mu-lu-zu-dè mu-da-ab-ḫa-lam-ma
35. ^{d}Aba (AB)-ba$_6$-bànda mu-lu-zu-dè mu-da-ab-ḫa-lam-ma
36. i-bí-bar-ša$_6$-ga-né mùš nam-ba-e-ga-ga
37. ka-bar-ša$_6$-ga-né mud na-an-ni-bar-re
38. ^{túg}ám-bàra-ga-na ur ba-e-nú
39. mu-lu-mà rig$_7$-ga-na uga^{mušen} ba-e-dúr
40. gi-di-da-ni tum$_{10}$-e àm-me
41. mu-lu-mà èn-du-ni tum$_{10}$-mi-ir-re àm-me

---

41 ér-šem$_5$-ma-^{d}Dumu-zi-da

[The beaten (?) bull lives no more]. The beaten (?) bull lives no more.
[Dumuzi, the beaten (?) bull,] lives no more. The beaten (?) bull lives no more.
[. . .] the one . . . lives no more. The beaten (?) bull lives no more.
[. . .], my spouse, lives no more.
My Amaušum lives no more.
Amaušumgalanna lives no more.
The lord of Arali lives no more.
The lord of Badtibira lives no more.
The shepherd, the lord Dumuzi, lives no more.
The lord of Dušuba lives no more.
The spouse of Inanna lives no more.
The lord of the Emuš lives no more.

The brother of Geštinanna lives no more.
The . . . faced one of the nation lives no more.
The mighty lord of the nation lives no more.
Bull, thus do you lie down! How the ewe (and) its lamb sleep!
Bull, thus do you lie down! How the goat (and) its kid sleep!
I shall ask the hill.
I shall ask the hill of the bison.
"Where is the young man, my man?" shall I say to it.
"My one who eats no more?" shall I say to it.
"My one who drinks no more?" shall I say to it.
"My beautiful young girl?" shall I say to it.
"My beautiful [young man]?" shall I say to it.
The bison has taken your man up to the mountains.
The bison has taken your [young man] up to the mountains.
Bison of the mountains with the beauteous countenance!
Bison of the mountains with . . .!
Bison, leave! Leave!
Leave my one who eats no more,
leave my one who drinks no more,
leave my beautiful young girl,
leave my handsome young man,
leave the young man whose acquaintances have forgotten him,
the young Ababa, who(se) acquaintances have forgotten him.
His loving glance has ended.
. . .
The dog lies upon his spread garment.
The raven perches in my man's fold.
The wind plays his reed pipe.
The northwind sings my man's songs.

---

41 (lines) An eršemma of Dumuzi.

In addition to these eršemmas concerning Dumuzi, there is preserved one eršemma in which the object of the demons' pursuit is Nergal. This work is tantalizing in that, except for our eršemma, we know nothing of this tale. Our composition may be based upon the tale of Nergal's becoming lord of the netherworld, as recounted in Akkadian recensions of the composition entitled "Nergal and Ereškigal." If this suggestion is valid, our eršemma might portray Ereškigal's attempt to have Nergal brought down to the netherworld as a punishment for being disrespectful to Namtar, Ereškigal's vizier. Another possible reference to the events depicted in our eršemma occurs in "Inanna's Descent to the Netherworld." When Inanna is questioned by Neti, the chief gate-keeper of the netherworld, as to the motive behind her visit, Inanna answers that she has come to attend the funerary rites for the husband of Ereškigal, Gugalanna, who had been killed. Gugalanna here might well be another name for Nergal and thus this reference might just conceivably refer to the tale upon which our eršemma is based.

The eršemma may be outlined as follows: The poet or Nergal's mother is asking what has become of the powerful god, Nergal, the strongman, the mighty wrestler. The answer: Nergal is lying helplessly upon the ground, his face bloodied and cut. Explaining his plight, Nergal addresses himself to his mother, to the royal household who misses its wrestler, i.e., Nergal—Nergal may well have symbolized the actual wrestlers who performed in the palace for the court's amusement—and to the people in the street, who have been disheartened since his disappearance. The demons, relates Nergal, have attacked him, cutting up his face and fettering him. The remainder of the composition is the wail over Nergal by his mother. Her allusion to Nergal as the "poplar-of-Gilgameš" is unclear to us.

Eršemma no. 164

Text: BM 22741 (*CT* 15 pl. 14). Collated: S. N. Kramer, *RA* 65 24.

1.	[ù lú-lirum-m]a	lirum ta me-⸢a⸣
2.	[e-lum ù lú-liru]m-ma	lirum ta me-a
3.	[ur-sag umun ^{d}Nè-eri$_{11}$]-gal	ù lú-lirum-ma
4.	[^{d}Mes-lam-ta-è]-⸢a⸣	ù lú-lirum-ma
5.	[kala-ga-mu mu-lu-ám-gi]-ra	ù lú-lirum-ma
6.	[ám-gi-ra gešpú]-⸢gìr⸣-ra	ù lú-lirum-ma
7.	⸢x⸣[. . .]⸢SÌG⸣	ù lú-lirum-ma
8.	nu-⸢x⸣[. . .]	ù lú-lirum-ma
9.	en ^{d}⸢SAG.PISAN-unu⸣^{ki}-ga	ù lú-lirum-ma
10.	lirum IŠ-bar-ra	sa bi-ak
11.	tu-bar-ri-ma$_{\text{túg}}$-pa-rim$_4$-ma^{túg} ba-rí-na KI.MIN	sa bí-KU-KU
12.	te [ba-]šub$^{\text{(ub)}}$-bé-en	te ba-zi-ge-en
13.	ù-mu-un-mu su-zi	ki e-ne bí-u$_5$
14.	i-bí-zi-da-zu	zi-ib$_{\text{zíb}}$ NI ba-an-gíd$^{\text{gi-id}}$
15.	guruš gáb-bu-zu	uri$_3$-e ba-an-si
16.	⸢du$_5$⸣-mu lirum nu-zu-ra	mu-un-na-an-gi$_4$-gi$_4$
17.	é-gal-la gešpú nu-zu-ra	mu-un-na-an-gi$_4$-gi$_4$
18.	sila ešemen nu-zu-ra	mu-un-na-an-gi$_4$-gi$_4$
19.	me-e gal$_5$-lá-bé i-bí-mu mu-un-TAR	kiri$_4$-mu mu-un-TAR
20.	zà-si-mu gal$_5$-lá-ḫul-du-e	te ba-dúr-ru-ne-eš
21.	ama-⸢ugu-ni⸣ ⸢x⸣ (x) KID-na-ka	šir mu-un-na-ra
22.	⸢x⸣[. . .]⸢x⸣-ám-ta u$_4$-šú-a-ni	šir mu-un-na-ra
23.	[. . .]⸢x⸣ al ⸢x x⸣ enmen-a-ni	šir mu-un-na-ra

24.	[. . . šu-dù]-⌜a⌝-[na]	túg-da ga-ra-BA-mu$_{x}$(KU)
25.	[. . .]⌜x⌝ ám-gi-ra-na	túg-tan$_{x}$(GÁxTAG$_{4}$(?)) ga-ra-da-mu$_{x}$(KU)
26.	ki-kal li-bi-ir-re ak-a-na	túg-da ga-ra-da-mu$_{x}$(KU)
27.	ki li-bi-ir-re ⌜kin⌝ ŠÈ ak-a-na	túg-tan$_{x}$ ga-ra-da-mu$_{x}$(KU)
28.	ki e-ne-ra eden-bi-⌜re⌝ i-[i]	túg-da ga-ra-da-mu$_{4}$
29.	KAL-KAL DI mu-ub-DU	a mu-lu-mu ga-àm-⌜du⌝$_{11}$
30.	guruš EN-bàn-da gur-ru-na-ta	gudu$_{4}$-e gù^{gu}-dé^{de}
31.	ér-ra nam-ba-da-tuš-ù-dè	ér-da tuš-ma-da
32.	ér-da a-nir-da tuš-ma-da	ér-da tuš-ma-da
33.	šà-nu-ḫúl-le-dè tuš-ma-da	ér-da tuš-ma-da
34.	bar-nu-zal^{za}-la-ge-da tuš-ma-da	ér-da tuš-ma-da
35.	^{giš}ildág ^{d}Bil$_{4}$-ga-meš tuš-ma-da	ér-[da tuš]-ma-da
36.	a guruš ⌜šu⌝-zu nu-uš-bí-in-tuk	bar-zu ⌜né-eš-mi⌝-in-gál
37.	^{giš}ildág ^{d}Bil$_{4}$-ga-meš šu-zu nu-uš-bí-in-tuk	bar-zu né-eš-mi-ni-gál

---

37 ér-šem$_{5}$-ma-^{d}Nè-eri$_{11}$-gal

* * *

[Woe the strongman!] What is strength!
[The honored one! Woe the strongman!] What is strength!
[The warrior, the lord Ner]gal, woe the strongman!
[Meslamtaea], woe the strongman!
[My powerful one, the killer], woe the strongman!
[The killer], the mighty [wrestler], woe the strongman!
[. . .], woe the strongman!
[. . .], woe the strongman!
The lord Pisansagunuga, woe the strongman! (What is strength!)

The strongman has been *netted(?)* in the . . . mountain.
A . . . garment, the *net(?)* just *lies* there.

Why have you been cast down? Why have you been hurled up?
My lord, terror has ascended . . . place.
Your right eye has been gashed!
Young man, your left one is filled with blood!

The son answers him who no longer knows the strongman.
He answers him in the palace who no longer knows the wrestler.
He answers him in the street who no longer knows dancing.
"As for me, this demon has cut up my face, cut off my nose.
Why . . . the evil demon . . . my side . . . sit(?)?"

His mother, over the . . . of her . . ., struck up a lament for him.

[She who used to provide for] his hunger struck up a lament for him.
[She who used to provide for] his thirst struck up a lament for him.
"[Upon the place where he was bound] I shall dress you(?) with a cloak.
Upon [the place] of his murder I shall dress you(?) with a clean cloak.
Upon his bare ground where the demon has (thus) acted I shall dress you(?) with a cloak.
Upon his place where the demon has . . . I shall dress you(?) with a clean cloak.
The place . . . for him . . . that steppe . . . I shall dress you(?) with a clean cloak.
. . . I shall say "Oh my man!"
Ever since the young man, the . . . lord, has turned away(?), the gudu-priest (has been) crying out.

I cannot endure sitting in tears. Sit by me with tears!
Sit by me with tears and with sighs! Sit by me with tears!
Sit by me, whose heart is unhappy! Sit by me with tears!
Sit by me, whose mood is gloomy! Sit by me with tears!
. . . poplar . . . Gilgameš sit by me! Sit by me with tears!
Oh young man, if only I could hold your hand! If only your body(?) were here!
. . . poplar . . . Gilgameš, if only I could hold your hand! If only your body(?) were here!"

37 (lines) an eršemma (of) Nergal

The following work is an eršemma of Gula, who is identified with Ninisina, the goddess of the city Isin, which attained a degree of hegemony in Sumer during the first century and a half of the second millennium B.C.E. We caution that the meaning or nuance of many of the words and phrases in this eršemma is unclear or unknown. Therefore, the following interpretation of the work must be viewed with extreme caution.

The eršemma begins with Ninisina identifying herself by her various epithets and titles, adding that that which belongs to her is great. But in lines 8–18 we are informed of the dramatic change in her fortune. In an attempt to remedy her plight Ninisina determines to go to Enlil, to him who has decided her cruel fate, despite her fears that Enlil will not be sympathetic to her. Nonetheless, she goes to the house where the fates are determined and knocks upon the door, calling Enlil by the appropriate epithet, "decider of the fates." In a rather difficult passage, it appears that Enlil opens the door for Ninisina and dutifully removes for inspection those tablets of fate pertinent to her. He carefully locks up the housing for the other tablets. He then informs her that these tablets decree a fate of adversity and destruction for her. Having stated this, Enlil appears to ignore her. Ninisina then informs Enlil that she refuses to succumb to this destiny and, in what appears to be a sarcastic speech, she dares Enlil to gloat over her misfortune. Apparently, her pleas are in vain for she states "He (i.e., Enlil) who used to know me has forgotten me." Feeling persecuted and sorry for herself Ninisina threatens to leave Enlil and go to the steppe, a place of loneliness and death. Not only does Enlil call her bluff, but he actually chases her out of the Enamtar. Now in the steppe she cries out to her mother, claiming that since she has been living in the steppe, no one has cared enough to look for her or even to ask about her. Her statement "the *asakku*-demon is here" perhaps signifies the misery and terror she experiences in the steppe. Her mother listens to her child and suggests to Ninisina that she should make herself alluring for Enlil, so that he will change her fate. But Ninisina replies that she has already tried this without success. Thereupon, her mother says that she herself will talk to Enlil on behalf of her daughter. In the closing soliloquy Ninisina's mother cries that her child has died.

Ninisina's very presence in the steppe signifies death, since the steppe, a place of misery and deprivation, was equated with the land of the dead. And another name by which the land of the dead was known was Arali. This, of course, brings us back to the opening line of the eršemma in which Ninisina is called "the one of Arali."

The restored portions of the text are based upon *CT* 42 no. 16, an eršemma of Inanna.

Eršemma no. 171

Text A A 6742
B BM 15793 (*CT* 42 no. 7) cols. i to iii

1. a-ra-li-[me-e]n[1] a-ra-li-me-en ám-mu ám-gal-la-àm
2. mu-lu-a-ra-li-me-en[1] ám-mu ám-gal-la-àm
3. sa$_{12}$-du$_{5}$-maḫ ga-ša-an-Ì-si-in-na-mèn
4. ama-uru-sag-gá ga-ša-an-tin-u$_{9}$-ba-mèn
5. dumu-é-e[1] ga-ša-an-mèn-gu-nu-ra

6a. ama-é-e[1] ^{d}Ezenu ^{d}Kù-su$_{x}$(BU)[2]-mu ám-mu ám-gal-la-àm
6b. [1]^{d}TUM.DIB-kù ama-é-šà-ba-mèn
6c. en-á-nun ama-kurku(KA.AN.NI.SI)-mèn
6d. ga-ša-[an]-ni$_{x}$-mar-ra-ki-kù-ga-mèn
6e. ga-[ša-an-a]š-te ga-ša-an-La-ra-ak^{ki}-mèn
7. á[m]-mu ám-gal-la[1] me-mu me-gal-la-àm[2]

8. [ám]-⸢ma⸣-al-ma-al ám-mu kúr-ra-àm
9. ![é]-zi-da i-lu ma-al-ma-al i-lu-mu kúr-ra-àm
10. [na-á]m-tar ma-al-ma-al-la! na-ám-tar-mu kúr-ra-àm
11. [me]-⸢e⸣ ⸢urú⸣-a mi-ni-ib-ge$_{16}$-le-èm-mèn-na-mu
12. [x]⸢x⸣KA-mu mu-un-gar!-ra-mu
13. [(x) x]⸢x⸣ i-ra ma!-ra-i-ra-mu
14. [usar-r]a sal-la ma-la-ra sal-la!
15. [. . .]-mu usar-ra gú ki-šè ma-ni-mar-ra-mu
16. [. . .]-⸢mu⸣(?) ma-la-ra ⸢á⸣-sìg éš ba-ni-íb-sìg-ge-na-mu!
17. [^{d}Mu-ul-líl]-ra ga-na-ab-du$_{11}$ in-šè! mu-un-dúb-bé
18. [a-a ^{d}Mu-ul-líl-r]a ga-na-ab-du$_{11}$ ás-se! mu-e
19. [. . .] ù nu-⸢ku⸣-ku!
20. [. . .]-TIL.TIL é-ba nu-ub-gi$_{4}$
21. [. . .-b]u(?)-uš ⸢na⸣-nam bar-mu-uš na-dúb-bé
22. [. . .]na-nam me! na-ùr-ùr-re
23. [. . .]⸢mu⸣-dub-dub-ba na-nam me! na-búr-búr-re
24. [. . .]-⸢šè⸣(?) nu-NE-a-mu-dè
25. ga-[ša-an]-Ì-si-in^{ki}-na-mèn nu-ḫúl-la! nu-du$_{11}$-ga-mu-dè[2]
26. a-a-zu-ta é-na-ám-tar-re-da a-gin$_{7}$ im-da-an-ku$_{4}$-re-en!
27. ^{d}Mu-ul-líl-da é-na-ám-tar-re-da a-gin$_{7}$ im-da-an-[ku$_{4}$-re]
28. é-di-da-ka é-ka-aš!-a-ka a-gin$_{7}$ im-da-ku$_{4}$-re
29. SU-bar-ra-na-ám-lú-ulù-ka a-gin$_{7}$ im-da-an-ku$_{4}$-re-en!
30. ^{giš}ig-e šu-mà mu-un-⸢ús⸣ na-ám-tar é gál-lu!
31. ⸢a-a-ugu-mu⸣ ⸢na⸣-ám-tar é gál-lu a-gin$_{7}$ mu-na-du$_{11}$
32. [. . .]⸢a⸣-gin$_{7}$ mu-na-du$_{11}$
33. [a-a-mu-me-en na-ám ì-tar-tar-re mu-e] ⸢mu-na-KU-⸣en
34. ^{d}Mu-ul-líl-ra na-ám ì-[tar-tar-re mu-e mu-un-na-KU-en]
35. i-bí-mu al-tar-re al-ma-[ma mu-e mu-un-na-KU-en]
36. ⸢bar⸣-mu al-tar-re al-ma-[ma mu-e mu-un-na-KU-en]
37. lú-dam-ra dam mu-na-ab-[zé-èm-mèn mu-e mu-un-na-KU-en]
38. lú-dumu-ra dumu mu-na-ab-[zé-èm-mèn mu-e
mu-un-na-KU-en
39. na-ám-tar šu im-ta-gar-ra-ta ⸢i⸣-[bí-ni mu-un-ši-in-bar]
40. é-na-ám-tar-ra mu-un-kéš-da-⸢ta⸣ [ma-ra gù mu-un-di]
41. na-ám-tar-ra ki-⸢pél-pél-la⸣-bi ú[r-mà mu-gá-g]á
42. ki-⸢pél⸣-la-bi ki-⸢ur$_{5}$⸣-ra-bi úr-m[à mu-gá-g]á
43. ki-mu-lu-da-ba-an-da-šub-ba-bi úr-mà m[u-gá]-gá
44. na-ám-tar-ra ⸢ŠÈR⸣-ra nu-me-a zà-da ⸢ba⸣-da-⸢an⸣-gub
45. ma-da-gá-gá ma-da-gá-gá šà im-ta-ab-è-⸢dè⸣
46. na-ám-tar da-mà ma-da-gá-gá šà im-[. . .]
47. na-ám-di-bi-⸢dib⸣-ba ma-da-gá-gá šà im-[. . .]
48. na-ám-ge$_{16}$-le-èm ‹da›-mà ma-da-gá-gá šà im-ta-⸢ab⸣-è-⸢dè⸣

49. ne-šè! ám-ma-al na-ma-da-ab-bé šà im-
50. i-bí na-an-ni-bar-re na-ma-da-ab-bé šà im-ta-ab-è-⸢dè⸣
51. ma e-re-da ma e-re$_7$-da im-ma-al ⸢i⸣-bí-ni in-bar
52. na-ám-tar ám-gig ma e-re-da im-
53. na-ám-di-bi-dib-be$_5$ ma e-re-da im-
54. kù-šu-mu-gin$_7$ ma e-re-da im-
55. za-gìn-gú-mu-gin$_7$ ma e-re-da im-ma-al i-bí-⸢ni⸣ [in]-bar
56. na-ám-tar-ba! i-bí-ḫúl-bar-ra KA-⸢mud$_5$⸣ ⸢mud$_5$⸣-me-ma[r-ra]
57. na-ám-di-bí-dib-ba i-bí-⸢mud$_5$⸣(?)-bar-ra KA-mud$_5$ MIN
58. dam an-tuk-tuk ám-GAM-ma mud-me-mar-ra
59. dumu an-ù-tu ám-GAM-ma mud-me-mar-ra
60. na-ám-tar-ba gi$_4$-in-bi ‹nu›-me-en šu-šè ba-ab-tuš-en
61. na-ám-di-bí-dib-bi gi$_4$-in-bi nu-me-en šu-šè
62. gi$_4$-in še-er-nu-ma-al-bi nu-me-en šu-šè
63. im-dù-dù-e im-BÚR-BÚR-re šu-šè
64. ì-tuš-en sag-‹mà› mu-da-ab-sìg-ge šu-šè
65. ⸢síg-sag⸣-mà sag-mà mu-ub-BIZ šu-šè
66. ⸢su⸣-bar-mà bar-mà mu-ub-BIZ ⸢šu-šè⸣
67. ám-⸢la⸣-LUM-gin$_7$ i-bí mu-ub-kúr [. . .]
68. mu-lú-zu-da-mu mu-da-ab-ḫa-lam-m[a (. . .)]
69. [mu]-⸢lú-su-za⸣(?)-mu gú-mu ⸢gaba⸣-ra-è ⸢x⸣[. . .]⸢x⸣[. . .]
70. ⸢na(?)-ám(?)-tar⸣(?)[úr-mà] ⸢a⸣!-ne ‹im›-ma-al eden-šè
ga-⸢ba-e⸣-da-⸢gin⸣
71. [na-ám-ge$_{16}$-le-è]m úr-mà! a-ne im-ma-al eden-šè
72. [a(?)-ne(?) n]a-ám-díb-ba im-ga-da-⸢x⸣-ma-al eden-šè
73. ⸢i$_7$⸣ nu-⸢zu⸣-mà e$_4$-bi ga-nag eden-šè
74. a-šà nu-zu-mà še-bi ga-gu$_7$ eden-šè
75. kaskal nu-zu-mà ga-gin eden-šè ga-ba-⸢e⸣-da-gin
76. ambar-gin$_7$ ⸢mušen⸣-buru$_5^{\text{mušen}}$ e-ne mu-un-sar-sa[r-en(?)]
77. ma-a na-ám-tar-mu ma-ab-gig-ga-ta ⸢ama-e⸣ ga-à[m-du$_{11}$]
78. ma-a na-ám-di-bí-mu ma-ab-gig-ga-ta ⸢ama⸣-e ga-àm-⸢du$_{11}$⸣
79. ama na-ám-e nu-un-tar!-ra-e á-sàg ba-ni-ma-al
80. aš na-ma-tar! ⸢ki⸣ ⸢na⸣-ma-⸢kin⸣-gá-gin$_7$ á-sàg
81. ensi-ma-šè! la(?)-ma-gin-na-gin$_7$ á-sàg
82. a-ra-na-šè la(?)-ma-⸢gin⸣-na-gin$_7$! á-sàg
83. ⸢gidim-ma⸣ inim nu-mu-ni-ib-bé-a-gin$_7$ á-sàg
84. gidim-eden-na inim nu-⸢mu⸣-ni-ib-bé-a-gin$_7$ á-sàg
85. a-a-ugu-mu ⸢tùr⸣ al-di-da-ni aš na-ma-tar-re
86. ù-mu-un ^{d}Mu-ul-líl amaš ḫé-dib-bé-da-ni aš na-ma-tar-re
87. ⸢dumu⸣ -mu ḫé-sig$_7$-ge ḫé-sa$_6$-⸢ge⸣ ér-ra a-na-bi-me-en
88. ù ḫé-sig$_7$-ge ù ḫé-sa$_6$-⸢ge⸣ ér-ra a-na-bi-me-en
89. šim-bi ḫé-du$_8$-du$_8$ ḪI⸢x⸣(x) ⸢NI⸣(?) ér-ra a-na-bi-me-en

90. ⌜unú-šuba⌝ DAB$_5$-bé-éš ḫa-ta-lá! ér-ra a-na-bi-me-en
91. sig$_7$-ga-mu-⌜e⌝ sig$_7$-ga-mu-e šà-bé a-na mu-e-zu
92. e$_4$-tu$_5$-a nu-⌜su⌝-ub-ba-mu-e šà-bé
93. i-bí šim-bi-zi ma-al-mu-e šà-bé
94. túg-tan$_x$ (GÁxTAG$_4$(?))-tá-na mu-ra-mu-e šà-bé ⌜a-na⌝ mu-e-zu
95. za-gìn ⌜gá(?)-ág-da-mu-e
96. me-e mu-lu-da im-da-tuš-en balag-šà-mà kúr-ra
97. na-ám-e mu-lu-da im-da-tuš-en balag-
98. šà-mà i-LI$_9$-na dar-a-e balag-
99. šà-mà ^{giš}tašgari(TÚG)-mul-la dar-a-mèn balag-šà-m[à kúr-ra]
100. mu-lu i-bí-mu i-bí bí-in-du$_8$-a-re m[ùš-àm na-ma-ab-bé]
101. mu-‹lu› dingir-mu i-bí-mu i-bí bí-in-du$_8$-a-re [mùš-àm na-ma-ab-bé]
102. i-bí lul-la ⌜šu⌝(?)-àm al-⌜pe⌝(?)-pe-[el-la-mu mùš-àm na-ma-ab-bé]
103. šu-um-du-um lu[l-la-àm al-di-di-in mùš-àm na-ma-ab-bé]
104. mu-gi$_{17}$-ib [mu-lu-na-ám-tar-gig-ga-ke$_4$ ga-TUŠ ga-àm-ga-TUŠ]
105. mu-lú-zu-m[u gù mu-un-na-ra ga-TUŠ ga-àm-ga-TUŠ]
106. GÁ(?) mu-lu-zu m[u-lu-na-ám-tar-gig-ga-ke$_4$ nì-ga-mu-e ba-ug$_5$]
107. mu-gi$_{17}$-ba mu-lu-⌜na-ám-tar-gig-ga⌝-[ke$_4$ nì-ga-mu-e ba-ug$_5$]
108. egí KA KA egí-gal-ù-mu-un-na-ke$_4$! [nì-ga-mu-e ba-ug$_5$]
109. ù-tu-da (x) en ^{d}Bil$_4$-ga-meš-[e nì-ga-mu-e ba-ug$_5$]

---

109 ér-šem$_5$-ma-^{d}Gu-⌜la⌝-[kam]

* * *

1. 1) A:-m[èn
2. 1) A:-m[èn
5. 1) A:-a instead of -e
6a. 1) A:-a instead of -e 2) A omits from here to end of line
6b. 1) lines 6b-6e according to text A
7. 1) A adds -àm 2) A omits -àm
9. 1) A inverts the line order of 9 and 10
10. 1) A omits -la
12. 1) A:-ma- instead of -gar-
13. 1) A:mu-
14. 1) A has different line: [. . .]-e ám-mu ám-gal-àm
16. 1) A: [m]a-ni-in-si-ge
18. 1) A: áš-a-šè
19. 1) A:[. . .]-ku$_7$(?)-ku$_7$(?) ám-mu ám-gal-àm
22. 1) A: me-e
23. 1) A: me-e
25. 1) A: e-ne-ḫúl instead of nu-ḫúl-la 2) A omits -dè

26. 1) A omits -en
28. 1) A:-kaš-
29. 1) A omits -en

I am of Arali. I am of Arali. My possessions are great possessions.
I am the one of Arali. My possessions are great possessions.
I am the exalted land registrar, Ninisina.
I am the mother of the chief city, Nintinugga.
I am the child of the house, the lady Gunura.
I am the mother of the house, Ezenu-kusu.
I am the holy . . ., the mother of the Ešaba.
I am Enanun, Amakurku.
I am the lady of the storehouse, of the holy place.
I am Gašanašte, the lady of Larak.
My possessions are great possessions. My "me's" are great "me's."

The possessions which are there, my possessions, are altered.
In the faithful house, the wails which are there, my wails, are strange.
The fate which is there, my fate, is changed.
[These "me's"] of mine which I am forgetting in the city!
My [. . .] which had been placed there!
My [. . .]which has been carried off from me!
Going wide for a comrade, going wide for a girl friend,
my [. . .] which brought me low to the comrade!
My [. . .] which has beaten me with a sling-stone and rope for my girl friend!
I will tell this to [Enlil], (but) he will hurl insults.
I will tell this to [father Enlil], (but) he will utter curses.
[. . .] never sleeps.
[. . .] does not turn it away in that house.
Indeed [. . .] . . . shake because of me.
Indeed [. . .] . . . drag about.
Indeed [. . .] pile up. . . . strew about.
When I (. . .) do not [. . .],
when I, Ninisina, do not rejoice,
so I enter unto my[!?] father, into the house where the fates are determined.
So I enter unto Enlil, into the house where the fates are determined.
So I enter into the house of judgments, the house of decisions.
So I enter . . . of mankind.

I laid my hand on the door. "Namtar, open the house!"
"My father, Namtar, open the house!" So I spoke to him.
"[. . .]" So I spoke to him.

[I . . .] to him: ["You, my father, decide the fates."]
[I . . .] to Enlil: "[You decide all] the fates."
[I . . . to him]: ". . ."
[I . . . to him]: ". . ."
[I . . . to him: "You are the one who gave] the spouse to her who is married."
[I . . . to him: "You are the one who gave] the child to the parent."

After he removed the (tablets of) fate, [he looked at me].
After he closed shut the housing for the (tablets of) fate, [he spoke to me]:
"(Your) fate is placed in this . . . place, my lap.
It is placed in this . . . place, this . . . place, my lap.
It is placed in the place . . ., my lap.
(Your) fate is no longer *locked up*; it is right next to me.
It is here with me. It is here with me." . . .
"The fate is here beside me." . . .
"*Adversity(?)* is here with me." . . .
"Destruction is here beside me." . . .

. . . he doesn't say anything to me. . . .
He does not look up. He says nothing. . . .

"Me into a slave, it has made me into a slave!" He looks up.
"The wretched fates have made me into a slave!" He looks up.
"*Adversity (?)* has made me into a slave!" He looks up.
"Like the silver (about) my hand, it has made me into a slave!" He looks up.

"Like the lapis-lazuli (about) my neck, it has made me into a slave!" He looks up.
"Be happy over this fate! Be joyous . . .
. . . over this *adversity(?)*! Be joyous . . .
Be joyous over the subjugation (of) her who has a husband!
Be joyous over the subjugation (of) her who has born a child!"

"I am not the slave of that fate!" . . .
"I am not the slave (of) *adversity(?)*!" . . .
"I am not its slave, its servant!" . . .
"I walk—I . . ." . . .
"I sit down—I shake(?)." . . .
"The hair of my head . . . on my head." . . .
"The flesh of my body . . . on my body." . . .

Like . . .
He who used to know me has forgotten me. (. . .)

He has caused (this) fate to be [in my lap]. "I shall go away from you to the steppe!"
He has caused [destruction] to be in my lap. "I shall go away from you to the steppe!"
[He] has caused also *adversity(?)* to be with me. "I shall go away from you to the steppe!"
"I shall drink the water of a river I know not. I shall go away from you to the steppe!"
"I shall eat the grain of a field I know not. I shall go away from you to the steppe!"
"I shall travel a road I know not. I shall go away from you to the steppe!"
As if (in) a swamp he chased me out (like) a flock of birds.

Since my fate has harmed me, I cry out "Oh mother!"
Since my *adversity(?)* has harmed me, I cry out "Oh mother!"
"Oh mother who had no part in deciding this fate! The *asakku*-demon is here!

It is as if no one inquires about me, no one is looking for me. The *asakku*-demon is here!
It is as if no one goes to the dream interpretess. The *asakku*-demon is here!
It is as if no one goes anywhere for me! The *asakku*-demon is here!
It is as if (I am) a ghost about whom no one says a word. The *asakku*-demon is here!
It is as if (I am) the ghost of the steppe about whom no one says a word.
The *asakku*-demon is here!
When my father goes about the cattle pen, he does not inquire about me.
Indeed when the lord Enlil passes by the sheepfold, he does not inquire about me."

"My child, may you beautify yourself! May you make yourself attractive! What good have tears done you?
Not only may you beautify yourself, but also may you make yourself attractive! What good have tears done you?
May you adorn yourself with antimony! . . . [. . .] What good have tears done you?
May a decoration of šuba-stone hang . . .! What good have tears done you?
Beautify yourself! Beautify yourself! What do you know about this matter?
Go bathe and scrub! What do you know about this matter?
Put antimony on the eyes! What do you know about this matter?
Dress yourself in clean clothes! What do you know about this matter?

. . . lapis-lazuli . . .!"

"As for me, I already did sit with the man. The harp-song of my heart is strange.
(Concerning) this fate I already did sit with the man. The harp-song of my heart is strange.
Inside me a . . . is busting out. The harp-song of my heart is strange.
Inside me I am a gleaming boxwood tree busting out. The harp-song of my heart is strange.
This man who looked at me [does not say to me "It is enough!"]
. . . who looked at me [does not say to me "It is enough!"]
My face which I had cheapened in vain! [He does not say to me "It is enough!"]
[I move] (my) lips [about in] vain. [He does not say to me "It is enough!"]"

"Hierodule, [oh one of a wretched fate! I shall . . . I shall also . . .]
[I shall cry out to] him whom I know. [I shall . . . I shall also . . .]
. . ., [oh one of a wretched fate! Oh my possession! She has died!]
Oh the hierodule, one of a wretched fate! [Oh my possession! She has died!]
. . ., oh the great daughter-in-law of the lord! [Oh my possession! She has died!]
Oh one who has born the en Gilgameš! [Oh my possession! She has died!]"

---

109 (lines) [It is] an eršemma of Gula.

The following eršemma is also of Gula/Ninisina. Although the tone of the work is decidedly negative in the first twenty-nine lines, the composition concludes in a most positive mood with an exhortation for the reactivation of Ninisina's temple, presumably the Egalmaḫ in Isin.

Eršemma no. 159

Text: BM 96940 (*CT* 36 pl. 41–42). Collated: S.N. Kramer, *Iraq* 36 101

1.	[. . .]⌈x⌉ é⌈x⌉[. . .]	
2.	[sa_{12}-du_5-m]aḫ	ga-ša-an-In-si-n[a-mèn]
3.	[ama-u]rú-sag-gá	ga-ša-an-tin-u_9-ba-⌈mèn⌉
4.	[T]UM-dib-kù	ama-é-šà-ba-mèn
5.	ga-ša-an-aš-te	ga-ša-an-La-ra-ak^{ki}-mèn

ama-é-e ^{d}Ezinu ^{d}Kù-sù-mèn
dumu-é-e ga-ša-an-mèn ^{d}Gu-nu-ra
ga-ša-an-ni$_{x}$-gar-ra ki-kù-ga-mèn
é-e ú-zé-ba nu-gu$_{7}$-a-mu
é-e e$_{4}$-zé-ba nu-nag-a-mu
é ki-tuš-zé-ba nu-dúr-ru-na-mu
é ki-nú-zé-ba nu-nú-a-mu
é bur-kù-ga nu-mu-un-gu$_{7}$-a-mu
é zabar-kù-ga nu-mu-un-nag-a-mu
é ^{giš}banšur-kù-ga nu-mu-un-íl-la-mu
ti-lim-da-kù-ga e$_{4}$ nu-dé-a-mu
^{kuš}ub-kù-ga nu-mu-un-gar-ra-mu
balag-kù-ga nu-mu-un-du$_{12}$-a-mu
šem$_{5}$-kù-ga ad nu-ša$_{4}$-ša$_{4}$-mu
me-zé-kù-ga nu-zé-zé-ba-mu
gi-di-da-mu ur$_{5}$ nu-ša$_{4}$ḪUR-mu
mu-gù-di-dè nu-mu-un-ta-ba-e-mu
gala-e šà-mu nu-šed$_{7}$-dè-mu
gudu$_{4}$-mu sil$_{6}$-lá nu-mu-ni-ib-bé-un-du$_{11}$-ga-mu
é-mu dam-ḫúl-la nu-mu-da-ti-la-mu
é-mu dumu-zé-ba nu-mu-da-tuš-a-mu
é-mu me-e ga-ša-an-bi gal-bi ba-ra-ni-íb-⌜dib⌝
gal-bi ba-ra-ni-íb-dib gal-bi ba-ra-ni-im-ma-al
a-a-mu ḫé-en-ge-me-na ḫé-en-ge-me-AKA(?)
a-a-mu ^{d}Mu-ul!-líl ḫé-en-ge-me-na ḫé-en-ge-me-AKA(?)
me-e é-mu ga-ku$_{4}$ ga-ku$_{4}$ ga-nú ga-nú
me-e erìm-ma-mu ga-ku$_{4}$ ga-ku$_{4}$ ga-nú ga-nú
me-e é-mu ù-sá-bi ga-ku ù-sá-bi zé-ba-àm
me-e é-mu mu-nú-bé ga-nú mu-nú-bi zé-ba-‹àm›
me-e é-mu aš-te-bé ga-tuš aš-te-bi zé-ba-àm

ér-šem$_{5}$-ma-^{d}Gu-la
igi-kár èš?-[UD.KIB.N]UN^{ki}

[. . .] house [. . .]
I am the exalted [land registrar], Ninisina.
I am the [mother] of the chief city, Nintinugga.
I am the holy . . ., the mother of the Ešaba.
I am Gašanašte, the lady of Larak.
I am the mother of the house, Ezinu-kusu.
I am the child of the house, the lady Gunura.
I am Gašannigara of the holy place.

Oh house, my tasty food which is not being eaten!
Oh house, my sweet water which is not being drunk!
My house of the good seat where no one is sitting!
My house of the good bedchamber where no one is lying down!
My house of the holy plate where no one is eating!
My house of the holy bronze (vessel) where no one is drinking!
My house of the holy offering table which no one carries!
My (house) of the holy vessel where no one libates water!
My (house) of the holy kettledrum where it is not set up!
My (house) of the holy balag-instrument which no one plays!
My (house) of the holy halhallatu-drum which does not resound!
My (house) of the holy manzu-drum which does not *sound sweet*!
My reed pipe which does not *thunder forth*!
My instruments which are not being distributed!
My gala-priest who no longer soothes my heart!
My gudu-priest no longer speaks happily!
My house! My happy spouse who no longer is present there!
My house! My sweet child who no longer is present there!
My house! I, its lady, do not majestically pass through it.
I do not majestically pass through it. I am no longer majestically present there.

May my father . . .
May my father Enlil . . .

I shall enter my house! I shall enter! I shall lie down (there)! I shall lie down (there)!
I shall enter my treasure-house! I shall enter! I shall lie down (there)! I shall lie down (there)!
I shall sleep at my house! That sleep is sure to be good.
At my house I shall lie upon its bed! That bed is sure to be good.
At my house I shall sit upon its throne! That throne is sure to be good.

---

an eršemma of Gula
collated (at) the shrine Sippar

This next eršemma of Baba, the chief goddess of Lagaš, laments Enlil's destruction of Girsu, Lagaš, Nina, Sirara and Guabba, a string of cities directly to the east of the southernmost end of the Tigris River. The composition is constructed upon the use of antithesis. In the opening portion the cities and shrines are described as jewels, yet in the next passage we are informed that the gems are now dull and crushed. Moreover, the storm, which should be kept out of the city, is inside the city; whereas the protective Lama-genie has been forced to live outside the city. The poet then relates that all the accoutrements of lordship were present in the city, yet in the following lines the lady of the city has abandoned it. The final contrast involves the loving care tendered by Enlil when founding the city. Yet now it is Enlil who destroys it.

We have two Old Babylonian recensions of this eršemma with so many differences that they merit separate editions.

Eršemma no. 166.1

Text: BM 85005 (*CT* 15 pl. 22)
Collated: S. N. Kramer, *RA* 65 26

1. uru a gi$_{16}$-sa bar-mu ba-e-ga-àm
2. uru-mu Gír-su^{ki} a gi$_{16}$-sa bar-mu ba-e-ga-àm
3. še-eb-ki-Lagaš^{ki} a gi$_{16}$-sa bar-mu ba-e-ga-àm
4. èš é-ninnu-mu a gi$_{16}$-sa bar-mu ba-e-ga-àm
5. du$_{6}$ Nina^{ki}-na-mu a gi$_{16}$-sa bar-mu ba-e-ga-àm
6. še-eb-Sirará^{ki}-mu a gi$_{16}$-sa bar-mu ba-e-ga-àm
7. eden-bar-Lagaš^{ki}-a a gi$_{16}$-sa bar-mu ba-e-ga-àm
8. uru-mu gi$_{16}$-sa-bi ba-bir-bir-re
9. Gír-su^{ki} za-gìn-tur-tur ba-sùḫ-sùḫ-e
10. uru šà-bi-ta u$_{4}$ in-ga-àm-du$_{11}$
11. Gír-su^{ki} bar-bi-ta ^{d}Lama-ki-kù-ga-mu
12. šà-ba bára-babbar-ra na-mu-un-ma-al
13. mu-dúr -ru-na-mu šu na-mu-un-ma-al
14. àm-mu-uš ⌜húl-la⌝-šè mu-un-ma-al
15. dam-ur-sag-gal-a-šè mu-un-ma-al
16. ga-ša-an ‹uru›-bi-ta nam-ba-ra-è
17. ga-ša-an-gu-la é-bi-⌜ta⌝ ba-ra-⌜è⌝
18. ^{e}-gi^{e}gí-uru-me-a gù ga-à[m-ra]
19. ama ga-ša-an-sún-na gù ga-à[m-ra]
20. imim^{im}-šè DI.DI im-du$_{8}$ ⌜x⌝-[. . .]
21. [uru]-mu a-a-mu sag-rig$_{7}$-⌜eš⌝ [. . .]
22. [kur]-gal ^{d}Mu-ul-líl-e mí⌜x⌝[. . .-du$_{11}$]
23. urú-mu gú-KU-a mu-ni-i[b-ḫa-lam-a]
24. Gír-su^{ki} gú-KU-a mu-ni-ib-ḫa-[lam-a]
25. Lagaš gú-KU-a mu-ni-ib-ḫa-lam-⌜a⌝
26. Sirará^{ki} gú-KU-a mu-ni-ib-ḫa-lam-a
27. Nina^{ki} gú-KU-a mu-ni-ib-ḫa-lam-a
28. sipa-šub-bé ba-ni-ib-te-en
29. sipa-šub-šub-bé ú ba-ni-ib-te-en-te-en

mu-lu-šìr-ra a uru-mu a é-mu a-na gál-lu-bi

ér-šem$_5$-ma-^{d}Ba-ba$_6$-kam

* * *

City! Oh jewel-work! Because of me it was pillaged.
My city Girsu! Oh jewel-work! Because of me it was pillaged.
Brickwork of "the place" Lagaš! Oh jewel-work! Because of me it was pillaged.
My shrine Eninnu! Oh jewel-work! Because of me it was pillaged.
My mound Nina! Oh jewel-work! Because of me it was pillaged.
My brickwork of Sirara! Oh jewel-work! Because of me it was pillaged.
. . . Lagaš! Oh jewel-work! Because of me it was pillaged.

My city (now) scatters its jewel-work.
Girsu makes the small lapis-lazuli (stones) dull.
From the midst (of) the city the storm has spoken out.
(While) my Lama-genie of the holy place (is) outside of Girsu!

Inside she(?) had placed a shining throne.
She(?) had placed a scepter(?) there.
She(?) placed a third one there for joy.
She(?) placed it there for the consort of the great warrior.
(Now) the lady has left this city.
The supreme lady has left this house.
"Princess of our city!" shall I cry out.
"Mother Ninsun!" shall I cry out.

Going to the clay, [fashioning(?)] the walls,
my father [had presented] my [city to me] as a gift.
The great [mountain], Enlil, [had taken] care [of it].

He destroys my city . . .
He destroys Girsu . . .
He destroys Lagaš . . .
He destroys Sirara . . .
He destroys Nina . . .

. . . shepherd . . . fallen . . .
. . . shepherd(s) . . . fallen . . .
Singer of songs, oh my city! Oh my house and whatever else there be!

It is an eršemma of Baba.

Eršemma no. 166.2

Text: VAT 617 (*VAS* 2 2) rev. iv 10 ff.

1. [urú a gi$_{16}$-sa] bar-mà ba-e-ga
2. [. . .] a gi$_{16}$-sa
3. [. . .] a gi$_{16}$-sa
4. [. . .]-⸢x⸣ a gi$_{16}$-sa
5. [še-eb-ki]-La-ga-sa a gi$_{16}$-sa
6. [é-tar-sí]r$^{!}$-sír-ra a gi$_{16}$-sa
7. ⸢ma⸣-gú-en-na a gi$_{16}$-sa
8. du$_{6}$ ⸢urú⸣-Mi-na a gi$_{16}$-sa
9. še-eb-Si-ra-ra a gi$_{16}$-sa
10. èš gú-ab-ba a gi$_{16}$-sa
11. urú-mu gi$_{16}$-sa-bi ba-bi-ib-re
12. Gír-su^{ki} za-tur-tur-bi ba-si-is-ḫe
13. urú-mu an-zu-ta an-zu-gi$_{6}$-ga
14. Gír-su^{ki} an-zu-ta an-zu-babbar-ra
15. šà-bar$_{6}$-bar$_{6}$-ba-ra na-mu-un-ri
16. mu-duru$_{5}$-u$_{4}$-sur-ra na-mu-un-ma-al
17. mi-úš ḫúl-la-šè na-mu-un-ma-al
18. dam-ur-sag-gal-la-šè na-mu-un-ma-al
19. gu$_{4}$-dè tùr-ra šu ì-zu-zu
20. Gír-su gu$_{4}$-da-gin$_{7}$ šu nu-mu-un-da-zu-zu
21. egí-me-en urú-mà-a gu ga-am-ra
22. ga-ša-an-ki-La-ga-sa-mèn gu ga-am-ra
23. urú-mu a-a-mu sag-e-eš mu-ni-rig$_{7}$
24. Gír-su^{ki} ^{d}Mu-ul-líl-lá mí-zi mu-un-du$_{11}$
25. za-di$_{4}$-di$_{4}$-lá šu-mu ba-e-dab$_{5}$
26. za-gal-gal-la gú-mu ba-e-dab$_{5}$
27. urú-mu ám-gig-ga nu-šub-⸢šub-bé⸣
28. ám-i-bí-ur$_{5}$-ka ur$_{5}$-ra nu-šub-[šub-bé]
29. me gú im-me urú ad-[. . .]
30. gú im-me ú-ra ad-[. . .]
31. urú-mu gú-gú-bi mu-ni-i[b-ḫa-lam-a]
32. Gír-su^{ki} gú-gú-bi mu-n[i-ib-ḫa-lam-a]
33. ki-La-ga-sa gú-gú-bi m[u-ni-ib-ḫa-lam-a]
34. ⸢sipa⸣-šub u$_{4}$-tur-bi u$_{4}$ ba-[. . .]
35. ⸢sipa⸣-šub u$_{4}$-tur-bi ní-bi-a u$_{4}$ ba-[. . .]

* * *

1. [City! Oh jewel-work!] Because of me it was pillaged.
   [. . .] Oh jewel-work!

[. . .] Oh jewel-work!
[. . .] Oh jewel-work!
[Brickwork of "the place"]-Lagaš! Oh jewel-work!
Etarsirsira! Oh jewel-work!
Maguenna! Oh jewel-work!
Mound Nina! Oh jewel-work!
Brickwork of Sirara! Oh jewel-work!
Shrine Guabba! Oh jewel-work!

(Now) my city smashes its jewel-work.
Girsu makes its small precious stones dull.
My city . . .
Girsu . . .

Inside she(?) had placed a shining throne.
She(?) had placed a scepter there for the measure of one's days.
She(?) had placed a third one there for joy.
She(?) placed it there for the consort of the great warrior.

The ox in the cattle pen . . .
(But) Girsu cannot (even) . . . like that(?) of(?) an ox.
"In our city you are the princess!" shall I cry out.
"You are the lady of 'the place'-Lagaš!" shall I cry out.
My father had presented my city to me as a gift.
Enlil had taken care of Girsu.
My hand had laid hold of the small precious stones.
My neck had laid hold of the large precious stones.
My city did not fall in sickness.
That which was *in front of a pit* did not fall in.

. . . the city [. . .]. . .[. . .].
. . . the city [. . .]. . .[. . .].
[He destroys] my city . . .
[He destroys] Girsu . . .
[He destroys] "the place" Lagaš . . .
. . .
. . .

B. Eršemmas Preserved in Both Old Babylonian and First Millennium B.C.E. *Copies*

This eršemma of Enlil is a plea to him that he witness for himself the havoc wrought by his wrath.

There are marked differences between the Old Babylonian recension (1.1) and the First Millennium B.C.E. recension (1.2). In 1.1 the cities Nippur, Ur and Larsa are mentioned, whereas in 1.2 the cities are Nippur, Babylon (=Tintir), Sippar, and Borsippa, with one text including Isin. These references can help us in assigning a date of adaptation or composition. The Old Babylonian recension would appear to have been written or adapted for use during the hegemony of Larsa (ca. 1932–1763 B.C.E.). 1.2, however, is centered upon the more northerly centers, thereby suggesting adaptation for this area, which probably did not occur any earlier than 1800 B.C.E. The most puzzling feature is the addition in one text of the city Isin. Isin was conquered in 1793 B.C.E. by Rim-Sin, king of Larsa. Yet the recension of this eršemma was probably not adapted before this time, as previously stated. In fact, Isin had lost control of Nippur by the close of the first century of the Second Millennium B.C.E. The question then is whether this inclusion of Isin in a text mentioning Babylon and Nippur, was made for the First Dynasty of Isin or possibly for the Second Dynasty of Isin (1156–1025 B.C.E.). (Note however the prevalent orthography PA.ŠE for Isin in this latter period, whereas our text uses Ì-si-in. However, our texts are late copies, and changes in orthography do occur.)

The other main difference between the two versions is that 1.2 has been expanded by inserting city names to 1.1:21–22, thereby making it into a refrain (1.2:28–35). The other points of divergence, such as 1.2:51 and the varying verbal forms, could be expected in two recensions copied during the same period.

Eršemma no. 1.1

Text: BM 29623 (*CT* 15 pl. 12–13)
Collated: S. N. Kramer, *RA* 65 24
Most recent treatment: R. Kutscher, *YNER* 6 pp. 61ff.

1. dilmun nigín-ù	urú-zu u$_{6}$ ⸢u⸣(?) b[í-du$_{11}$]
2. alim-ma dilmun nigín-ù	urú-zu u$_{6}$ b[í-du$_{11}$]
3. ù-mu-un-kur-kur-ra-ke$_{4}$ nigín-ù	urú-[zu u$_{6}$ bí-du$_{11}$]
4. ù-mu-un-du$_{11}$-ga-zi-da nigín-ù	urú-[zu u$_{6}$ bí-du$_{11}$]
5. ^{d}Mu-ul-líl a-a-ka-na-ág-gá [nigín-ù]	[urú-zu] u$_{6}$ bí-[du$_{11}$]

6. sipa-sag-gi$_6$-ga nigín-ù urú-[zu u$_6$ bí-du$_{11}$]
7. i-bí du$_8$ ní-te-na nigín-ù urú-[zu u$_6$ bí-du$_{11}$]
8. am erén-na di-di nigín-ù urú-[zu u$_6$ bí-du$_{11}$]
9. ù-lul-la ku-ku nigín-ù urú-[zu u$_6$ bí-du$_{11}$]
10. urú-zu Nibru^{ki}-zu nigín-ù [urú-zu u$_6$ bí-du$_{11}$]
11. še-eb-é-kur-ra-ta nigín-ù [urú-zu u$_6$ bí-du$_{11}$]
12. ki-ùr ki-gal-ta nigín-ù [urú-zu u$_6$ bí-du$_{11}$]
13. du$_6$-kù ki-kù-ta nigín-ù [urú-zu u$_6$ bí-du$_{11}$]
14. šà-é-dìm-ma-ta nigín-ù [urú-zu u$_6$ bí-du$_{11}$]
15. é-ká-maḫ-ta nigín-ù [urú-zu u$_6$ bí-du$_{11}$]
16. é-*mà*-nun-maḫ-ta nigín-ù [urú-zu u$_6$ bí-du$_{11}$]
17. ma-mu-šú-a-ta nigín-ù u[rú-zu u$_6$ b]í-du$_{11}$
18. ma-é-gal-maḫ-ta nigín-ù u[rú-zu u$_6$ b]í-du$_{11}$
19. še-eb-Urí^{ki}-ma-ta nigín-ù urú-z[u u$_6$] bí-du$_{11}$
20. še-eb-Larsa^{ki}-ma-ta nigín-ù urú-zu u$_6$ bí-du$_{11}$
21. urú e$_4$-du$_{11}$-ga e$_4$-gi$_4$-a-zu
22. e$_4$-du$_{11}$-ga e$_4$-ta gar-ra-zu
23. urú še ku$_5$-da ki lá-a-zu
24. [ám]-gu$_7$!-nu-gu$_7$!-a u$_4$ zal-zal-la-ri
25. dam-tur-ra-ke$_4$ dam-mu mu-ni-ib-bé
26. dumu-tur-ra-ke$_4$ dumu-mu mu-ni-ib-bé
27. ki-sikil-e šeš-mu mu-ni-ib-bé
28. urú-ta ama-gan-e dumu-mu mu-ni-ib-bé
29. dumu-bàn-da a-a-mu mu-ni-ib-bé
30. tur-e al-è maḫ-e al-è
31. e-sír-e gub-ba mu-un-sar-re-dam
32. sal-la-bi ur-e àm-da-ab-lá
33. sig$_{11}$-bi mu-bar-re àm-da-ab-lá
34. ešemen-ba líl ba-e-sù

---

34 ér-šem$_5$-ma-^{d}En-líl-a-kam

* * *

1. Important one, go about! You have watched over your city.
Honored one, important one, go about! You have watched over your city.
Lord of the lands, go about! [You have watched over your] city.
Lord whose pronouncement is true, go about! [You have watched over your] city.
5. Enlil, father of the nation, [go about]! You have watched over [your city].

Shepherd of the black-headed, go about! [You have watched over] your [city].
He who witnesses (everything) first-hand, go about! [You have watched over] your [city].
Bull who causes the troops to wander, go about! [You have watched over] your [city].
He who sleeps a false sleep, go about! [You have watched over] your [city].
Go about your city, your Nippur! [You have watched over your city].
Go about in the brickwork of the Ekur! [You have watched over your city].
Go about in the Kiur, the great place! [You have watched over your city].
Go about Duku, the pure place! [You have watched over your city].
Go about the Šaedima! [You have watched over your city].
Go about the Ekamah! [You have watched over your city].
Go about the Eganunmah! [You have watched over your city].
Go about the Gagiššua! [You have watched over your city].
Go about the Maegalmah! [You have watched over your city].
Go about the brickwork of Ur! You have [watched over] your city.
Go about the brickwork of Larsa! You have watched over your city.

Your city which has been flooded, washed away,
Your (city) which has been flooded, which has been submerged beneath the waters,
Your city which must (carefully) check the weight of the grain (whose supply) has been cut off,
(Where) the glutton spends the day without eating, (go about)!

She who has a new spouse says, "My spouse!"
She who has a little child says, "My child!"
The young girl says, "My brother!"
From the city the mother says, "My child!"
The young child says, "My father!"
These youngsters go mad; these adults go mad,
so that those standing in the street become restless.
The dogs carry off those spread far and wide.
The wolves carry off those who are scattered.
In its dancing places ghosts are spread about.

---

34 (lines) It is an eršemma of Enlil.

Eršemma no. 1.2

Text		
	A BM 79-7-8, 70 (BL 80) 1–11	18–25, 28–29
	B K.2003+K.3466 (*4R*^{2} 28* 4) rev. 5–70	1–51
	C K.2789+K.4964+K.4966 1–21	29–34, 36–51
	D K.3506 1–17	29–33, 36–46, 48–51
	E K.5273 (BL 93) 1–13	1–13
	F K.6084 (BL 144) 1–7	1–7
	G K.8646 5–10	1–4
	H Sm.47 1–8	30–33, 36–39
	I Sm.528 6	1
	J *UET* 6/2 207 16–24	41–46, 48–50
	K VAT 37+(*SBH* 70) obv. 1–14	42–45, 48–51
	L VAT 245+(*SBH* 46) rev. 27–30	1, 51
	M VAT 2173+(*SBH* 85) 1–10	37–42
	N VAT 6427 (*VAS* 17 55) obv. 1–10	17–18, 21–22, 28, 33

1. dilmun^{ki} nigin-na[1] urú-zu u$_6$ gá-e-dè[2]
   kab-tum : ^{d}*En-líl na-as-ḫi-ram-ma ana* URU-*ka tu-ur :*
   URU-*ka ḫi-iṭ-ṭi*[3]
2. alim-ma dilmun^{ki} nigin-na[1] urú-zu
3. umun-kur-kur-ra nigin-na[1]
4. umun-du$_{11}$-ga-zi-da nigin-na[1]
5. ^{d}Mu-ul-líl a-a-ka-nag-gá nigin-na
6. sipa-sag-gi$_6$-ga nigin-na
7. i-bí du$_8$ ní-te-en[1]-na nigin-na
8. am erén-na di-di nigin-na
9. ù-lul-la ku-ku nigin-na
10. umun ^{d}Am-an-ki nigin-na
11. ur-sag ^{d}Asar-lú-hi nigin-na
12. umun ^{d}En-bi-lu-lu nigin-na
13. ur-sag ^{d}Mu-zé-eb-ba-sa$_4$-a nigin-na
14. umun ^{d}Di-ku$_5$-maḫ-a nigin-na
15. ur-sag ^{d}Ut-u$_x$-lu nigin-na
16. umun-an-uraš-a-ra nigin-na
17. urú-zu Nibru^{ki}-ta nigin-na[1]
    ana URU-*ka Ni-ip-pu-ru na-[as-ḫi-ram-ma]*[2]
18. še-eb-é-kur-ra-ta ki-ùr é-nam-ti-la
19. še-eb-Zimbir^{ki}-ta[1] nigin-na
20. èš é-babbar-ra[1] é-di-ku$_5$-kalam-ma
21. še-eb-Tin-tir^{ki}-ta nigin-na[1]
22. še-eb-é-sag-íl-la èš é-tùr-kalam-ma

23. še-eb-Barsip^{ki}-ta nigin-na
24. še-eb-é-zi-da-ta èš é-maḫ-ti-la
25. še-eb-é-te-me-an-ki èš é-dàra-an-na
26. [še-eb]-Ì-si-in^{ki}-na-ta[1] nigin-na
27. [èš] é-gal-maḫ èš é-rab-ri-ri
28. urú e$_4$-du$_{11}$-ga e$_4$-gi$_4$-a-za
a-lum šá naq-rù[1] ú-šá-nu-u[2] : a-ḫu-lap tu-ur-šú
29. Nibru^{ki} e$_4$-du$_{11}$-ga e$_4$-ta mar-ra-za
šá naq-ru-u ana me-e sa-lu-u
30. urú e$_4$-du$_{11}$-ga e$_4$-gi$_4$-a-za[1]
31. Zimbir^{ki} e$_4$-du$_{11}$-ga e$_4$-ta[1]
32. urú e$_4$-du$_{11}$-ga e$_4$-gi$_4$[1]
33. Tin-tir^{ki} e$_4$-du$_{11}$-ga e$_4$-ta[1]
šá ana me-e sa-lu-[u]
34. urú e$_4$-du$_{11}$-ga e$_4$-gi$_4$-[1]
35. Ì-si-in^{ki}-na e$_4$-du$_{11}$-ga e$_4$-ta
36. urú še ku$_5$-da ki lá-lá-a-zu
a-lum šá še-um ip-par-su-šú ud-di-tum iš-šaq-lu-šu
37. ám-gu$_7$ nu-gu$_7$-e[1] u$_4$[2] zal-zal-la-ri[3]
ak-ki-lu ina la a-ka-li uš-tab-ru-u
38. dam-tur-ra-ke$_4$ dam-mu mu-ni-íb-bé
šá mu-us-sà ṣe-eḫ-ru[1] mu-ti-ma i-qab-bi
39. dumu-tur-ra-ke$_4$ dumu-mu mu-ni-íb-bé
[. . .] ma-ri-ma i-qab-[bi]
40. ki-sikil-mu šeš-mu mu-ni-íb-bé
ar-da-tum a-ḫi-mi i-qab-bi
41. urú ama-gan-mu dumu-mu mu-ni-íb-bé
ina a-li um-mu a-lit-tu ma-ri-mi
42. dumu-bàn-da a-a-mu mu-ni-íb-bé
mar-tum ṣe-ḫer-tum a-bi-mi
43. e-sír-ra[1] gub-ba mu-un[2]-sar-re-e-ne
šá ina su-qí iz-za-az-zu uš-taḫ-mi-ṭú
44. tur-e[1] al-è maḫ-e al-è[2]
ṣe-eḫ-ru[3] i-maḫ-ḫi ra-bu-ú i-maḫ-ḫi
45. Nibru^{ki} tur-e al-è maḫ-[1]
46. Tin-tir^{ki} tur-e al-è maḫ-
47. Ì-si-in^{ki}-na tur-e al-è maḫ-
48. sal-la-bi ur-re[1] an-da-ab-lá[2]
qal-la-šu[3] kal-bu uš-⌜qa⌝-lil : na-ak-ru it-ta-ši[4]
49. sig$_{11}$-bi mu-bar-ra an-da-ab-lá
sà-ap-ḫu-us-su bar-ba-ru ú-šaq-lil[1]
50. ešemen líl-lá-àm e-si
me-lul-ta-šu[1] zi-qí-qam im-ta-la

51. e-sír[1] la-la-bi nu-gi$_4$-gi$_4$
su-ú-qu šá la-la-a[2] *la áš-bu-ú*

D: [ér]-šèm-ma-^{d}En-líl-lá(-kam)

Variants

UET 6/2 207 obv. 16–24:

16. (41) urú a-gal-gal dumu-mu mu-ni-íb-ba
17. (42) dumu-bàn-da a-a-mu mu-ni-íb-ba
18. (43) e!-si-ra-a gub-ba mu-un-sa-re-bi
19. (44) tur-ra GÌR(?) DIR(?) ab-ma-ḫu! i-má!-la
20. (45) Nibru^{ki} tur-ra i-má-la-⌈ma-ḫu⌉
21. (46) Tin-tir^{ki} tur-ra i-má-la-ma-ḫu
22. (48) sil-la-bi GIŠ mu-ra an-da-ab-la-al
23. (49) ⌈sig⌉$_4$(?)-⌈x⌉-ne mu-ba-ra an-da-ab-la-al
24. (50) KI.AN.NI.DA li-li-a-a e-su

1. 1) E.F:[nigin]-ù; I,L: nigín-ù 2) F: ga-e-dè; G: gá-e-du$_{11}$: -dè; L: ga-e-du$_{11}$ 3) G :*[na]-as-ḫi-ram-ma* URU-*ka ḫi-iṭ : a-mu-ur* / *[na]-as-ḫi-ram-ma ana* URU-*ka tu-ur;* L: *kab-tum na-às-ḫi-ram-ma* URU-*ka ḫi-i-iṭ*
2. 1) F: nigin-ù (:) -na; G: nigín-na
3. 1) G: nigín-[na]
4. 1) G: nigín-[na]
7. 1) E omits -en-
17. 1) N: nigín-[ ] 2) Akkadian according to N
19. 1) A:-ke$_4$ instead of -ta
20. 1) A: é-babbar-rù
21. 1) N: nigín-[ ]
26. 1) B:-ta according to collation
28. 1) A,N: *na-aq-ru* 2) A: *u*!*-[šá-nu-u]*; N: *ú-šá-an-[nu-u]*
30. 1) H:-zu
31. 1) C adds mar-ra-[za]; H: mar-a-zu
32. 1) C adds -a; H adds -a-zu
33. 1) C,N add mar-ra-[za]; H: mar-a-zu 2) Akkadian according to N
34. 1) C adds -a
37. 1) C:[. . .]-e ám-gu$_7$-e 2) D omits u$_4$ 3) H:-zu instead of -ri
38. 1) M:-*ri*
39. 1) Akkadian according to M
43. 1) C: e-sir-ra 2) C: -lu- instead of -un-
44. 1) K:[tur]-re 2) B,C: maḫ-e ‹‹e›› al-è 3) K: *[. . .] za*⌈x⌉*[. . .]*
45. 1) D adds -e

48. 1) D: ur-ra 2) D: an-da-ab-lá-e : -re 3) K: *qal-la-šú* 4) K:*[uš]-ta-qal-lil : [na]-ak!-ri i-ta-[ši]*
49. 1) K: *uš-⌈ta⌉-[qal]-lil*
50. 1) K: *me-lul-la-šú*
51. 1) C: e-sir 2) K: *la-la-šú*

Important one, go about! . . . watch over . . . your city.
Honored one, important one, go about! . . . watch over . . . your city.
Lord of the lands, go about!
Lord whose pronouncement is true, go about!
Enlil, father of the nation, go about!
Shepherd of the black-headed, go about!
He who witnesses (everything) first-hand, go about!
Bull who causes the troops to wander, go about!
He who sleeps a false sleep, go about!
Lord Enki, go about!
Warrior Asarluḫi, go about!
Lord Enbilulu, go about!
Warrior Mudugasa, go about!
Lord Dikumaḫa, go about!
Warrior Utulu, go about!
Lord of heaven and earth, go about!
Go about in your city, Nippur!
In the brickwork of the Ekur, (in) the kiur and the Enamtila
(and) in the brickwork of Sippar go about!
In the shrine Ebabbar, the Edikukalama
(and) the brickwork of Tintir go about!
In the brickwork of the Esagil, the shrine Eturkalama
(and) the brickwork of Borsippa go about!
In the brickwork of the Ezida, the shrine Emaḫtila,
the brickwork of the Etemenanki, the shrine Edaranna,
(and) the brickwork of Isin go about!
(In) the [shrine] Egalmaḫ and the shrine Erabriri (go about)!
In your city which has been flooded, washed away,
in your Nippur which has been flooded, which has been submerged beneath the waters,
in your city which has been flooded, washed away,
in your Sippar which has been flooded, which has been submerged beneath the waters,
in your city which has been flooded, washed away,
in your Tintir which has been flooded, which has been submerged beneath the waters,
in your city which has been flooded, washed away,

in your Isin which has been flooded, which has been submerged beneath the waters,
your city which must (carefully) check the weight of the grain (whose supply) has been cut off,
(where) the glutton spends the day without eating, (go about)!

She who has a new spouse says, "My spouse!"
She who has a little child says, "My child!"
My young girl says, "My brother!"
(In) the city my mother says, "My child!"
The young child says, "My father!"
They make those standing in the street restless.
These youngsters go mad; these adults go mad.
(In) Nippur these youngsters go mad; these adults go mad.
(In) Tintir these youngsters go mad; these adults go mad.
In Isin these youngsters go mad; these adults go mad.
The dogs carry off those spread far and wide.
The wolves carry off those who are scattered.
The dancing places are filled with ghosts.
The street is not sated with its joy.

[It is] an eršemma of Enlil.

This next work is also an eršemma of Enlil and it is preserved as an Old Babylonian syllabic recension (35.1) and as a First Millennium B.C.E. recension (35.2). The theme of the eršemma is the overpowering greatness of Enlil. The cities and temples which he has destroyed can only sigh in the face of his mere utterance, which can unleash complete devastation. Nature itself, symbolized by the majestic mesu-trees, does him homage. And it is before Enlil, portrayed as a fowler, for he ensnares in his nets and traps everyone, that the orphan and widow come to seek justice. This last reference to justice is apparently intended to indicate that everything instigated by Enlil, including the destruction of cities and temples, is just and not capricious.

The only notable difference between the two recensions is that 35.2 has inserted a list of northerly cities and their temples, thus lengthening the text.

Eršemma no. 35.1

Text: *TLB* 2 6 ii 14'-iii 13

[ú-ru] a-še-ra mi-na ⸢x⸣[x]⸢x⸣
⸢ú-ru⸣-mu Ni-ib-ru ⸢x-x⸣-gu-la

3. ⸢ši⸣-bi-kur-ra a-še-ra [. . .]⸢x⸣[. . .]
4. ki-ur ki-gal a-še-ra mi-na [. . .]
5. ši-bi-du-du-ba a-še-ra a-še-ra [. . .]
6. e-⸢si⸣-kur-zi a-še-ra mi-⸢na⸣ [. . .]
7. ú-ru a-še-ra ni-iš-bi-gu-la ka-ša-an ka-bi ba-an-ga
8. Ni-ib-ru a-še-re ni-iš-bi-gu-le ka-ša-an ka-bi ba-an-ga
9. ši-bi-kur-ra ni-iš-bi-gu-le ka-ša-an ka-bi ba-an-ga
10. ⸢ki-ur ki-gal⸣ ni-iš-bi-gu-le ka-ša-an ka-bi! ba-an-ga
11. ba-[an]-di-ri-ga ba-an-di-ri-ga ú-ru-ta ba-re-e
12. ú-[ru]-mu Ni-ib-ru ba-an-di-ri-ga ú-ru-ta ba-ra-e
13. ši-bi-kur-ra ba-an-di-ri-ga ú-ru-ta ba-ra-e
14. ⸢ki-ur⸣ ki-gal ba-⸢an-di-ri-ga⸣ ú-⸢ru⸣-[ta ba-ra-e]
15. ⸢im⸣-ma-al KU⸢x⸣[. . .] du-x [. . .]
16. a-ma-⸢mu⸣ [. . .]

(*Remainder of text not preserved*)

Eršemma no. 35.2

Text	A BM 132094 (*CT* 42 21)	1–39
	B K.3801 (BL 94)	20–29
	C K.8608 (BL 162)	12–16, 19–20
	D K.9309 (BL 63)	34–39
	E *UET* 6/2 205 obv. 8–14	26–31
	F VAT 14486 (*LKU* 10) obv. i	20–34?

1. [urú a-še-er-ra èn-šè ba-gul-e]
2. [urú-m]u ⸢Nibru^{ki}⸣ [a]-
3. [še-eb]-⸢é⸣-kur-⸢ra⸣ [a]-
4. [ki-ù]r ki-gal [a]-
5. [èš] ⸢é⸣-nam-ti-la ⸢a⸣-
6. [še-eb]-Zimbir^{ki} a-
7. [èš] ⸢é⸣-babbar a-
8. [še-eb-Tin]-tir^{ki} a-
9. [še-eb]-⸢é⸣-sag-íl-la a-
10. [še-eb]-Barsip^{ki} a-
11. [še-eb]-⸢é⸣-zi-da a-
12. [še-eb-é-maḫ]-ti-la a-
13. [é-te-m]e-an-⸢ki⸣ a-
14. [é-dàr]a-⸢an⸣-na a-
15. [urú a-še-er]-ra nu-uš-ba-an-gul-la! gasan ši-bi ba-an-!gi
16. [Nibru]^{ki} a-še-er-ra nu-uš-ba-an-gul-la! gašan
17. [ki-ùr ki-gal a-še-er]-ra nu-uš-ba-an-gul-la gašan!
18. [še-eb-é-kur-ra a-še-er]-ra nu-uš-ba-an-gul-la gašan!

19. [. . . im]-ma-al eden-na ^{ú}šumun$_x$(NUMUN$_2$)-bur-re[1] ^{ú}šu-mu-un-šè[2][. . .]
20. u$_8$ silá rig$_7$-ga-gin$_7$ na-an-gul-e ama$_5$ ér-bi na-an-gul-[e]
[. . . pu(?)-ha(?)]-⸢di⸣(?) ṣa-ab-tù⸢x⸣ [maš]-⸢ta-ki-šá⸣ ⸢x-x⸣ ul ⸢i⸣-[kal-la]
21. ùz máš tùr-ra-gin$_7$ na-an-gul-e ama$_5$ ér-bi na-an-gul-e
[. . .] ṣa-ab-tu$_4$ MIN
22. šilam amar-bi nigin-na-gin$_7$ na-an-gul-e ama$_5$
23. ⸢še⸣-en amar-bi gùd-gi-a-gin$_7$ na-an-gul-e ama$_5$
24. ba-an-diri-ga ba-an-diri-ga urú-ta ba-ra-è
25. e-ne-èm-an-gu-la ba-an-diri-ga urú-ta
26. e-ne-èm-^{d}Mu-ul-líl-lá ba-an-diri-ga urú-ta
27. urú-mu du-lum-gig šeg$_x$(KAxŠID) mi-ni-in-gi un-bi ba-[tu$_{10}$]-bé-eš
[. . . ni]-ši-šú ⸢ik-ka-ma⸣-ra
28. urú-mu ḫa-zí-in-na šeg$_x$ mi-ni-in-gi di$_4$-di$_4$-lá-‹bi› ba-
[. . .]-⸢x⸣ ṣe-eḫ-ḫe-ru-tu-šú
29. urú-mu ab-ba-a šeg$_x$ mi-ni-in-gi guruš-bi ba-
[. . . eṭ]-lu-tu-šú
30. [urú-mu . . . šeg$_x$ mi-ni-in-gi] dam-bi ba-
[. . . mu]-us-sa id-⸢DAK-*ki*⸣
31. [e-ne-èm-^{d}Mu-ul]-líl-lá-ke$_4$ šeg$_x$ mi-ni-in-gi KA.KA ba-
[. . .]⸢x⸣a⸢x⸣
32. [. . .]-si urú-mu bí-íb-bé [. . .] bí-íb-⸢x⸣
33. [x x]⸢x⸣-ba gú-ni bí-ni bí-íb-lá ^{giš}mes g[ú-ni bí-íb-lá]
34. [^{giš}mes]-di$_4$-di$_4$-lá-mu gú-ni bí-íb-lá ^{giš}mes[1]
35. [^{giš}mes]-gal-gal-la-mu gú-ni bí-íb-lá ^{giš}mes
36. [mu-]lu-šìr-re ^{giš}mes-di$_4$-lá-mu ^{giš}mes
37. ⸢mu⸣-lu-šìr-re ^{giš}mes-gal-gal-la-[1]mu ^{giš}mes
38. ⸢x⸣ba tar-ra mu-lu-é-[1]kur-ra-ke$_4$[2] urú-mu ba-nú-a[3]
39. [i]-bí mušen-dù nu-tuk-[1]la mu-lu-é-[2]kur-ra-ke$_4$ i-bí-a-né mu-un-gub

---

ér-šèm-ma-^{d}En-líl-lá-kam

Variants

UET 6/2 205 obv. 8–14:

8. (26) e-ne-èm-^{d}Mu-ul-líl-lá ba-an-diri-ga urú-ta ba-da-pàd
9. (27) ⸢uru⸣⸢uru-u⸣-ni gùmu-ḫúl-lu-gin$_7$ šèg me^{kum}-me lu in ⸢x⸣-nigi-mu un-⸢bi⸣(?) ⸢ba⸣(?)-tu$_{10}$-bé-eš
10. (28) urú-ni ḫa-zé-lá šèg me-nigi-mu di-di-lá ba-
11. (29) urú-ni mu-a-ab-ba-gin$_7$ šèg me-nigi-mu guruš-bi ba-
12. (30) urú-ni gú-e-ga-a-gin$_7$ šèg me-nigi-mu da-bi ba-

13. (31) e-na-ám-^{d}Mu-ul-líl-lá-ke$_4$ šèg me-nigi-mu [x]⸢x x x⸣[x]⸢x⸣ KA.KA ba-tu$_{10}$-bé-eš

15. 1) So A; C:-e
16. 1) So A; C:-e
17. 1) C omits line
18. 1) C omits line
19. 1) So A 2) C: [. . .]-ma-al eden-na ú-NUMUN$_2$-bu-re / ú-šu-NUMUN$_2$-bu-re
34. F has two lines we can't exactly place: [. . .] bu ka / [. . .]⸢bar$_6$⸣(?)-bar$_6$
37. 1) D: [. . .]-la RAT mu
38. 1) D omits -é 2) D:-ke$_4$(collated) 3) D omits -a
39. 1) D: sík instead of -tuk- 2) D omits -é-

[When will the city be able to hold back the sighing]?
When will my [city], Nippur, be able to hold back the sighing?
When will [the brickwork] of the Ekur be able to hold back the sighing?
When will [the kiur], the great place, be able to hold back the sighing?
When will [the shrine] Enamtila be able to hold back the sighing?
When will [the brickwork] of Sippar be able to hold back the sighing?
When will [the shrine] Ebabbar be able to hold back the sighing?
When will [the brickwork] of Tintir be able to hold back the sighing?
When will [the brickwork] of the Esagil be able to hold back the sighing?
When will [the brickwork] of Borsippa be able to hold back the sighing?
When will [the brickwork] of the Ezida be able to hold back the sighing?
When will [the brickwork] of the Emaḫtila be able to hold back the sighing?
When will the Etemenanki be able to hold back the sighing?
When will the Edaranna be able to hold back the sighing?

Were [the city] but able to hold back the sighing! The lady has silenced it.
Were [Nippur] but able to hold back the sighing! The lady has silenced it.
Were [the kiur, the great place], but able to hold back the sighing! The lady has silenced it.
Were [the brickwork of the Ekur] but able to hold back the sighing! The lady has silenced it.

[. . .] the cow in the steppe to the rushes and grasses [. . .]
As the ewe cannot hold herself back from the lamb in the fold, so the cella cannot hold back its tears.
As the goat cannot hold herself back from the kid in the pen, so the cella cannot hold back its tears.
As the cow cannot hold herself back from her calf in the enclosure, so the cella cannot hold back its tears.

As the swallow cannot hold herself back from her fledglings in the nest of reeds, so the cella cannot hold back its tears.

It is pre-eminent. It is pre-eminent. It goes forth from the city.
The word of great An is pre-eminent. It goes forth from the city.
The word of Enlil is pre-eminent. It goes forth from the city.

My city cried out in sickening misery. Its people were heaped up.
My city cried out (like the whir) of an axe. Its young ones were heaped up.
My city cried out (like the roar) of the sea. Its men were heaped up.
[My city cried out . . .]. Its spouses were heaped up.
[The word] of Enlil cried out. . . . were heaped up.
[. . .] says my city. [. . .] . . .

He . . . [. . .]. He . . . the mesu-trees.
He . . . my small [*mesu*-trees]. He . . . the mesu-trees.
He . . . my huge [*mesu*-trees]. He . . . the mesu-trees.
Oh singer of songs, he . . . my small mesu-trees. He . . . the *mesu*-trees.
Oh singer of songs, he . . . my huge mesu-trees. He . . . the *mesu*-trees.

[. . .] . . . my city lies down by him of the Ekur.
Before(?) the fowler, the *orphan* and the *widow* stand before him, him of the Ekur.

It is an eršemma of Enlil.

According to its colophon, this next work is also an eršemma of Enlil. However, the composition is addressed to Ninurta, Enlil's son, whose prowess is lauded throughout the work. There are continual references to Ninurta's relationship with Enlil: "the warrior of his father, the august child of Enlil, the plow operator of Enlil, granted strength by the lord of the Ekur, destroying the land rebellious against his father." Yet we are still surprised that this is not considered to be an eršemma of Ninurta.

The differences between the Old Babylonian recension (163.1) and the First Millennium B.C.E. recension are minimal.

Eršemma no. 163.1

Text A BM 29644 (*CT* 15 pl. 11–12), collated by S. N. Kramer, *RA* 65 24
B CBS 15089 obv. i
C VAT 617 (*VAS* 2 2) rev. iii 23 to iv 8

Previous Translation: A. Falkenstein, *SAHG* 77–79

1. A: en-zu sá-mar-mar mu-lu ta-zu mu-un-zu
C: en-zu sa-mar-[mar] lú ta-zu mu-un-zu
2. A: á-sum-ma-ù-⸢mu⸣-un-e-é-kur-ra
C: á-sum-ma-ù-⸢mu-un⸣-e-é-kur-ra
3. A: ù-tu-ud-da-ḫur-sag-gá ù-mu-un-e-é-ninnu
C: ù-tu-da-ḫur-sag-gá ù-mu-un-é-nin$_5$-ù
4. A: u$_4$ á-nun-gál-a-a-^{d}En-líl-lá
C: ù á-nu-gál-a-a-^{d}En-líl-lá
5. A: bulùg-gá-dìm-me-er-maḫ-a mè-šè ti-na gub-bu
C: bulùg-gá-dingir-maḫ me-e ⸢šen⸣! -na gub-bu-ú
6. A: kur zì-gin$_7$ peš-peš-e še-gin$_7$ gur$_{10}$ -a su-ub-bu
C: kur zi-gi$_4$-in peš-peš-e še-gi$_4$-in šip-ri su$_x$(BU)-pa
7. A: sag ì-mar ki-bal a-a-zu-šè
C: sa-mar e$_4$-ma-ru ki-bal-⸢a⸣ a-a-zu-šè
8. A: mu-e-te ḫur-sag-gul-la-zu-šè
C: ba-e-te ḫur-sag-⸢gu⸣-la-šè
9. A: kur-erím-šè gi-dili-dù-a-gin$_7$ sag ì-sìg!-sìg!-ge
C: kur-^{giš}eren-šè gi-dili-d[ù-a-gin$_7$ sa]g im-sìg-sìg ḫé-e-dù
10. A: kur-kur téš-a bí-íb-sì!-sì!-ge
C: kur-kur téš-a b[í-. . .]-ge$_4$
11. A: kur-kur bàd-gal-bi mà-e si-gar-bi-me-en
12. A: sag-an-ta-dè bí-íb-ra-ra-ra
B: [. . .]-an
C: gù-an-ta-dé [. . .]-⸢ra⸣
13. A: ^{giš}ig-an-na-ke$_4$ bí-íb-gub-gub-bé
B: [. . .]-gub-bé-en
C: ^{giš}ig-an-na-⸢ke⸣$_4$ [. . .]-⸢bé⸣
14. A: ^{giš}šu-de-eš-an-na-ke$_4$ bí-íb-gar-gar-re-dè
B: [. . .]-ib-gar-gar-re-me-en
C: ^{giš}šu-de-eš-an-na-ke$_4$ [. . .]-gar-re
15. A: ^{giš}sag-kul-an-na-ke$_4$ im-si-il-⸢le⸣-en
B: [. . . i]m-si-il-en
C: ^{giš}sag-kul-an-na-ke$_4$ bí-ib-si-il-e
16. A: ^{giš}si-gar-an-na-ke$_4$ im-su$_x$(BU)-[ud]-en
B: [. . .]-su$_x$(BU)-ud-e-en
C: ^{giš}si-gar!-an-na-ke$_4$ bí-ib-su-dè
17. A: kur nu-še-ga zar-re-eš ⸢sal-sal⸣-e-en
B: [. . .]-eš sal-sal-e-en
C: ⸢kur⸣ nu-še-ga zar-re-eš sal-e
18. A: ki-bal nu-še-ga ki-⸢bé⸣ nu-gi$_4$-gi$_4$
B: [. . .] nu-gi$_4$-gi$_4$-in
C: [ki]-bal nu-še-ga ni-ba ì-gul-e
19. A: en-me-en gù-téš-a-⸢si-ga⸣-zu èn-⸢šè⸣ nu-bad-dè-en

B: [. . .]-šè nu-bad-en
C: enmen gú-téš-a-sì-ga-zu-DÈ en-šè nu-bad-e

20. A: šà-íb-ba-zu a-ba íb-šed$_{10}$(MÙŠ.DI)-dè
B: [. . .].DI-dè
C: šà-íb-ba-zu a-ba ib-te-en-te-en

21. A: ka-ta-è-a-zu sig$_{11}$ nu-di-dam
C: ⌜ka⌝-ba-a-a-zu šen(?) nu-di-dè

22. A: za-da a-ba-a in-na-bal-e
C: za-e a-ba in-na-ab-bal-e

23. A: en-me-en ug-an-kù-ga-me-en nir-gál-kalam-⌜ma-me⌝-[en]
C: enmen kù-an-kù-ga-me-en nir-gál-kalam-ma-me-en

24. A: ku$_{6}$ aba$_{x}$(AB) asila-ak-a «mu» mušen (x) nu-ni-ri
C: [. . .] ⌜asila⌝(?)-ka mu-šè-en nu-šub-bu-me-en

25. A: engar «URU» gána ur$_{x}$(ÚRU)-ru-^{d}En-líl-[lá-me]-en

26. A: ù-mu-un-bulùg-gá ur-sag-g[á-a-a-na]-me-[en]

27. A: ⌜á⌝-zi-da-zu lú-er[ím . . .]

28. A: [. . .]⌜x⌝[. . .]

29. A: [. . .]⌜KA x⌝[. . .]

30. A: [kur(?) ka]-⌜ba⌝-zu ki-bé nu-⌜gi$_{4}$⌝-[gi$_{4}$]

31. A: [x x] ba-e-ku$_{5}$-da-zu lú nu-mu-[ni-ib-dib-bé]
C: [. . .]-bé

32. A: [dumu-ma]ḫ-di-dè-^{d}Mu-ul-[líl-lá-me-en]
C: [. . .]-⌜me⌝-en

33. A: (x)⌜x⌝-é-kur-ra á-sù-⌜sù⌝-[me-en]
C: [. . .]-⌜me⌝-en

34. A: ⌜x⌝[. . .]-dingir-re-e-ne-me-en
C: [. . .]-⌜me⌝-en

35. A: ⌜x⌝[. . .]-^{d}a-nun-ke$_{4}$-e-ne-me-en
C: [. . .]-⌜me⌝-en

36. A: [. . .]-⌜ra⌝-^{d}En-líl-lá-me-en
C: [. . . -^{d}Mu-ul]-⌜líl⌝-lá-me-en

37. A: ⌜x⌝[. . .]-^{d}a-nun-ke$_{4}$-e-ne-me-en
C: [. . .]-⌜ne⌝-me-en

38. A: en ^{giš}⌜x⌝ ra-^{d}En-líl-lá-me-en
C: [. . .-^{d}M]u-ul-líl-lá-me-en

A: 38 ér-šem$_{5}$-ma-^{d}En-líl-lá-kam
C: [. . .] mu-bi-im

Translation based upon text A:

1. Wise 'en,' planner, what has one known about you?
Granted strength (by) the lord of the Ekur,

born by the mountain, lord of the Eninnu,
storm, great strength of father Enlil,
reared by Dingirmaḫ, wildly poised for battle,
dispersing the mountains like meal, reaping (them) like grain,
you rushed headlong. To the land rebellious against your father
you approached. In order to destroy the mountain-land
you trample down the enemy land like a single planted reed.
You make all countries harmonious,
(saying), "I am the towering wall (of) the lands! I am their bolt!"
You beat down the mighty.
You dislodge the door of heaven,
strip away the bar of heaven,
tear off the lock of heaven,
and pull out the bolt of heaven.
You pile the disobedient land into heaps.
The rebellious land which does not hearken you do not restore.
You are the 'en.' *How long will the harmony you have instilled remain?*
Who can calm your angry heart?
There is none who can oppose the utterance of your mouth.
Who has it in him to rebel against you?
You are the 'en.' You are the lion of holy An. The respected one of the nation are you.
A fish frolicking in the sea, a bird (which) does not fall,
the farmer of Enlil who plows the fields are you.
The lord who has been reared to be the warrior [of his father] are you.
Your right hand [lets no] enemy [escape].
[Your left lets no evil-doer flee].
[. . .]
Your pronouncement does not restore [the mountain] to its place.
No one [passes by the rebellious land] which you have cursed.
[The august child] of Enlil are you.
[. . .] of the Ekur, you are the swift one.
You are the [. . .] of the gods.
You are the [. . .] of the Anunna-gods.
[. . .] of Enlil are you.
You are the [. . .] of the Anunna-gods.
You are the 'en,' the . . . of Enlil.

---

38 (lines) It is an eršemma of Enlil.

Eršemma no. 163.2

Text A K.8728 obv. a+5 to a+13
B K.11174 (*BA* 5/5 6) obv. 11–42 a+13 to a+28
C Rm.272 (*BA* 10/1 19) a+2 to a+9

1. [en-zu sá-mar-mar mu-lu ta-zu mu-un-zu]

(*perhaps a few lines missing*)

a+2. [alim-m]a a[n-šè . . .]

a+3. [ur-sag-ga]l ki-šè [. . .]

a+4. [ù-tu]-ud-da-urú-zé-eb-b[a . . .]

a+5. [u$_4$ á]-nun-gal-a-a-^{d}En-[líl-lá]

a+6. [bulùg-gá]-dìm-me-er-maḫ-a mè šen-šen-na ti-na ba-gub-[bé]
ṣa-pit ^{d}*Be-let*-DINGIR. MEŠ *šá ina qab-lim u ta-ḫa-zi da-ap-niš iz-[za-az-zu]*

a+7. [kur] zì-gin$_7$ peš$_6$-peš$_6$ še-gin$_7$ gur$_{10}$ su-[ub-bu]
[. . .] i-qam-mu-ú ki-ma še-im e-ṣi-[du]

a+8. sá mu-e-mar ki-bal a-a-zu-[šè]
tu-ṣa-am-me-er-ma a-na KUR *nu-kúr-tim šá a-[bi-ka]*

a+9. ba-e-te ḫur-sag-gul-la-[zu-šè]
te-eṭ-ḫi-ma ana KUR-*i a-ba-[ti]*

a+10. kur-erím-ma gi-dili-dù-a-gin$_7$ [. . .]
KUR *a-a-bi ki-ma qa-ni [. . .]*

a+11. kur-kur-ra [. . .]

a+12. kur-kur-ra [. . .]
ma-ta-[ti . . .]

a+13. gù-[an-ta-dé . . .]
[. . .] le-a-um [. . .]

a+14. [^{giš}ig]-an-na-bi bí-[íb]-g[ub-g]ub-[. . .]
⸢*da*⸣*-la-ti-šú šá-qa-ti tuš-bal-*⸢*ki*⸣*-[it]*

a+15. ^{giš}šu-de-eš-an-na-bi bí-íb-BI-mar-ma[r-. . .]
me-de-li-šá ta-aš-ḫu-⸢*uṭ*⸣

a+16. ^{giš}sag-kul-an-na-bi ba-e-si-il-si-⸢il⸣-[. . .]
sik-ku-ri-šá tu-šal-liṭ

a+17. ^{giš}si-mar-an-na-bi bí-su$_x$(BU)-su$_x$(BU)-⸢en⸣
ši-ga-ri-šá tu-na-as-si-⸢*iḫ*⸣

a+18. kur nu-še-ga zar-re-eš mu-un-sal-sal-[. . .]
KUR *la ma-gi-ri sar*$_6$*-ri-iš tu-ma-aṣ-ṣi*

a+19. ki-bal nu-še-ga ki-bal ì-gul-⸢e⸣
KUR *nu-kúr-ti šá la ma-gi-ri taq-qur tu-uš-bal-[kit]*

a+20. en-me-en gug-téš-a-sì-ga-zu en-šè nu-bad-bad-⸢e⸣
be-lum šá su-un!*-qu mit-ḫa-riš taš-ku-nu a-di ma-ti la in-[ne-su-ú]*

a+21. šà-íb-ba-zu a-ba íb-šed$_{10}$-dè
ag-ga ŠÀ-*ka man-nu ú-na-aḫ-šú*
a+22. umun-bulùg-gá ur-sag-a-a-na-mèn
be-lum šur-bu-ú qar-rad a-bi-šú [. . .]
a+23. á-zi-da-zu lú-erím nu-è-[dè]
ina im-ni-ka a-a-bu ul uṣ-ṣi
a+24. á-gáb-bu-zu ḫul-ma-al-la nu-⸢x⸣-[x]
ina šu-me-li-ka lem-nu ul ⸢i⸣-[. . .]
a+25. kur ka-ba-zu du$_6$(?)-du$_6$(?) [. . .]
ina e-piš pi-ka šá ⸢x⸣[. . .]
a+26. ki-bal-a na-ám-bi ku$_5$ ⸢x⸣[. . .]
KUR *nu-kúr-ti šá ta-ru-ru [. . .]*
a+27. ⸢šul⸣ ka-tar-ra-zu [. . .]
eṭ-la da-lil-ka [. . .]
a+28. ⸢dumu⸣-maḫ-⸢di-di⸣-[^{d}Mu-ul-líl-lá-me-en]
(*remainder of text not preserved*)

* * *

[Wise 'en,' planner, what has one known about you]?
(*perhaps a few lines missing*)
[Honored one], to the heavens [. . .]
Great [warrior], to the earth [. . .]
born by the *good city* (. . .)
[Storm], great [strength] of father Enlil,
reared by Dingirmaḫ, wildly poised for battle and war,
you plotted to grind [the mountains] like meal, to reap (them)
like grain. To the land rebellious against your father
you approached. In order to destroy the mountain-land
[you trample down] the enemy like a single planted reed.
[You make all the countries [harmonious],
(saying), "[I am the towering wall] of the lands! [I am their bolt]!"
[You beat down] the mighty.
You dislodge its door of heaven,
strip away its bar of heaven,
tear off its lock of heaven,
and pull out its bolt of heaven.
You pile the disobedient land into heaps.
You destroy the rebellious land which does not hearken.
You are the 'en.' For how long will the famine you inflict not go away?
Who can calm your angry heart?
The lord who has been reared, the warrior of his father are you.

Your right hand lets no enemy escape.
Your left hand lets no evil-doer [flee].
a+25. Your pronouncement [turns(?)] the mountains [into] ruins.
The curse of the rebellious land [which you have] placed [. . .].
He-man, your praise [. . .]
The august child [of Enlil are you].
(remainder of text not preserved)

Eršemma no. 160

Old Babylonian Text A N 3335 (rev. i 14'ff.)+N 4226 (ii 1' ff.) 1–5, 23–38
First Millennium Text B K.2789+4964+4966+14198 obv.22'-rev.14.1-36.

1. A: mušen-dù-e kur-ú[r-]
B: mušen-dù kur-úr-ra-na ⸢gu⸣ i-ni-in-lá
2. A: e-lum-e [ ]
B: e-lum-e [umun-kur-kur]-ra-ke_4
3. A: šà-sud-rá ⸢x⸣[ ]
B: umun-kur-kur-ra šà-sù-[da-ke_4 e-ne]-èm-zi-da-ke_4
4. A: ám-du_{11}-ga[ ]
B: ám-du_{11}-ga-na [nu-gi_4]-gi_4-dè
5. A: ⸢x x x⸣[ ]
B: ^{d}Mu-ul-líl inim-ka-[na šu nu]-bal-e-dè
6. é-na Nibru^{ki} [gu] i-ni-in-lá
7. še-eb-é-kur-ra gu
8. ki-ùr ki-gal gu
9. èš é-nam-ti-la gu
10. še-eb-Zi[mbir^{ki}] gu
11. èš é-[babbar] gu
12. še-eb-Tin-tir[^{ki}] gu
13. šé-eb-é-sag-[íl-la] gu
14. šé-eb-Bar[sip^{ki}] gu
15. še-eb-é-zi-da gu
16. é-maḫ-ti-la gu
17. é-te-me-an-ki gu
18. é-$dara_3$-an-na gu
19. umun-šà-ba-na ta-àm ma-al-la-bi
20. mu-uš ^{túg}PI-ga-na a-na-àm ma-al-la-bi
21. mu-uš-^{túg}PI-kù-ga-na ta-àm [an-ga-mu(-un)-ri-a-bi]
22. kur na-ám-ge_{16}-le-[èm]-mà im-ma-[ni-in-ma-al]
23. A: e_4-na-ám-g[e_{16}- . . .]
B: e_4-na-ám-ge_{16}-le-èm-mà i_7-da [i-ni-in-dé]

24. A: ú téš nu-zu [eden-na] bí-[in-mú]
B: ú téš nu-un-zu eden-na [bí-in-mú]
25. A: $^{e\ u\ e}$ sag-g[i$_6$-ga eden-na nu]mun-e-eš m[i-ni-ma-al]
B: sag-gi$_6$-ga eden-na numun-e-[eš mi-ni-ma-al]
26. A: dam-a-ni [šìr mu-na-an-ra] i-lu mu-na-ab-b[é]
B: dam-a-ni šìr mu-na-an-ra i-lu [mu-na-ab-bé]
27. A: ^{d}Mu-ul-líl [dam-a-ni] ^{d}Nin-líl-le
B: ^{d}Mu-ul-líl-lá dam-a-ni ^{d}[Nin-líl-le]
28. A: nin$_9$-gal-a-ni ga-ša-an-Kèš^{ki}-a-ke$_4$ i-lu mu-[n]a-ab-bé
B: nin$_9$-gal-a-ni gašan-é-maḫ-a-ke$_4$
29. B: kù-gašan-Nibru^{ki}-ke$_4$ i-lu mu-un-na-ab-bé
30. A: mušen-dù gúr-gurum-ma-zu [(x)]⸢x⸣ ba-DI-DI-dè-en
B: mušen-dù gúr-gurum-ma-zu-dè te ba-di-di-di-in
31. A: ^{d}Mu-ul-líl a-a [ka]-na-ág-gá [z]i-dè-eš ⸢x⸣-mu-dè
B: ^{d}Mu-ul-líl ka-nag-gá gúr-gurum-ma-zu-dè te
32. A: ù-mu-[un . . .]-DI-dè-en
B: umun-du$_{11}$-ga-zi-da gúr-gurum-ma-zu-dè te
33. A: [. . .] nu-e-dib
B: e$_4$ bí-lù ku$_6$ bí-dib
34. A: [. . .] in-ga-ur$_4$-ru
B: sa ba-e-nú buru$_5$^{mušen} bí-laḫ$_x$(DU.DU)
34a A: [. . .] mu-e-gul
35. A: [. . .] mu-e-BAD
B: ⸢x⸣ é-zi mu-un-gul-gul mu-lu-zi [ba-an]-tu$_{10}$(?)-bé-eš
36. A: [. . . -z]u nu-kúš-ù
B: a-a ^{d}Mu-ul-líl i-bí-zu nu-kúš-ù en-[šè ì-kúš-ù]
37. A: [. . .]-gi$_4$-gi$_4$
38. A: [. . .]-dè-en

The fowler has spread the net over the base of his mountain.
The honored one, the lord of the lands,
the lord of the lands whose thoughts are unfathomable, whose word is true,
whose orders no one can challenge,
Enlil, whose utterances are unalterable,
has spread the net over his house, over Nippur.
He has spread the net over the brickwork of the Ekur.
He has spread the net over the kiur, the great place.
He has spread the net over the shrine Enamtila.
He has spread the net over the brickwork of Sippar.
He has spread the net over the shrine Ebabbar.
He has spread the net over the brickwork of Tintir.

He has spread the net over the brickwork of the Esagil.
He has spread the net over the brickwork of Borsippa.
He has spread the net over the brickwork of the Ezida.
He has spread the net over the Emaḫtila.
He has spread the net over the Etemenanki.
He has spread the net over the Edaranna.

What does the lord have in his heart?
What does he have in mind?
What does he have in his pure mind?
He has destroyed the land.
He has poured the waters of destruction into the canals.
He has caused . . . plants to sprout in the steppe.
He has placed the black-headed people in the steppe like (scattered) seeds.

His wife strikes up a cry to him; she utters a wail to him.
Enlil's wife, Ninlil (utters a wail to him).
His older sister, the lady of the Emaḫ (utters a wail to him).
Holy Ninnibru utters a wail to him.

Fowler, when you stoop over, what (is able) to move about?
Enlil, when you stoop over the land, what (is able) to move about?
Lord whose word is true, when you stoop over, what (is able) to move about?
You roiled the waters and caught the fish.
You laid out a net and captured the flocks of birds.
. . . the faithful house has been destroyed; the faithful people were heaped up.
Father Enlil, your eye never tires. When will you grow weary?
[. . .] . . .
[. . .]

The First Millennium B.C.E. recension of eršemma no. 34 is the only extant eršemma which consists of three units. Unfortunately, although the Old Babylonian recension (34.1) is preserved, only the beginning of the composition is extant. Thus, we are unable to trace the development of this work into the highly unusual three unit eršemma. However, we are able to see that the Old Babylonian recension differed greatly from the later recension, for of the thirteen lines preserved in 34.1, five or six do not occur in 34.2.

This work is an eršemma of Inanna consisting entirely of praise, there being no narrative tale.

Eršemma no. 34.1

Text: VAT 613 (*VAS* 2 4 obv. ii 21 ff.)
(The numbers in parentheses represent the corresponding line number in 34.2)

1. (1) an-su-da-ág! zi-gi-mi-en [(. . .)] ki gi-ba zi ši-ga-ne-na
2. mu-gi-íb ka-ša-na-na an-su-da-[ág] zi-gi-mi-⌈en⌉
3. e-gi ka-ša-an-é-a-na an-su-da-á[g] zi-gi-mi-en
4. (2) mu-gi-íb an-su-da-ág gu-ba-mu-[dè]
5. (3) ki-gi ri-ba zi ši-⌈ga⌉-ne-⌈na⌉
6. mu-gi-íb ki-a gu-⌈ba⌉-mu-⌈dè⌉ ki-gi ri-b[i(?) (. . .)]
7. mu-gi-íb si(?)-a gu-ba!-m[u-dè] ki-gi ri-b[i(?) (. . .)]
8. (4–5) za-aš si-la-⌈zi⌉-de šu im-mi-[. . .] ⌈lú⌉(?) kur-kur-ra-m[i(?) (. . .)]
9. za-⌈aš⌉ [x]-zi-de šu im-mi-[. . .] lú-ši kur-kur-ra-m[i(?) (. . .)]
10. (6) [ur]-⌈ba⌉-ra si-la šu-tu-a [. . .]
11. (7) ⌈ur⌉-ma-ḫe šu(?)⌈x⌉[. . .]
12. (8) ù-da NE⌈x⌉[. . .]
13. ká(?) NE ra ⌈ù⌉⌈x⌉[. . .]

(*remainder of text not preserved*)

* * *

Celestial luminary, you are like the fire! Verily you . . . the earth.
Hierodule Inanna, celestial luminary, you are like the fire!
Princess, lady of the Eanna, celestial luminary, you are like the fire!
Hierodule, celestial luminary, when I(?) am standing,
you are as surpassing as the earth.
Hierodule, when I(?) am standing on the earth, (you are) as surpassing as the earth.
Hierodule, when I(?) am standing on the . . . (you are) as surpassing as the earth.
In the faithful street (the people) bless you. When you enter a man's [. . .]
In the faithful [. . .] (the people) bless you. When you enter a man's [. . .]
[you go as] a wolf snatching a lamb.
[. . .] a lion [. . .]
If . . . [. . .]
. . .[. . .]

(*remainder of text not preserved*)

Eršemma no. 34.2

Text	A	K.7670	9–13
	B	K.16740	12–14
	C	MLC 1881 (*BRM* 4 10)	10–21, 25–33
	D	Sm.954 (Delitsch AL^3 34–36)	1–40
	E	VAT 159 (*SBH* 53) rev.	1–40

(transliteration according to text D):

1. an-sù-ud-ág[1] izi-gin$_7$ mú ki-ta za-e ši-in-ga-me-en-ne
   nu-úr AN-*e ša*[2] *ki-ma i-šá-tim*[3] *i-na*[4] *ma-a-tim nap-ḫat at-ti-ma*
2. mu-gi$_{17}$-ib ki-a gub-ba-zu-dè
   iš-ta-ri-tum[1] *i-na*[2] *er-ṣe-ti*[3] *i-na*[2] *ú-zu-zi-ki*[4]
3. ki-gin$_7$ rib-ba za-e ši-in-ga-me-en-ne[1]
   šá ki-ma er-ṣe-tim šu-tu-qat[2] *at-ti-ma*
4. za-e sila-zi-da šu [1]mi-ni-íb-mú-mú
   ka-a-ši[2] *su-le-e kit-ti*[3] *i-kar-rab-ki*
5. é-mu-lu-e ku$_4$-ku$_4$-ra-zu-dè
   a-na[1] É *a-me*[2]*-lim i-na*[3] *e-re-bi-ki*[4]
6. ur-bar-ra silá šu-ti-a DU-a-mèn
   bar-ba-ru[1] *šá a-na*[2] *le-qé-e pu-ḫa-di šu-lu-ku*[3] *at-ti*[4]
7. ur-maḫ šà-túm-ta DU-a-mèn
   né-e-šú šá ina qir-bé[1]*-ti it-ta-na-al-la-ku at-ti*
8. u$_4$-da lú-ki-sikil an-na ḫé-du$_7$-ra
   u$_4$*-mu ar-da-tum ú-su-ma*[1] AN-*e*
9. ki-sikil ^{d}Inanna-^{na}[1] an-na ḫé-du$_7$-ra
   ar-da-tum ^{d}*Iš-tar ú-su-ma* AN-*e*
10. unú-la šuba-lá an-na ḫé-du$_7$-ra
    šá šu-kut-ti[1] *šu-bi-i šak-na-ta*[2] *ú-su-ma* AN-*e*
11. ám-ú-rum ^{d}Utu «ra» an-na ḫé-du$_7$-ra
    ta-lim-ti[1] ^{d} UTU[2] *ú-su-ma*[3] AN-*e*
12. mu-ni-šè gub-ba dili-du gub-ba
    a-na[1] *šu-ta-bu-ul*[2] *te-re-e-ti*[3] *az-za-az*[4] *git-ma-liš az-za-az*[5]
13. a-a-mu ^{d}Suen-na-ra mu-ni-šè gub-ba dili-du gub-ba
    a-na[1] *a-bi-ia* ^{d}Sin [2]*šu-ta-bu-ul*[3] *te-re-e-ti az-za-az git-ma-liš az-za-az*
14. šeš-mu ^{d}Utu-ra mu-ni-šè gub-ba dili-du gub-ba
    a-na[1] ŠEŠ-*ia*[2] ^{d}UTU [3]*šu-ta-bu-ul*[4] *te-re-e-ti*[5] *az-za-az git-ma-liš az-za-az*
15. ma-ra a-a[1] u$_4$-sar-ra[2] mu-un-na-gub-ba[3] mu-ni-šè gub-ba dili-du gub-ba
    [4]*ia-a-ši a-bi*[5] ^{d}*Na-an-na-ru*[6] *ul-zi-iz-za-an-ni* [7]*šu-ta-bu-ul te-re-e-ti az-za-az*

16. mu-gi-gi-ir-ra-ke$_4$[1] mu-ni-šè gub-ba dili-du gub-ba
ina AN-*e ed-de-šu-ti*[2] [3]*šu-ta-bu-ul*[4] *te-re-e-ti az-za-az git-ma-liš az-za-az*

---

17. el-lu ár-re-mu el-lu[1] ár-re-mu
i-na[2] *ri-šá-a-ti ta-na-da-tu-u*[3]*-a i-na ri-šá-a-ti*[4] *ta-na-da-tu-u-a*

18. a ù-li-li mu-gi$_{17}$-ib mu-lu an-na ši-im-du
i-na[1] *ri-šá-a-ti*[2] *iš-ta-ri-tum ana-ku šá-qí-iš al-lak*

19. gašan-an-na an-na an[1]-usan-na-mèn
^{d}*Eš*$_4$*-dar i-lat ši-me*[2]*-tan ana-ku*

20. gašan-an-na an-na u$_4$-zal-la-mèn
^{d}*Eš*$_4$*-dar*[1] *i-lat še-re-e-ti*[2] *ana-ku*

21. gašan-an-na si-gar-kù ri-ri[1]-mu ár-re-mu
[2]^{d}*Iš-tar pe-ta-at ši-gar* AN-*e el-lu-ti*[3] *ta-na-da-tu-u*[4]*-a*

22. an al-dúb ki al-sìg ár-re-mu
AN-*e ú-ra-ab*[1] *er-ṣe-tum*[2] *ú-nar-raṭ*[3] *ta-na-da-tu-u-a*

23. an al-dúb-dúb ki al-sìg-sìg ár-re-mu
mu-rib-bat AN-*e mu-nar-ri-ṭa-at* KI-*tim ta-na-da-tu-u-a*

24. ul-ḫé-šè [1]mú kur-kur-ra zà-šè[2] mu-bi ár-re-mu
šá ina šu-pu-uk AN-*e nap-ḫat*[3] *ina da-ád-mi*[4] *zi-kir-šá*[5] *šu-pu-u ta-na-da-tu-u-a*

25. ušumgal-an-na-ke$_4$ elam-ma^{ki} ḫu-bu-úr-ra ḫa-ma-ab-bé[1] ár-re-mu
šar-rat AN-*e e-liš u šap-liš u šap-liš liq-qa-ba-a ta-na-da-tu-u-a*

26. kur-kur-ra téš-bi bí-íb-sì-sì-ge ár-re-mu
šá[1]*-di-i il*[2]*-te-niš a-sap-pan ta-na-da-tu-u-a*

27. kur-kur-ra bàd-gal-bi bí-me-en[1] za-e ^{giš}si-mar-bi bí-me-en[2] ár-re-mu
ša ša -di-i du-ur-šú-nu ra-bu-u[3] *ana-ku ši-gar-šú-nu* GAL-*ú*[4] *ana-ku ta-na-da-tu-u-a*

---

28. šà-zu ḫé-en-ḫun-e[1] bar-zu ḫé-en-šed$_7$-dè
lìb-ba-ki[2] *li-nu-uḫ*[3] *ka-bat-ta-ki*[4] *lip-šaḫ*

29. [1]umun an-gal-e šà-zu ḫé-en-ḫun-e[2]
be-lum ^{d}*A-nù* GAL-*ú lìb-ba-ki li-ni-iḫ*

30. umun kur-gal ^{d}Mu-ul-líl bar-zu ḫé-en-šed$_7$-dè
be-lum šá-du-u GAL-*ú* ^{d}*En-líl ka-bat-ta-ki li-pa-aš-ši-iḫ*

31. mu-gi$_{17}$-ib gašan-an-na šà-zu ḫé-en-ḫun-gá
^{d}*iš-ta-ri-tum be-let* AN-*e*[1] *lìb-ba-ki*[2] *li-nu-uḫ*

32. egí gašan-an-na bar[1]-zu
ru-ba-a-ti be-let AN-*e*[1]

33. [1]egí gašan-é-an-na ša[2]-zu
ru-ba-a-tú be-let É-an-na

34. egí[1] gašan-ki[2]-Unu^{ki}-ga[3] bar[4]-zu
ru-ba-a-ti be-let Ú-ruk[5]
35. egí[1] gašan-ki-Zabalam^{ki} šà-zu
36. egí[1] gašan-ḫur-sag-kalam-ma bar-zu
37. egí[1] gašan-é-tùr-kalam-ma šà-zu
38. egí[1] gašan-Tin-tir^{ki}-ra bar-zu
39. egí[1] gašan-mu ^{d}Na-na-a šà-zu
40. gašan-é-a gašan-dìm-me-er-e-ne bar-zu

ér-šèm-ma-^{d}Inanna-ke$_4$(var. E:-kam)

Variants

1. 1) E: an-sù-ud-da-ág 2) E: *šá* 3) E: *i-šá-tú* 4) E omits *i-na*
2. 1) E: *iš-ta-rit* 2) E: *ina* 3) E: KI-*tim* 4) E: *ú-zu-uz-zu-[ki]*
3. 1) E:-⌜na⌝ 2) E: *šu-tu-qa-tum*
4. 1) E adds àm- 2) E:-*šu* 3) E:-*tum*
5. 1) E: ⌜*ana*⌝ 2) E:-*wi-* 3) E: *ina* 4) E:-*ka*
6. 1) E:-*ri* 2) E: *ana* 3) E:-*ki* 4) E:-*ta*
7. 1) E adds -*e-*
8. 1) E: *ú-su-um*
9. 1) E omits -na
10. 1) C:-*tim* 2) E:-*at*
11. 1) C: *ta-lì-mat* 2) C:^{d}UTU-*ši* 3) C: *ú-su-um*
12. 1) E: *ana* 2) C,E:-*lu* 3) E:-*tú;* C: *te-ret* 4) C:-*zu* 5) E:-*zu*
13. 1) E: *ana* 2) C: *a-na*; E: *ana* 3) C:-*lu*
14. 1) C: *a-na;* E: *ana* 2) C,E: *a-ḫi-ia* 3) C: *a-na;* E: *ana* 4) C:-*lu* 5) C: *te-ret*
15. 1) C,E omit a-a 2) C: dingir-meš instead of u$_4$-sar-ra 3) C omits -ba 4) E: *šá* 5) C,E omit *a-bi* 6) C: DINGIR.MEŠ; E: *na-an-na-ri* 7) E: *ana*
16. 1) C:[mu]-gi$_4$-gi$_4$-ra-ke$_4$ 2) C:-*ta* 3) C adds *a-na* 4) C:-*lu*
17. 1) C,E omit el-lu 2) C,E: *ina* 3) C,E:-*ú-* 4) C,E omit *i-na ri-šá-a-ti*
18. 1) E: *ina* 2) E:-*tum*
19. 1) C omits an- 2) C,E:-*mi-*
20. 1) E: ^{d}Iš-tar 2) C: *še-e-re-ti;* E:-*tú*
21. 1) C,E: tag$_4$-tag$_4$- 2) C:*[. . .] la-pa-ni šá* AN-⌜*e*⌝*[. . .]* 3) E:-*tim* 4) E:-*ú-*
22. 1) E: *ú-rab-bi* 2) E: KI-*tim* 3) E: *ú-nar-ra-aṭ*
24. 1) E adds mu- 2) E: zà-du 3) E: *nap-ḫa-tum* 4) E:-*me* 5) E:-*šú*
26. 1) E:*šá* 2) E:*iš-*
27. 1) E:bàd-gal-bi-me-en 2) E:^{giš}si-mar-bi-me-en 3) E:-*ú* 4) E omits GAL-*ú*
35–39. 1) E omits egí; C begins line 35 [egí] gašan-an-na [. . .]
40. 1) E adds ḫé-en-šed$_7$-dè

You are the celestial luminary blazing like fire upon the earth.
Hierodule, when you bestride the earth,
you are as surpassing as the earth.
In the faithful street (the people) bless you.
When you enter a man's house,
you go as a wolf snatching a lamb.
You are a lion roaming through the fields.

If the young girl, the fitting one of heaven,
the young girl, Inanna, the fitting one of heaven,
wearing the ornament of šuba-stone, the fitting one of heaven,
the *devoted one* of Utu, the fitting one of heaven,
(is) standing *in regard to him,* (she is) standing as an equal.
"Standing *in regard to* my father Suen, standing as an equal!"
"Standing *in regard to* my brother Utu, standing as an equal!"
"(When my) father causes the moonlight to stand by me, standing *in regard to him,* standing as an equal!"
". . . standing *in regard to him,* standing as an equal!"
Jubilation! My praising! My praising!
Oh joy! Hierodule, who proceeds up above,
Inanna, in the heavens you are the twilight.
Inanna, in the heavens you are the dawn.
Inanna, my opener of the holy bolt, my praising!
(Akk: Ištar, opener of the holy bolt of heaven, my praising!)
The heavens rumble; the earth shakes. My praising!
(Akk: She causes the heavens to rumble, the earth to shake. My praising!)
The heavens rumble; the earth shakes. My praising!
(Akk: She who causes the heavens to rumble, the earth to shake my praising!)
Lighting up (even) to the vault of heaven, in all the lands that name is to the very limits. My praising!
May Ušumgalanna speak to you in Elam and Ḫubur! My praising!
You have overthrown all the lands at once. My praising!
You are the towering wall of the lands; you are its bolt. My praising!

May he pacify your heart! May he calm your liver!
May the lord, great An, pacify your heart!
May the lord, the great mountain Enlil, calm your liver!
Hierodule Inanna, may he pacify your heart!
Princess Inanna, may he calm your liver!
Princess, lady of the Eanna, may he pacify your heart!
Princess, lady of "the place"-Uruk, may he calm your liver!

Princess, lady of "the place"-Zabalam, may he pacify your heart!
Princess, lady of Ḫursagkalama, may he calm your liver!
Princess, lady of the Eturkalama, may he pacify your heart!
Princess, lady of Tintir, may he calm your liver!
Princess, lady of Nanâ, may he pacify your heart!
Lady of the house, lady of the gods, may he calm your liver!

It is an eršemma of Inanna.

The eleventh and final kirugu of the Old Babylonian recension of the balag- lamentation to Enlil, e-lum gu$_4$-sún, was adapted into an eršemma of Marduk. For a more detailed analysis of this development and its significance, I refer the reader to the Introduction.

Old Babylonian Parallel to Eršemma 13 (11th kirugu of e-lum gu$_4$-sún)

Text: NBC 1315 (*RA* 16 208) reverse 15–24

15. ù-mu-un-mu za-e u$_4$-urú-mà ur-sag-gá-me-en
16. šub$_x$(ŠUBA)-bi-mu ù-mu-un-guruš-a ur-sag-gá-me-en
17. ù-mu-un-guruš-a ur-sag-gá-me-en kala-ga na-me-en
18. ^{d}Utu-gin$_7$ za-e zé-⸢en⸣-na-an-ni-ku$_4$-ku$_4$-dè-[en]
19. ^{d}Nanna-gin$_7$ šu-!sulug-zu na-an-búr-re-en
20. ù-mu-un-mu inim-zu lú-ra na-an-na-ab-zé-[mèn]
21. inim-zu lú-ki-bal-ra na-an-na-ab-zé-[mèn]
22. inim-zu lú-EN.NA nu-še-ra na-an-na-ab-zé-[mèn]
22a. EN.NA ^{d}En-líl-ra nu-še-ra na-an-na-ab-zé-[mèn]
23. ù-mu-un-mu a-mú-sar-ra-kam urú-zu-a è-ì
24. a-a ^{d}Mu-ul-líl ki-bulùg TA bulùg TA urú-zu-a è-ì

* * *

You are my lord. Light of my city, you are a warrior.
My shining one, Umunguruša, you are a warrior.
Umunguruša, you are a warrior. Indeed you are powerful.
Like the sun you *whirl about* (in) the clouds.
Like the moon you spread forth your light.
My lord, you give notice to a man.
You give notice to the rebellious man.
You give notice to the insubordinate and unsubmissive man.
You give notice to the insubordinate to Enlil, to the unsubmissive.
My lord, inspect the watercourses(?) in your city!
Father Enlil, inspect the earth which has *grown up* in your city!

Eršemma no. 13

Text: *STT* vol. ii 155

1. [umun-mu za-e] umun-urú-mu [ur-sag-mèn]
[be-lí at] -⌜ta⌝ be-el URU*-ia qa[r-ra-du at-ta]*
2. [alim-m]a ur-sag ^{d}As[ar-lú-ḫi]
[kab-t]u qar-ra-du ^{d}[Marduk]
3. [umun ^{d}En]-⌜bi⌝-lu-⌜lu⌝ ⌜dumu-sag⌝-^{d}En-[ki-ke$_4$]
*[be]-⌜lum⌝ ^{d}[*MIN*]* ⌜*mar*⌝ *reš-[tú šá ^{d}É-a]*
4. alim-ma [x(-x)] ^{d}⌜x⌝[. . .]
*kab-⌜tu⌝ (x)⌜x⌝*KIT ⌜*be*⌝*(?)-[lum . . .]*
5. umun-⌜é⌝-sag-íl-la umun-é-[zi-da]
be-lum É-sag-gíl be-lum [É-zi-da]
6. alim-ma ur-⌜sag⌝ ^{d}⌜Mu-zé-eb⌝-[ba-sa$_4$-a]
kab-tu q[ar-r]a!-du ^{d}Nà
7. ⌜umun⌝ ^{d}En-zà-⌜ge⌝! ^{d}Šed-⌜dù-ki⌝-šár-ra
be-lum ^{d}En-⌜zag⌝ pa-qid kiš-[šá-t]i
8. [alim]-ma umun-Barsip^{ki}
kab-tu be-lum Bar-si-pa
9. á-bàd-é-zi-da ibila-é-sag-íl-la
ta-bi-in É-zi-da a-pìl É-sag-gíl
10. ⌜sipa⌝-an-mu sipa-sag-gi$_6$-ga
re-ʾu-u šá-qu-u re-ʾu-u ṣal-mat qaq-qa-di
11. kala-ga umun ^{d}Asar-lú-ḫi-i-mèn
dan-nu be-lum ^{d}Marduk at-ta
12. [umun] ^{d}Asar-⌜lú⌝-ḫi ur-s[a]g-mèn kala-ga na-mèn
be-lum ^{d}Marduk ⌜qar-ra⌜-du at-tú dan-nu at-[tú]
13. ^{d}Utu-gin$_7$ zé-zé⌜x⌝[(x)] na-an-ku$_4$-ku$_4$-dè-en
*ki-ma ^{d}*UTU *ina ú-pe-e la te-⌜ri⌝-i*
14. ^{d}Nanna-gin$_7$ pa-è-zu-àm na-an-na-ab-bu-⌜re⌝-en
ki-[ma] ^{d}Sin šá-ru-ur ṣe-e-ti-ka la ta-⌜šap⌝-pi
15. [e]-⌜lum-e⌝ ^{d}Nanna-gin$_7$ pa-è-zu na-
⌜*kab-tu*⌝ ⌜*ki-ma*⌝ *^{d}Sin šá-ru-ur ṣe-⌜e⌝-ti-ka*
16. [umun-mu inim-z]u mu-lu-r[a] [n]a-⌜x-x⌝-zé-⌜e⌝?-[x]
[. . .]⌜x⌝ana ka-[. . . la] ⌜*ta*⌝*-nam-*⌜*din*⌝
17. [inim]-zu mu-lu-ki-bal-a-ra na-
⌜*a-ma-at-ka*⌝ *ana* KUR *nu-kúr-ti la ta-nam-din*
18. inim-zu mu-⌜lu⌝-EN-nu-še-ga na-
pi-i-ka ana la ma-gir be-lum la ta-nam-din
19. [mu-lu-EN-nu]-še-ga-^{d}Asar-lú-ḫi
la ⌜ma⌝-gir be-lum ^{d}Marduk la ta-⌜nam-din⌝
20. [umun]-mu [a]-mú-sar-ra-a-⌜na⌝(?) urú-zu-a! è-ì
be-⌜lum⌝ šá ⌜e⌝-mu-⌜qí⌝-šú ra-⌜ba⌝-a URU*-ka ḫi-ṭi*

21. ^{d}Asar-[lú-ḫi] ki-bulùg-⸢gá⸣-bulùg-gá urú-zu
^{d}Marduk šar-ḫu ⸢tar⸣-bu-u URU-*ka ḫi-ṭi*

---

22. šà-[zu] ⸢ḫé-en⸣-ḫun-gá bar-zu ḫé-en-šed$_7$-dè
[lib-ba]-ka li-nu-uḫ ka-bat-ta-ka lip-šaḫ
23. a umun-e an de-⸢èm⸣-mà-⸢ḫun⸣-gá
ú-a ⸢be⸣-lum AN-*ú li-ni-ḫu-ka*
24. ⸢ur-sag⸣ ^{d}⸢Asar-lú⸣-ḫi šà-zu ḫé-en-ḫun-gá
⸢qar⸣-ra-du [^{d}]Marduk lib-ba-ka li-nu-uḫ
25. mu-ud-na-‹ki›-ág-zu ^{d}Pa$_4$-nun-na-ki [a]-ra-zu dè-ra-ab-bé
⸢ḫi⸣-ir-tú na-ra-‹am›-ta-ka ^{d}Ṣar-pa-[ni]-tum tes-le-tú liq-bi-ka
26. [sukk]al-zi ^{d}Mu-zé-eb-ba-sa$_4$-a a-ra-zu
27. [é]-gi$_4$-a dumu-sag-an-uraš-a a-ra-zu
28. [egí]-zi-da gašan-gù-téš-a-sì-ga-ke$_4$ a-ra-[zu]
29. ⸢egí⸣-gu-la gašan-zu ^{d}Na-na-a a-ra-[zu]
30. ⸢urú-⸣zu na-an-šub-bé-en dè-ra-ab-bé a-[ra-zu]
31. [me]-⸢na⸣-šè Tin-tir^{ki} na-an-šub-bé-en dè-ra-[ab-bé] a-ra-zu dè-[ra-ab-bé]

ér-šèm-ma-^{d}Marduk-[kam]
èr-šem-ma-e-lum-[ma]

* * *

1. [You are my lord]. Lord (of) my city, [you are a warrior].
Honored one, warrior, Asarluḫi,
Lord Enbilulu, first-born of Enki,
Honored one, [. . .]
5. Lord of the Esagil, lord of the Ezida,
Honored one, warrior Mudugasa,
Lord Enzag, Šeddukišara,
Honored one, lord of Borsippa,
Roof of the Ezida, heir to the Esagil,
10. My elevated shepherd, shepherd of the black-headed,
Mighty one, you are the lord Asarluḫi.
Lord Asarluhi, you are the great warrior. Indeed you are powerful.
Like Utu you *whirl about* in the clouds.
(Akk.: Like Šamaš you do not *whirl about* in the clouds.)
Your appearance is like Nanna-Sîn. Indeed you cause it to shine forth.
(Akk.: Like Sîn you do not cloud the splendor of your rising.)
15. Oh honored one, indeed you cause the radiance of your appearance to shine forth like the moon.

(Akk.: Honored one, like the moon you do not cloud the radiance of your rising.)
[My lord], you give [notice] to a man.
You give [notice] to him of the rebellious land.
(Akk.: You do not give your word to the hostile land.)
You give notice to the insubordiante and unsubmissive.
(Akk.: You do not give your utterance to him who is disobedient to the lord.)
To the insubordiante and the unsubmissive to Asarluḫi you give notice.
(Akk.: You do not give (your word) (to) him who is disobedient to the lord Marduk.)
My [lord], inspect among his (?) watercourses(?) in your city!
(Akk.: Lord whose might is great, inspect your city!)
Asarluḫi, inspect the earth which has *grown up* in your city!
(Akk.: Marduk, majestic and lofty one, inspect your city!)

May he pacify [your] heart! May he calm your liver!
Oh lord, may heaven pacify you!
Warrior Asarluḫi, may he pacify your heart!
May your beloved spouse, Panunanki, utter a prayer to you!
May the faithful vizier, Mudugasa, utter a prayer to you.
May the daughter-in-law, the first-born of heaven and earth, utter a prayer to you!
May the faithful princess, Ningutešasiga, utter a prayer to you!
May the supreme princess, your lady, Nanâ, utter a prayer to you!
"You should not desert your city!" may he utter to you! May he utter a prayer to you!
"You should never desert Tintir!" may he utter to you! May he utter a prayer to you!

It is an eršemma of Marduk.
An eršemma of the honored one

C. Eršemmas Preserved Only in First Millennium B.C.E. *Copies*

According to its colophon this eršemma, preserved only in First Millennium B.C.E. copies, is an eršemma of Nintinugga, a goddess frequently identified with Ninisina. However, the deity mentioned throughout our work is Baba, the chief goddess of Lagaš. Since Baba was frequently identified in turn with Ninisina, ultimately in our eršemma she became identified also with Nintinugga.

In this work, the poet declares his anguish over the misfortune that has befallen Lagaš. But the interesting passage is lines 20–23, spoken by either the poet or Baba herself. The speaker of this section claims that the misfortune unleashed by Enlil has not affected him/her directly. It is for the other parties, not for him/herself, that the speaker feels sorrow. This is in direct contrast to eršemma no. 171 wherein Ninisina personally experiences the insults and harm resulting from Enlil's actions.

Eršemma no. 10

Text:	A	K.2442 (*SBH* 49a)	17–29
	B	K.4629 (*SBH* III) col. iv	6–28
	C	Rm. 132 (5*R* 52 no. 1) col. iii 30–iv 3	1–4, 28–39
	D	VAT 16+(*SBH* 49)	1–13, 17–29
	E	BM 79037 rev. ii 1–5	31–39

1. me-er-ra-mu-⌈dè⌉ a-ba mu-un-šed$_7$-dè
ina e-ze-zi-ia man-nu ú-na-aḫ-ḫa-an-ni
2. me-er-ra-[mu-dè][1] gašan-mu ^{d}Ba-ba$_6$-mèn me-er-ra-mu-dè
3. ama ^{d}Aba$_x$(AB)-ba$_6$-mèn me-er-
4. ^{d}Lama-é-an-na-mèn me-er-
5. gašan-mu gašan-sikil-la-mèn me-er-
6. ^{d}Nab dumu-sag-an-na-mèn me-er-
7. egí-maḫ-gú-en-na-mèn me-er-
8. dumu[1]-kù gašan-MAR^{ki}-mèn me-er-
9. egí ^{d}Lama-é-šà-ba-mèn me-er-
10. é-u-dul-[1]urú-kù-ga me-er-
11. èš é-ninnu me-er-
12. EDEN.BAR-Lagaš^{ki}-mèn me-er-
13. íb-ba na-ám-urú-ni im-me-ir-ra-mu[1]
ina ug-ga-ti aš-šum URU*-šá šá iš-šal-lu*[2]
14. íb-ba na-ám-é-ni im-me-ir-ra-mu
ina ug-gat aš-šum É-šá

15. a urú-mu a é-mu im-mi-du$_{11}$-ga-ta
a-ḫu-lap URU-*ia a-ḫu-lap É-ia i-na qa-bé-e*

16. a dam-mu a dumu-mu im-mi-du$_{11}$-ga-ta
a-ḫu-lap mu-ti-ia a-ḫu-lap ma-ri-ia [i-na qa-bé]-e

17. é gù gi$_6$-a mu-⌈un⌉-dé-dé-e
ina É *ri-ig-ma ina m[u-ši i-šá]-as-su-*[1]*u*

18. [a]-⌈še⌉-er gi$_6$-a mu-un-dé-[dé]-⌈e⌉(?) mu-un-mar-ra-ta
ta-ni-ḫa šá ina[1] *m[u-ši i]-⌈šá⌉*[!]*-as-su*[2]*-ú*

19. gašan ki-mar-mar-ra ì-su$_8$-su$_8$-ge-eš
kan-šá-a-tum iz-za-az-za-ni

20. me[1]-er-ra e-lum-e šu ba-an-gi
kab-tu ina[2] *e-ze-zi-šú ú-šal-li-man-ni*[3]

21. me[1]-er-ra kur-gal-e šu ba-an-gi

22. umun ^{d}Mu-ul-líl-lá šu ba-an-gi
be-lum ^{d}*En-líl*[1]

23. ù-u$_8$ ba[1]-ab-bé ù-u$_8$ ba-ab-bé ir DU na nam ur$_5$-re[2] nu[3]-mu-un-ḫúl-la[4]
ú-a a-qab-bi MIN[5] *ana šá iš-šal-lu*$_4$ *ana šat-tim*[6] *ki-a-am*[7] *ul*[8] *a-ḫad-du*[9]

24. é-mu gul-la-bi ér na-ám-mà-ni šà-kúš-ù na-ám-mà-ni
bi-ti[1] *ab-tu*[2] *bi-ki-ta*[3] *ub-lam-ma* ŠÀ-*šú ta-ni-ḫa ub-lam-ma*[4]

25. urú-mu ḫul-a[1]-bi ér na-ám-mà-ni šà-kúš-ù na-ám-mà-ni
a-li šul-pu-tu$_4$ *bi-ki-tum ub-lam-ma* ŠÀ-*šú ta-ni-ḫa ub-lam-ma*

26. tùr-gul-gul-la-bi ér na-ám-mà-[ni] šà-

27. amaš-bu-bu-ra-bi ér na-ám-mà-ni šà-

28. é-a ge$_{16}$-le-èm-mà-ni ér na-ám-mà-ni[1] a-ba mu-un-šed$_7$-dè
bi-ti ina šaḫ-lu-uq-ti bi-ki-tum[2] *ub-lam-ma man-nu ú-na-aḫ-ḫa-an-ni*

---

29. [šà-zu] ⌈ḫé-en⌉-ḫun-e bar-zu ḫé-en-šed$_7$-dè
[lìb-ba-ka li-nu-uḫ] ka-bat-ta-ka lip-šaḫ

30. [umun ^{d}Di]-ku$_5$-maḫ-àm — šà-zu ḫé-en-ḫun-e
31. [umun]-⌈é-⌉rab-di$_5$-di$_5$ — šà-zu
32. gašan-tin-u$_9$-ba — šà-zu
33. gašan-Ì-si-in^{ki}-na — šà-zu
34. gašan-é-gal-maḫ — šà-zu
35. gašan-é-rab-di$_5$-di$_5$ — šà-zu
36. gašan-mu ^{d}Ba-ba$_6$-mu — šà-zu
37. egí ama ^{d}Ba-ba$_6$ — šà-zu
38. ^{d}Ba-ba$_6$ nu-nuz$_x$-ša$_6$-ga — šà-zu
39. mu-gi$_{17}$-ib gašan-an-na — šà-zu

ér-šèm-ma-^{d}Nin-tin-ug$_5$-ga-ke$_4$ ér-šèm-ma mu-tin nu-nuz$_x$ dím-ma

Variants

2. 1) D:[x(-x)]-x, no room for me-er-ra-mu-dè
8. 1) So B; D: gašan (perhaps read dumu$^{!}$)
10. 1) So B; D: dul(?) instead of é-u-dul
13. 1) So B; D: im-ma$^{!}$-ir$^{!}$-ra-[mu] 2) So B; D:-*lu*$_4$
17. 1) So B; D:-*sú*-
18. 1) So A; according to size of break B omits *ina mu-ši*; D: *ana* 2) So B; D:-*sú*-
20. 1) So D; A: mi- 2) So A,B; D omits *ina* 3) B: *e-ze-*⌜*zi ú*$^{!}$⌝*-šal-li-man-ni*
21. 1) So D; A: mi-
22. 1) Akkadian according to B
23. 1) So A,B; D: ba$^{!}$- 2) So B; D-ra 3) So B; D omits nu- 4) So B; D:-le 5) So A,B; D: *ú-a a-qab-[bi]* 6) So B; D: *šat-ti-šú* 7) So B; D: *ki-i* 8) So B; D omits *ul* 9) So B; D: *a-ḫa-ad-‹du›*
24. 1) So A,B; D: É 2) So A,B; D:-*tum* 3) So A,B; D:-*tum* 4) So B; D omits -*ma*
25. 1) So B; A,D:-la-
28. 1) So D; C adds -ir 2) So D; C:-*ti*

* * *

When I am angry, who can calm me?
When I am angry, (who can calm me)? You are my Baba. When I am angry, who can calm me?
Mother Ababa are you. When I am angry, who can calm me?
The genie of the Eanna are you. When I am angry, who can calm me?
My lady, Ninsikila, are you. When I am angry, who can calm me?
Nab, the first-born of An, are you. When I am angry, who can calm me?
The exalted princess of the throne room are you. When I am angry, who can calm me?
The holy child, Ninmara, are you. When I am angry, who can calm me?
The princess, the genie of the Ešabba, are you. When I am angry, who can calm me?
Eudul of Urukug, when I am angry, who can calm me?
Shrine Eninnu, when I am angry, who can calm me?
The . . . of Lagaš are you. When I am angry, who can calm me?

My anger because of the pillaging of her city!
My anger because of the pillaging of her house!
While uttering, "Oh my city! Oh my house!"
while uttering, "Oh my spouse! Oh my child!"
(at) the house she pours out cries in the night.
She pours out sighing in the night. After . . .
. . . stand . . . lady.

In (his) anger the honored one has dealt kindly with me.
In (his) anger the great mountain has dealt kindly with me.
The lord Enlil has dealt kindly with me.
I say, "Woe!" I say, "Woe!" For those who have been taken away—it is over this—I do not rejoice.

My destroyed house! Tears on her behalf, heart felt sighs on her behalf!
My ruined city! Tears on her behalf, heart felt sighs on her behalf!
Its destroyed cattle pens! Tears on her behalf, heart felt sighs on her behalf!
Its uprooted sheepfolds! Tears on her behalf, heart felt sighs on her behalf!
His(?) destroying of the house! Tears on her behalf! Who can calm me?

May he pacify [your heart]! May he calm your liver!
May the lord Dikumaḫam pacify your heart!
May [the lord] of the Erabdidi pacify your heart!
Nintinugga, may he pacify your heart!
Ninisina, may he pacify your heart!
Lady of the Egalmaḫ, may he pacify your heart!
Lady of the Erabdidi, may he pacify your heart!
My lady, my Baba, may he pacify your heart!
Baba, beautiful woman, may he pacify your heart!
Hierodule, Inanna, may he pacify your heart!

An eršemma of Nintinugga. The eršemma (for the lamentation) mu-tin nu-nuz dím-ma

In our transliteration of eršemmas nos. 45, 53 and 59, all in CT 42 12, we have omitted the cuneiform signs which indicate the pronunciation of the Sumerian, or that serve as instructions regarding the recitation of the work. In no. 45 and no. 53 a pronunciation of the incipits has been provided directly below the incipits, no. 45: a-ur-sag-ut-tu-lu-u-u-e-ma-ru-u and no. 59: i-lu-u na-gi-in-e-ra-a i-lu-u-u-ak-ke-e (note the inverted order of this syllabic rendering of the opening line).[208]

(208)Another example of the syllabic rendering directly below the opening line is CT 42 no. 1:1–2 (incorrectly read by Kutscher, *YNER* 6 *1):

⌜umun⌝-e ḫu-luḫ-ḫa-zu a šà-íb-ba!-zu èn-šè nu-šed₇-dè

ᵃše-še-e nu-si-i!-du ᵃiš-še-en-ni : !Uú ḫu-luḫ-ḫa-zuú eš-še nu-si-du MIN

(še-še-e, iš-še-en-ni and eš-še are renderings of èn-še, nu-si(-i)-du for nu-šed₇-dè.) Note the inversion of the line where the beginning of the line occurs in the last half of the syllabic line: U/umun ḫu-luḫ-ḫa-zu.

Guides to the pronunciation also occur in the margins: $^{\text{a-lim}}$alim-a-a (line 3); ^{AN}alim-ma-^{a} (line 11). Guides to the pronunciation occur within the Sumerian line itself: ur-sag^{qa} (lines 1, 10); e$_4$-ma-ru^{u} (line 1); ur-sag-ut-u$_{18}$-lu^{u} (line 3); é-u$_6$-nir-ki-tuš-maḫ^{ḫu} (line 7); rib-ba-zu-dè^{e}(line 12); i-lu^{u} (line 31); i-lu-ke$_4$$^{\text{i-lu-ke}_4}$-e (line 31); e-lu$^{\text{li-lu-ke}_4}$ (line 29); ^{d}Ba-ba$_6$^{a} (lines obv. 18, rev. 20); umun^{un} (lines obv. 6, rev. 16).

As for the instructions, note in no. 45:5 the instructions to recite u-e-ma-ru-u (for a-ma-ru) before the line. The MIN-sign in the margin before lines 6–25 indicates that a-ma-ru is to be recited before all these lines. Perhaps the KI.MIN in the right margin with the subsequent MIN-signs in lines 6–13 indicate that a-ma-ru is also to be repeated at the end of each line. The instruction for the end of each line in the heart-pacification unit is ambiguous, ér-ḫun-gá-ta-a or a-lim ḫun-gá-ta-a. This same repetition occurs in no. 59; wherein, line 33 has in the left margin i-lu-ak-ke-e, the following lines have MIN. In no. 53, only two lines begin with a phrase from the incipit (lines 21 and 24): zag-ga-dib-ba-a-ni-ír-ra. For the u-sign before šà in the heart-pacification unit see the commentary to no. 45:15.

Eršemma no. 45

Text A BM 132093 (*CT* 42 no. 12) obv. 1–26
B Metropolitan Museum 86.11.288 obv. 1–24

1. ur-sag ut-u$_{18}$-lu e$_4$-ma-ru na-nam
2. alim-ma ur-sag ut-u$_{18}$-lu
3. umun-irigal-la ur-sag
4. umun-Kiš^{ki}-a-ta umun-é-kišib-ba
5. umun-é-me-te-ur-sag umun-é-u$_6$-nir-ki-tuš-maḫ
6. ^{d}^{giš}Ig-alim-ma-ta$^{!}$-ra ^{giš}ig-gu-NU-ra
7. umun ^{d}Sukkal-maḫ-àm sukkal ^{d}Pap-sukkal
8. ur-sag dili-maḫ-àm ur-sag ^{d}Lú-ḫuš-àm
9. alim-ma ur-sag ut-u$_{\text{x}}$-lu
10. an-gin$_7$ ki-gin$_7$ rib-ba-zu-dè
11. ur-sag ki-bal di-da-zu-dè

---

12. u$_4$ šà-ab ḫun-e-ta u$_4$ bar ḫun-e-ta	
13. šà-ur-sag-gal	šà-ab ḫun-e-ta
14. šà-$^{\text{d}!}$Ut-u$_{18}$-lu	šà-ab
15. šà-umun-^{d}Di-ku$_5$-maḫ-àm	šà-ab
16. ša-^{d}Ba-ba$_6$ nu-nuz$_{\text{x}}$-ša$_6$-ga	šà-
17. šà-gašan-tin-u$_9$-ba	šà-
18. šà-gašan-Ì-si-in^{ki}-àm	šà-

19. šà-gašan-gù-téš-a-si-ke[1]-ke$_4$ šà-
20. šà-gašan-mu ^{d}Na-na-a šà-
21. šà[1]-gašan-ḫur-sag-kalam-ma šà-
22. šà[1]-gašan-é-tùr-kalam-ma šà-
23. šà[1]-gašan-Tin-tir^{ki}-ra šà-

ér-šèm-ma-^{d}Nin-urta-kam

Variants

6. 1) B omits -ta-
14. 1) B omits ^{d}
19. 1) B: -ga- instead of -ke-
21–23. 1) B adds -egí-

Warrior, southstorm, verily a flood!
Honored one, warrior, southstorm!
Nergal, warrior, southstorm!
Lord of Kiš, lord (of) the Ekišibba!
Lord (of) the Emeteursag, lord (of) the Eunirkitušmaḫ!
Igalimatara! Iggunu!
Lord Sukkalmaḫ ! Vizier Papsukkal!
Warrior who alone is exalted! Warrior who is Luḫuš!
Honored one, warrior, southstorm!
When you are as surpassing as heaven and earth, (verily a flood)!
When you are the warrior goring the rebellious land, (verily a flood)!

So that the heart (of) the storm be pacified; so that the exterior (of) the storm be pacified!
So that the heart (of) the great warrior be pacified!
So that the heart (of) Utulu be pacified!
So that the heart (of) Dikumaḫ be pacified!
So that the heart of Baba, the beautiful woman, be pacified!
So that the heart of Nintinugga be pacified!
So that the heart (of) Ninisina be pacified!
So that the heart of Ningutešasiga be pacified!
So that the heart (of) my lady Nanâ be pacified!
So that the heart (of) the lady (of) Ḫursagkalama be pacified!
So that the heart (of) the lady (of) the Eturkalama be pacified!
So that the heart (of) the lady of Tintir be pacified!

It is an eršemma of Ninurta.

Eršmma no. 53

Text	A	BM 132093 (*CT* 42 no. 12) rev. 7ff.	1–27
	B	K.3506 19–24	1–6
	C	Metropolitan Museum 86.11.288 rev. 1–18	1–28
	D	BM 83-1-18, 444	7–21

1.	kur-gal a-a ^{d}Mu-ul-líl zà-dib-ba [a-nir-ra][1]	
2.	a-a ^{d}Mu-ul-líl[1]	umun-kur-kur-ra
3.	a-a ^{d}Mu-ul-líl[1]	umun[2]-du$_{11}$-ga-zi-da
4.	[1]a-a ^{d}Mu-ul-líl	a-a-ka-n[ag-gá]
5.	umun-ka-nag-gá	sipa-sag-gi$_{6}$-ga
6.	a-a ^{d}Mu-ul-líl[1]	i-bí du$_{8}$ ní-te-na
7.	a-a ^{d}Mu-ul-líl[1]	am erén-na di-di
8.	umun-ka-nag-gá	ù-lul-la ku-ku
9.	umun-Kiš^{ki}-a-ta	umun-é-kišib-ba
10.	umun-é-me-te-ur-sag	umun-é-u$_{6}$-nir-ki-tuš-maḫ
11.	$^{d\,\text{giš}}$Ig-alim-ma-ta-ra[1]	^{giš}ig-gu-NU-ra
12.	umun ^{d}Sukkal-maḫ-àm	sukkal ^{d}Pap-sukkal
13.	ur-sag dili-maḫ-àm	ur-sag ^{d}Lú-ḫuš-àm
14.	an-gin$_{7}$ ki-gin$_{7}$ rib-ba-zu-dè	
15.	ur-sag ki-bal di-da-zu-dè	

16.	u$_{4}$ šà-ab ḫun-e-ta u$_{4}$ bar ḫun-e-ta	
17.	šà-[1]ur-sag-gal	šà-[2]
18.	[1]šà-^{d}Ut-u$_{18}$-lu	šà-
19.	šà-umun-^{d}Di-ku$_{5}$-maḫ-àm	šà-
20.	šà-^{d}Ba-ba$_{6}$ nu-nuz$_{x}$-ša$_{6}$-ga	šà-
21.	šà-gašan-tin-u$_{9}$-ba	šà-
22.	šà-gašan-Ì-si-in^{ki}-na	šà-
23.	šà-gašan-gù-téš-a-sì-ga-ke$_{4}$	šà-
24.	šà-gašan-mu ^{d}Na-na-a	šà-
25.	šà-gašan-ḫur-sag-kalam-ma	šà-
26.	šà-gašan-é-tùr-kalam-ma	šà-
27.	šà-gašan-Tin-tir^{ki}-ke$_{4}$	šà-

ér-šèm-ma-^{d}En-líl-lá-kam

Variants

1. 1) Line restored according to A rev. 33: zà-dib-ba a-nir-ra; C: ne-ra
2. 1) C: -lá
3. 1) C: -lá 2) C adds -na-

4. 1) C omits line
6. 1) C:-lá
7. 1) C:-lá
11. 1) C omits -ta-ra; E omits -ta-
17. 1) C,E add -ab- 2) C adds ab-ḫun-e-ta
18. 1) C skips 18–27: egí-gašan-Tin-tir^{ki}-ra šà- 9 MU.MEŠ GU_4.UD.MEŠ

* * *

Great mountain, father Enlil, unsurpassed one, [in lament]!
Father Enlil, lord of the lands!
Father Enlil, lord whose pronouncement is true!
Father Enlil, father of the nation!
Lord of the nation, shepherd of the black-headed!
Father Enlil, he who witnesses (everything) first-hand!
Father Enlil, bull who causes the troops to wander!
Lord of the nation, he who sleeps a false sleep!
Lord of Kiš, lord of the Ekišibba!
Lord (of) the Emeteursag, lord of the Eunirkitušmaḫ!
Igalimatara! Iggunu!
Lord Sukkalmaḫ! Vizier Papsukkal!
Warrior who alone is exalted! Warrior who is Luḫuš!
When you are surpassing as heaven and earth, (unsurpassed one, in lament)!
When you are the warrior goring the hostile land, (unsurpassed one, in lament)!

So that the heart (of) the storm be pacified; so that the exterior (of) the storm be pacified!
So that the heart (of) the great warrior be pacified!
So that the heart (of) Utulu be pacified!
So that the heart (of) the lord Dikumaḫ be pacified!
So that the heart of Baba, the beautiful woman, be pacified!
So that the heart of Nintinugga be pacified!
So that the heart (of) Ninisina be pacified!
So that the heart of Ningutešasiga be pacified!
So that the heart of my lady, Nanâ, be pacified!
So that the heart (of) the lady (of) Ḫursagkalama be pacified!
So that the heart (of) the lady (of) the Eturkalama be pacified!
So that the heart of the lady of Tintir be pacified!

It is an eršemma of Enlil.

Eršemma no. 59

There are two differing recensions of eršemma no. 59. Although both contain the same opening unit, the heart-pacification unit differs.

Text A BM 132093 (*CT* 42 no. 12) obv. 29–40
B MLC 382 obv. 1–12
C Metropolitan Museum 86.11.288 obv. 25–33

1. i-lu-ke$_4$ i-lu-ke$_4$ i-lu na-ám-in-ra[1]
2. mu-gi$_{17}$-ib i-lu-ke$_4$ i-lu-ke$_4$[1] i-lu na-ám-i[n-ra][2]
3. mu-gig-an-na gašan-an-na-ke$_4$[1]
4. kur-gul-gul gašan-ḫur-sag-kalam-ma-ke$_4$
5. an al-dúb-ba gašan-é-tùr-kalam-ma-ke$_4$
6. ki-sìg-ga gašan-é-ḪUR-šà-ba-ke$_4$[1]
7. ^{d}Líl-lá-en-na gašan-[tùr-amaš-a-ke$_4$][1]
8. ama-é-a ^{d}Da-da[1] nu-nuz$_x$-ša$_6$-ga
9. ^{d}Na-na-a dumu-sag-é-a-ke$_4$
10. mu-gi$_{17}$-ib i-lu-ke$_4$[1] i-lu-ke$_4$

Text B:

11. u$_4$ šà-ab ḫun-e-ta u$_4$ bar ḫun-e-ta
[. .] u-mu lu-nu-úḫ
12. [šà-egí-gašan-an-na u$_4$]
13. [šà-egí-gašan-é-an-na u$_4$]
14. [šà-gašan-ki-Unu^{ki}-ga u$_4$]
15. [šà-egí-gašan-ki-Zabalam^{ki} u$_4$]
16. [šà-egí-gašan-ḫur-sag-kalam-ma u$_4$]
17. šà-[egí-gašan-é-tùr-kalam-ma u$_4$]
18. šà-[egí-gašan-Tin-tir^{ki}-ra u$_4$]
19. šà-[egí-gašan-mu ^{d}Na-na-a u$_4$]
20. šà-[gašan-é-a gašan-d]ìm-me-er-e-ne u$_4$]

É[r-šèm-ma-^{d}Inanna-kam]

Text C:

11. u$_4$ šà-ab ḫun-e-ta u$_4$ bar ḫun-e-ta
12. [ša[3]]-ur-sag-gal šà-ab ḫun-e-ta[1]
13. [šà-^{d}Ut-u$_{18}$-lu šà-ab
14. šà-umun-^{d}Di-ku$_5$-maḫ-àm šà-ab
15. šà-^{d}Ba-ba$_6$ nu-nuz$_x$-ša$_6$-ga šà-ab
16. šà-gašan-tin-u$_9$-ba šà-ab
17. šà-gašan-Ì-si-in^{ki}-àm šà-ab
18. šàgašan-gù-téš-a-sì-ga-ke$_4$ šà-ab

19. šà-gasan-mu ^{d}Na-na-a šà-ab
20. egí-gašan-ḫur-sag-kalam-ma šà-ab
21. egí-gašan-é-tùr-kalam-ma šà-ab]
22. egí gašan-Tin-tir^{ki}-ra šà-

ér-šem̀-ma-^{d}Inanna-ke$_4$

Variants

1. 1) So C; A:na-a-ám-in-[ra]; B:nam-ra
2. 1) A omits i-lu-ke$_4$ 2) B omits refrain i-lu nam-ra; C omits na-ám-in-ra
3. 1) C omits lines 4–8: mu-gig-an-na 5 MU.MEŠ GU$_4$.UD.MEŠ gašan-an-na-ke$_4$
6. 1) So B; A omits line
7. 1) So A; B:ama-é-a gašan-é-x-x-AB^{ki}
8. 1) A omits ^{d}
10. 1) So A; B omits -ke$_4$
12. 1) C omits 13–21: egí-gašan-Tin-tir^{ki}-ra šà- 9 MU.MEŠ GU$_4$.UD.MEŠ

She of lament, she of lament struck up a lament.
The hierodule, she of lament, she of lament struck up a lament.
The hierodule of heaven, Inanna,
the devastatrix of the mountain, the lady of Ḫursagkalama,
she who causes the heavens to rumble, the lady of the Eturkalama,
she who shakes the earth, the lady of the Eḫuršaba,
Lillaenna, the lady [of the cattle pen and sheepfold],
the mother of the house, Dada, the beautiful woman,
Nanâ, the first-born of the house,
the hierodule, she of lament, she of lament (struck up a lament).

Text B:

So that the heart (of) the storm be pacified! So that the exterior (of) the storm be pacified!

[So that the heart (of) the princess, Inanna, the heart (of) the storm be pacified!

So that the heart (of) the princess, the lady of the Eanna, the heart (of) the storm be pacified!

So that the heart (of) the lady of "the place"—Uruk, the heart (of) the storm be pacified!

So that the heart (of) the princess, the lady of "the place"—Zabalam, the heart (of) the storm be pacified!
So that the heart (of) the princess, the lady (of) Ḫursagkalama, the heart (of) the storm be pacified!
So that] the heart [(of) the princess, the lady (of) the Eturkalama, the heart (of) the storm be pacified!
So that] the heart [(of) the princess, the lady of Tintir, the heart (of) the storm be pacified!
So that] the heart [(of) the princess, my lady Nanâ, the heart (of) the storm be pacified!
So that] the heart [(of) the lady of the house, the lady] of the gods, the heart (of) the storm be pacified!

[It is an] e[ršemma of Inanna].

Text C:

So that the heart (of) the storm be pacified! So that the exterior (of) the storm be pacified!
So that [the heart] (of) the great hero be pacified!
[So that the heart (of) Utulu be pacified!
So that the heart (of) the lord Dikumaḫ be pacified!
So that the heart of Baba, the beautiful woman, be pacified!
So that the heart of Nintinugga pacified!
So that the heart (of) the lady of Isin be pacified!
So that the heart of Ningutešasiga be pacified!
So that the heart of my lady Nanâ be pacified!
So that the heart (of) the princess, the lady (of) the Ḫursagkalama, be pacified!
So that the heart (of) the princess, the lady (of) the Eturkalama, be pacified!
So that the heart (of) the princess, the lady of Tintir be pacified!

An eršemma of Inanna

PART III

Commentary

Eršemma no. 23.1

(1)According to the spacing of the signs in the first line, there may be a verb after an-z[à-šè]. For the possible restoration of the verb as either gál or pa-è see A. Poebel, *ZA* 37 245 ff. wherein references to mu an-zà-šè gál and mu an-zà-šè pa-è are cited. Another possible restoration is maḫ-àm; for an-zà-šè maḫ-àm see J. vDijk, *SGL* 2 142; W. Römer, *Königshymnen* 168. Cf. also Å. W. Sjöberg, *Studia Geo Widengren oblata* E. J. Brill, Leiden, (1972) 61 line 16'.

(2)alim-ma has been restored on the basis of 23.2:2.

(4)For the readings of IM^{ki} as Karkara, the city of Iškur, Muru(m), the city of Ningirin, or Enegi, the city of Ninazu, see Å. W. Sjöberg, *TCS* 3 99 with previous literature.

(9)We have transliterated úg-gal-la rather than pirig-gal-la since lines 8 and 9 appear to be intentional homonyms: u$_4$-gal-la / ùg-gal-la. Moreover, see Å. W. Sjöberg *TCS* 3 6 for úg-gal-gin$_7$ with variant u$_6$-gal-gin$_7$.

(11)We do not expect the verbal infix -n-, rather mu-du$_7$-du$_7$-du$_7$(-e). For du$_7$-du$_7$ meaning "to gore" governing the locative see W. Heimpel, *Tierbilder* 300-301. See also Å. W. Sjöberg, *TCS* 3 p. 144 commentary to line 510 for DU$_7$-DU$_7$ governing the locative wherein Sjöberg, based upon context, suggests a translation "to fall upon," due to the variant ra-ra. Perhaps the infix -n- is for -ni-, thus mu-ni-du$_7$-du$_7$-du$_7$.

(12)For dul$_{1/4/5}$ governing the locative, see A. Falkenstein, *AnOr* 29 p. 107, wherein our line is quoted. As in line 11 above we do not expect the verbal infix -n-, but rather im-mi-dul.

(13)In our line we expect the ergative (^{d}Mu-ul-líl-e) to govern the phrase sag sìg, for which we see J. Krecher, *Kultlyrik* 214 with previous literature.

(15)The compound verb á-ág includes the expected commitative infix in the verbal chain. Thus we expect ^{d}Iškur(-da) rather than ^{d}Iškur-ra.

(16)We are unaware of any appropriate meaning for si-si in our passage.

(18)For TUMXEŠ compare *CT* 12 23 BM 41499 32: [NI]NDÁxEŠ = *ṣi-in-[du]*, which is cited by CAD Ṣ 197 sub *ṣimdu* B and by AHw 1102 sub *ṣimdu(m)* II (= *ṣ*. I?). According to the context of our passage, this lexical entry should be cited sub *ṣimdu* A mng. 2) "team (of draft animals)" rather than under *ṣimdu* B "three seahs" or a "measure of three seahs' capacity." The sign NINDÁxEŠ (read ḫáš) as well as TUMxKÀD may also designate a part of a wooden implement (see CAD E 153 sub *emšu*). This further meaning of NINDÁxEŠ is an additional indication that NINDÁ(or TUM)xEŠ = *ṣimdu* should be cited sub *ṣimdu* A, since the related noun *ṣimittu* (CAD Ṣ 198) may mean either a team of animals or the crosspiece of a yoke (thus a wooden implement).

(21)For ul used adverbially cf. C. Wilcke, *Das Lugalbandaepos* 24: ul ti-a "der froh dasitzt." Note the homonymous variant ul_4 "hurry!" in no. 168:9, 10.

(23-25)We are unaware of any other references to the term na_4-TUM_{10}, possibly "wind-stones." Could na_4-ní-tur-tur be a variant for na_4-nì-tur-tur = MIN(*aban*) *ṣeḫḫerti* (*MSL* 10 32 96)? It is possible that the term na_4-IM-tur-tur in this eršemma may have resulted from a fusing of the terms IM-di_4-di_4-lá and na_4-tur-tur which are juxtaposed in eršemma 185:16–18. If this is the case, then IM may represent a variant for na_4 rather than serving as a modifier of na_4.

(29)For bàn-da, "fierce (said of animals)", see CAD E 62 sub *ekdu*.

(30)For KA.ḪUR see Å. W. Sjöberg, *TCS* 3 84–85 with previous literature and *Studies Kramer* 426. Add *YOS* 15 6 (= Garrett Theological Seminary 6):

KA.ḪUR ak / *gu-ru-du-um*

ib-ši-in-du_{11} / *il-te(?)-su-ú*

Our reading -mur in our passage is based upon the syllabic orthography GÙ-mu-ra in eršemma 184:27.

Eršemma no. 23.2

(6–12)These lines have been translated on the basis of eršemma 23.1:6–12.

(13)This line appears to be a combination of 23.1:13–14.

(27–28)For a discussion of the term ki-sì-ga see *YNER* 3 81–82 wherein Hallo and vDijk state: "ki-sì-ga does not always mean 'offerings for the dead' or the place where such offerings were brought. The ki-sì-ga is often found in the desert and the ritual against illnesses was performed there." Because of our not being able to understand the background or context of the reference to ki-sì-ga in our text, we have left the term untranslated.

(31)gul-gul in our context clearly seems to be a variant for gu-ul-gu-ul, "to make great." See Sjöberg, *Mondgott* 159–160 for another possible instance wherein, gul-gul could be interpreted as being a variant for gu-ul-gu-ul.

Eršemma no. 168

(7)According to collation -luh- might be an erasure. We expect a finite verb.

(9)Note the homonymous variants ul_4 "hurry" in our line and ul "joyfully" in no. 23.1:21.

(34)For síg-bar-ra du_8, "to let the hair hang freely down the neck," see Sjöberg, *JCS* 21 278 wherein our passage is quoted. Note *VAS* 2 66 rev. 11: ap-ka-le sig-ba-ra du-a-ge.

(36)The parallel lines in eršemma 184:40 and eršemma 185:32 contain še-karadin nu-me-a, "although not piles of grain." Note also *VAS* 2 66 rev. 12:]-⌈x⌉ še-ù-ra du-a-ge which occurs parallel to line 34 above. še-mu-ra-gin_7/dím appears to be a variant for še-karadin. However, lacking nu-me-a in our text we have chosen to translate še-mu-ra on its own merits. še-mu-ra quite possibly is an Emesal orthography for še-giš-ra. For še-giš-ra, "threshed grain," see *MSL* 12 164 204: lú še-giš-ra = *ša* ⌈*na-ar-pa-ás*⌉*-t[im]*. For giš-ra becoming Emesal mu-ra cf. eršemma no. 60.1.
ur_5-re appears on the basis of the parallel lines to be a variant for u_4-dè, resulting from the "d" and "r" interchange.

(37)Could TÚG be a mistake for -šè? Cf. the parallel line in eršemma 23.1:26: gáb-bu-zu ù-mu-e-sì.

(38–39)The writing ur-sag-gá is presumably for the ergative ur-sag-e, as is seen in its paralleling ^{d}Iškur-e in the next line. For the reading and meaning of these two lines, see C. Wilcke, *Das Lugalbandaepos* 162.

(40)For IM.A.A read $šeg_x$ (= *zunnu* "rain"), see Å. W. Sjöberg, *TCS* 3 117. The orthography IM.MA.A.A need not be viewed as proof of an alternate reading im-a-a. This unusual orthography may have resulted from the scribe having repeated the sound "imaa" to himself as he copied the signs constituting the value $šeg_x$.

We have interpreted ra-ra-mu-ni and zi-ga-mu-ni as being unusual variants for ra-ra-mu-dè and zi-ga-mu-dè. Note the parallel ending to eršemma 185:35–36. This highly unusual variant -ni for -dè(NE) is occasionally attested, e.g. *CT* 42 no. 9 obv. iii 16: u_5-a-zu-ni for u_5-a-zu-dè. See also footnote 51.

(41)For the reading e_4-ma-ru rather than a-ma-ru see Krecher, *WO* 4 266.

Eršemma no. 184

(6)Note the orthography tum_{10}-mu for tum_{10}-u_x(ULÙ).

(7)the beginning of this line is atested in *SBH* 23 obv. 23 with homonymous variant ki-^{giš}ḫa-lu-úb-da-ri-ta.

(9)For lú-ḫi as an epithet of Iškur, see Th. Jacobsen, *Image of Tammuz,* p. 22, wherein Jacobsen suggests a translation "man-drenching."

(10)For e_4-silim, "health-giving waters," compare Gudea Cyl. B iv 18. It is also possible that e_4-di-da is a variant for e_4-dé-da (see E. Gordon, *Sumerian Proverbs* 1.38 wherein Gordon translates "libation").

(13)We expect ^{d}En-líl-le.

(14)The form um-me-en-šè-si-sá for si um-me-en-šè-sá would be highly unusual in the Old Babylonian period. Thus, we doubt that this verbal form is intended to represent si sá = *ešèru.* Rather it may serve as a variant for si-si as in eršemma 23.1:16–17.

(17)For sír = *šapû(m)* II 1)"to be thick (said of clouds)," see *AHw* 1177.

(21)šu um-mi-ta may be for šu um-mi-tag as in the next line, or for šu um-mi-te as in 23.1:23–24.

(27)For GÙ-mu-ra see the commentary to 23.1:30

(29)NÍ-ta-na may derive from ní-ta-na ‹ní-te-a-na. Cf. ní-te-na in 185:33–34.

(31)For sag gi/gi_4 = *ḫâšu* see Castellino, *Two Šulgi Hymns* (BC) Univ. of Rome, Rome, 1972, p. 144.

(32)On the basis of context, we have assumed nimgir to be a variant for nim-gír.

(34–35)For ur and me-er used in parallel see Krecher, *Kultlyrik* 141 ff.

(37)Note the variant -me- for -mè-.

(39)For gú ki(-še) gál/ma-al see Krecher, Kultlyrik 222 no. 640; Cohen, *ELA* commentary to line 225.

(40)Presumably še-ga-ra-di nu-me-a ‹še-garadin nu-me-a. However, note no. 185:32 for še-garadin-da nu-me-a and note 168:36 for še-mu-ra-gin$_7$ instead of še-garadin nu-me-a. We have interpreted la-ḫe as being syllabic for laḫ (=*abālu* B). Note 168:36 for laḫ$_4$.

(41)Perhaps ZÚ ku-ku is a variant for zú ku$_5$(-ku$_5$) = *našāku,* "to bite." Even were we to take this assumption, the meaning of our line would be unclear.

(44–48)For these lines occurring in other compositions, see M. Cohen *WO* 8 29. Presumably níg-e-rib-ba is a variant orthography for ní-gìr-rib-ba as in *WO* 8 29:174.

(50–51)Note the variant è-da-sá in the common phrase a-ba e-da-sá.

Eršemma no. 185

Our translation is based upon reconstructing each line on the basis of the following correspondences:

line	6–7	=	23.1:13–14; 168:6–7
	8	=	168:8; 184:13
	9–10	=	23.1:21–22
	11	=	cf. 184:19
	12	=	23.1:18; 184:15
	14	=	23.1:19; 184:16
	15	=	23.1:20
	16–18	=	23.1:23–25; 184:21–22
	19	=	23.1:27; 184:25
	20	=	23.1:26; 184:23
	21–22	=	23.1:28–29
	29–32	=	168:34–36; 184:40–43
	33–36	=	168:38–41

(35)The parallel passage 168:38–41 has the verbal form ra-ra-mu-ni. The phrase an-gin$_7$ rib-ba is common (see 53:14). Yet the verbal form in our line appears to be too corrupt as to allow an emendation.

Eršemma no. 79

The following seven lines occur at the bottom of the tablet. Their great similarity with the beginning of our text suggests that these seven lines were from a variant text.

1′. munus-zi-mèn i-lu ga-nú lú nam-mu-un-zi
2′. ul-e ⌜pa⌝-pa-al-la ga-nú
3′. ul-e ki-kù-mu ga-nú
4′. ki-kù ki-⌜kin⌝(?)-na ga-nú

5′. ki-ám-me-⌈e⌉-gar-ra-mu ga-nú
6′. kù a-a-mu ba-til-la-ta
7′. za a-a-mu ba-til-la-ta
1′. I, the faithful lady, lie down in laments. No one can arouse (me).
I lie down . . . among the shoots.
I lie down . . . my holy place,
I lie down at the holy place, the sought after place.
5′. I lie down at my place of silence.
Since(?) (my) silver, oh my father, has been destroyed,
since (?) (my) precious stones, oh my father, have been destroyed,

(1)For various interpretations of the difficult phrase ul-e ba-nú see Alster, Dumuzi's Dream commentary to lines 15–16, wherein the variants i-lu and u_x-lu are cited in this context. Alster has suggested translating ul-e as "to rest" on the basis of ul = *ulṣu* "pleasure." Alster quotes Kramer's interpretation of ul-e as "among buds" and Jacobsen's interpretation of ul-e as "in the southwind," Jacobsen preferring the orthography u_x-lu.

(3)For Inanna's epithet kur-gul-gul "devastatrix of the mountain," see W. W. Hallo and J. vDijk, *YNER* 3 83.

(5)The epithet ᵈUn-mà-i-bí-ma-al means "the wise one among the people."

(10)Note the syllabic Emesal orthography ám-me-e-gá-ar for nì-me-gar / *qūlu,* "silence" (*AHw* 927). If our suggested translation is correct, we don't expect the verbal infix -n-, but rather ba-a_5-en-a, which in our text has become ba-a_5-an-na.

It is not unusual in eršemmas for part of the opening line to be understood at the close of the ensuing passage. Note for example eršemma no. 171 wherein ám-mu ám-gal-la-àm occurs at the end of line 6; no. 1.1 wherein the suffix -ri in line 24 indicates the repetition of at least part of line 1. And cf. nos. 45, 53 and 59 for the closing line of the first unit.

(11)For other occurrences of the phrase lú-di ama-mu-ra du_{11}-ga-na-ab, see M. E. Cohen, "The 'Monkey-Letter': A Different Perspective," *OrNS* 45 (1976) 270–274.

(16)For tu_9 as a variant for $tu_{10/11}$ = *kamāru,* "to heap up," see J. Krecher, *Kultlyrik* 106–107.

(18–19)Note the verbal form ba-til-la-ta in line 7′ at the bottom of the tablet in the same context as ba-ti occurs in our text.

(20–21)For èš-da, "barrel," see vDijk, *SGL* 2 127 ff.

(20–23)These four lines contain verbs in the same order as in the lamentation é tùr-gin$_7$ nigin-na-àm a+31 to a+34 (*CT* 42 no. 8 obv. i 3–6):

še-eb-⸢urú-zé-ba^{ki}	ba-gul⸣-šè
é-^{d}Am-an-ki-ga	ba-⸢ḫul-lu⸣-a-šè
é-^{d}Dam-gal-nun-na	ba-pe-el-la-šè
é-^{d}Asar-lú-ḫi	ba-i-ra-šè

(24)We have understood nu-a-še as being a syllabic orthography for nú-a-šè, thus, "at (the lament) of the reposing one," presumably a reference to the position of the mourner who has instructed the messenger to talk to Nanna. Note the variant text quoted above lines 1′–5′ wherein the speaker is clearly lying down.

(32)The transliteration zi-dè-e[s] is not definite, a transliteration zi bí-i[n-. . .] being also possible.

(33–35)Note the following two couplets which parallel our lines 33–35: *CT* 42 8 i 13–14:

šu-ni EL-lá im-ta-zur$_5$-zur$_5$ ér-gig ì-še$_8$-še$_8$
gaba-ni ^{kuš}ub$_5$-kù-ga ì-sìg-ge ér-gig ì-še$_8$-še$_8$

Ur Lament 299–300:

lú munsub-ni ^{ú}numun-bur-gin$_7$ šu mu-ni-in-dub-dub
gaba-ni ub$_5$-kù-ga-àm ì-sìg-ge a urú-mu im-me
"The man pulls out his hair like a rush.
He strikes his chest like a holy uppu-drum. 'Oh my city!' he says."

zur-zur, which occurs in line 33, usually is equated with Akkadian *kunnû, kutennû* "to treat with care." Note also CAD D 34 sub *dakāku* B for zur-zur = *dakāku*. Noting the syllabic orthographies in our text perhaps zur-zur is a variant for zur$_5$-zur$_5$ as in *CT* 42 8 i 13 quoted above. See CAD E 341 sub *eṣēlu* for šu LA "to immobilize, to become heavy of movement." EL may be related to e-la-lu et.al., "cries of mourning" (see CAD L 47 sub *lallarātu;* Krecher, *Kultlyrik* n. 433). Perhaps Ningirgilu is described as raising her hands to the sky in wailing, thus causing her hands to become heavy.

For ^{ú}numun-sar-ra see MSL 10 107 18a and 18b for ^{ú}numun-sar = *zi-ru-u ki-ri, a-zu-pí-ru.*

(37)šu ni-me-en is presumably a syllabic orthography for šu nigin. For Nergal, Ereškigal's husband, with the epithet EN-bàn-da see eršemma no. 164:30. For EN-bànda see also *VAS* 10 149:5 EN-bàn-da-^{d}Nin-x-x-ke$_4$ and W. W. Hallo, *Studies Kramer,* p. 216, *AOAT* 25 216 line 16 for dumu with variants EN-bànda/tur and NIG.TUR(?).

(38)For Ningirgilu with the epithet kù-zu-mu, "my wise one," see *SBH* IV 126–127: kù-zu-mu(^{d})Gašan-gir-gi-lum / *e-muq-tum (^{d})Nin-gir-gi-lum.*

Eršemma no. 32

(8)The epithet dumu-šag$_5$-é-e is a variant for the expected epithet dumu-sag-é-a. For Nanâ as dumu-sag-é-a, see eršemma 59:9; BL 62:8 (collated): [^{d}Na-n]a-a dumu-sag-[. . .].

(9)The deity ^{d}EN-gal-DU.DU is listed in the second tablet of AN = ^{d}*A-nu-um* (*CT* 24 pl. 26: 126) as nimgir-kur-ra-[ke$_4$], "herald of the netherworld." Because of this deity's relationship with the netherworld, as well as the goddess Inanna's being called EN-gal-DU.DU, we suggest the reading uru$_x$(EN)-gal, this being a variant for urugal (ABxGAL) / *erṣetu,* "netherworld," or *qabru,* "grave." uru$_x$-gal-DU.DU would then be "she who roams the netherworld." The identification of uru$_x$-gal DU.DU as the herald of the netherworld thereby comes clearer. This epithet is also fitting for Inanna, probably referring to her ill-fated descent to the netherworld. The use of this epithet in our eršemma implies that the ruination of the Eanna complex may have indirectly resulted from Inanna's being in the netherworld, away from her city. For the personal name uru$_x$-gal-DU.DU, see Jestin *Tablettes Sumeriennes de Shuruppak,* Paris, Boccard, 1937, 302 rev. v 3.

(10)ù-tuk may be an orthography for udug / *utukku.* For another syllabic orthography for udug note Gudea cyl. A iii 20: ú-dug$_4$.

(11)Noting the syllabic orthography gi$_4$-ge for gig-ge in line 37 below, we suggets that gi$_4$-ra is syllabic for gir$_5$-ra. For gir$_5$(-gir$_5$), "to sink," see J. Krecher, Kultlyrik 176; *AHw* 940a sub *rabû(m)* IV. The imagery is quite apt, for in line 10 the house is described as being so tall that it spans the entire distance between heaven and earth. Here, in line 12, its great size is further described, the brickwork being so long that it sinks below the horizon.

(20)sig$_7$-igi, literally "eyebrow," most likely refers to the upper part of the gate of the Enamtara mentioned in the previous line. For other references to sig$_7$-igi of the door or gate see A. Salonen, *Die Türen,Helsinki Suomalaisen, Kiyailisunden kairtjapaino, 1960,* 55 wherein Salonen translates "Türsturz," "lintel."

(22)We have no suggestion as to the meaning of the phrase uš ù-mu-un-di-ka-na-ág-d[a(?)].

(23)For kun-sag see Å. Sjöberg, *Mondgott* 117 n. 119 with previous literature. We expect šà-bé, "to its midst."

(37)gi$_4$-ge is syllabic for gig-ge.

(40–41)For our restoration of the line cf. K.58 (courtesy E. Sollberger and the Trustees of the British Museum) obv. 16–17:

[é]-la-ga-me nu-me-a-mu
[urú]-la-ga-me nu-me-a-mu

For la-ga = *sarru,* "false, treacherous," see *AHw* 1030. Possibly -me, "our," in our line includes Inanna and Enlil or perhaps Inanna is speaking on behalf of herself and the people of her city.

(42–48)For these lines, see J. Krecher, *Kultlyrik* 141–144 with previous literature. The locative infixes in the verbal forms in lines 42–43 probably refer to "in the house" and "in the cella."

(53)šu ir in our passage may be related to šu túm literally "to bring the hand (against someone)," thus, "to attack."

(54)For šu lá with the meaning "to defile," see CAD L 258 sub *lu'û;* 83 sub *lapātu* for Nabnitu G_1 ii 104: ⌜šu⌝-lá-lá = [*lu-up-pu-tu*] (perhaps *lupputu* in this instance has its meaning "to make unclean" (cf. mng. 4g). Cf. The Lamentation over the Destruction of Sumer and Ur (Ms. Kramer) 311:
kin-sig unú-gal-dingir-re-e-ne-ke_4 šu ba-e-lá-lá.
"The evening meal at the banquet hall of the gods was *defiled*(?)."

(55)For UN ní-te cf. S. N. Kramer, "Death of Ur-Nammu," *JCS* 21 (1967) 112 line 5: ukù-e ní bí-in-te.

(56)Perhaps ba-an is syllabic for bán. For ba-an syllabic for [gìš]bán in a literary text, see A. Falkenstein, "Fluch über Akkade" (*ZA* 57) line 181.

(a+62–63) For mir-sig = *šarbillu* "a king of wind," see *MSL* IV Emesal Voc. III 90.

Eršemma no. 106

(1)The suffix -mu after the non-finite verbal form renders the exact translation of this clause, which contains an interrogative question, difficult.

Lines 4–22 of our eršemma occur in four other texts:

A: *STVC* 30 ii
B: *SBH* 31 obv. 7 ff.
C: K.41 (*PSBA* (1895) 17)
D: K.58 (courtesy E. Sollberger and the Trustees of the British Museum)

(4)B 21: é ma-mú-da ma-dù-a-mu
22: É *šá ki-ma šu-ut-tim in-né-ep-šá-am:* É *šá te-diš-tim*
D 33: é ma-[. . .]

Text B gives two variant Akkadian translations of ma-mú-da, namely, the expected *šuttim* and the unexpected *tēdištim.* Apparently *tēdištim* is based upon mú-mú(-da) = *edēšu, uddušu,* "to become new, to renew" said of the moon (see CAD E 30 sub *edēšu* bilingual passage section and p. 32b for STC 2 pl. 49:12 wherein the Akkadian has inverted its translation; the expected equations are *uddušu* = mú-mú-da, *banâ* = ù-tu-ud-da).

(5)Text B provides no variants.

(6)Texts B and D provide no Sumerian variants, but D does have an Akkadian translation:

É *šá ki-ma tar-ba-ṣu u su-pu-ru du-uš-šu-ú*

(7)Texts B and D provide no Sumerian variants, but B does have an Akkadian translation:

[ki-m]a ṣe-e-ni ina su-pu-ru du-uš-šu-ú

This Akkadian translation is apparently inaccurate, for we would expect the corresponding Sumerian to be: e-zé amaš-a-gin_7 lu-lu-a

(8)B 11: [bur-gu]l[!]-e bur gul-la-mu
12: *šá pur-kul-lum pu-ra iq-qú-ru*
D 28: [bur]-gul-e bur [. . .]-la-mu

(9)B 13: zá-dím-ma zá ba-an-dím[!]-ma-mu
14: *šá za-dim*[!]*-ma ab-nu ib-nu-ú*
D 29: zá-dím-ma [. . .]-ma-mu

(10)A 4: ká-bi-ta ki-u_6-di-mu
B 15: ká-bi-ta ki-u_6-di-mu
16: *ba-ab-ba a-šar tab-ra-a-ti-ia*
D 30: e_4 ká-bi-ta [. . .]

The addition of e_4 in text D is not unexpected. e_4 would be a variant for é, "house," which is assumed to be at the beginning of the line in the other passages.

(11)A 5: ki-šu-me-eš-na-ám-lu-lu-mu
B 17: é-zi ki-šu-⌈peš⌉-na-ám-mu-lu-a-mu
18: É *ki-i-ni ma-ḫa-zi šá ni-ši-ia*
D 31: e-zí ki-šu-pe[š - . . .]

For ki-šu-peš / *māḫāzu* as in text B, see J. Cooper, *OrNS* 43,83–86. The Old Babylonian variants ki-šu-me-eš and ki-šu-me-$ša_4$ might suggest a derivation of šu-me-$ša_4$ in the temple name é-šu-me-$ša_4$ from šu-peš. The possible relationship between these two terms has been discussed by Th. Jacobsen, *Image of Tammuz,* 373 n. 19 wherein our passage is cited. (See *NRVN* for names of the form DN-me-DU. Note *MSL* 2 154 12′:

me-duKA.ME.DU = *ma-ga-[rum].*Could -me- DU in these personal names be a writing for *magir,* thus DN-*magir?*)

(12)A 6: ma-ni$_{x}$-gar-ra-kur-kur-ra-mu
B 19: é-ni$_{x}$-mar-ra-kur-kur-ra-mu
20: É *nì-gá-ru šá ma-ta-ti*
D 32: é-ni$_{x}$-[. . .]

(13)A 7: ì-dù-àm kúr in-ga-dù-àm
B 3: é-mu ì-dù-àm kur in-ga-dù-a
4: É *šá in-né-ep-šu-ma ma-a-tum in-né-ep-šú*
C 3: [. . . ma]-da in-ga-dù-a
4; *[. . .] ma-a-ti in-né-ep-pu-uš*

(14)A 8: ba-gul-gul kúr ba-da-gul-gul
B 5: é-mu ba-gul-gul kur ba-[da]-gul-gul
6: É *it-ta-'-bat ma-[ ]-ti-šú-ma it-ta-'-bat*
C 5: [. . . ku]r ba!-da-gul-gul
6: *[. . .] ma-a-ti ú-tab-bat*

(15)A 9: dam-ša$_{6}$-ga kúr-re ba-da-ab-GAM
B 7: é-a dam-sig$_{5}$-ga [kúr-re b]a-da-ab-ga
8: *šá* É *mu-tú* ⌈*dam-qa*⌉ *[nak-r]u iš-ta-lal*
C 7: [. . .] kúr-re ba-da-ab-GAM
8: *[. . .] nak-ri iš-ta-lal*

(16)A 10: du$_{5}$-mu-ša$_{6}$-ga kúr-re ba-da-ab-GAM
B 9: é-a dumu-sig$_{5}$-ga
9: *: šá* É *ma-ru dam-qa*
C 9: [. . .] kúr-re
9: *ma-ri dam-qa* MIN

(17)A 11: ezen-gal-bi šu nu-du$_{7}$-du$_{7}$
B 10: ezen-[gal-bi] šu! nu-um-du$_{7}$-du$_{7}$
11: *i-si[n-nu-šú ra-bu-ú-t]i ul uš-tak-li-lu*
C 10: [. . .] šu nu-um-du$_{7}$-du$_{7}$
11: *[. . .] ul uš-tak-la-lu*

(18)A 12: me-kal-kal-bi é àm-gi$_{4}$
B 12: me-⌈sag⌉(?)(-gá?)-bi é-a àm-gi
[par-ṣ]u ma-[aḫ-ru-ú]-ti ina É *pe-ḫu!-ú*
C 12: [. . .] é-a àm-gi$_{4}$
13: *[. . .] ina* É *pe-ḫu-u*

(19)A 13: me-bi al-ur$_{4}$-ur$_{4}$ ‹ub›-bé ba-ra-gub
B 14: [me-bi al-ur-u]r-ra ub-ba ba-da-gub

15: *[. . .] ḫa-am-mu-ma ina tub-qí šu-uz-zu-zu*
C 14: [. . .] ub-bé ba-da-gub
15: *[. . .] ina túb-qí šu-uz-zu-zu*

(20)A 14: [bill]udu-a-bi ám ba-da-kúr bala-bi ba-kúr-kúr
B 16: [billudu-bi] ám kaš ⌜ba⌝(?)-da-bar bala-[bi b]a-da-kúr-re
17: *[pil-lu]-du-šú u-par-ri-[su] ⌜iq-ta(-ta)⌝ pa-lu-ú!-šú it-te-ki-ir*

If our suggested reading of text B is correct, then the Sumerian states: "[Its rites], that which has been decided, and its terms of duty does he alter." The Akkadian: "He has *ended* its rites which he had decided; he has altered its terms of duty."

(21)A 15: [é]-zi-da bala-bi bala-kúr-ra šu-bal ba-ni-ib-⌜ak⌝
B 18: é-zi-dè bala-⌜bi⌝ ⌜ba⌝-da-kúr-re ⌜šu⌝-bal ba-ab-ši-in-ak
19: *šá É ki-ni pa-lu-[ú] pa-lu-⌜ú⌝-šú(?) nak-ri uš-te-pe-le*

Note the variant ba-da-kúr-re in text B for bala-kúr-ra as in text A and our eršemma. Yet the Akkadian translation in B is based upon bala-kúr-ra.

(22)For the many variants to this line and a discussion of the difficulties in this passage see Krecher, *Kultlyrik* 178 f. We have suggested a translation based upon our variant, but by no means are we sure that this translation is valid for all variants to this line.

Eršemma no. 97

(1)For the restoration [e]-en in text B note catalogue entry B_2 39: e-en gig-ga-bi. For (e-)en gig-ga-bi, "How horrible!" see the commentary to no. 88.1.

We have preferred not to translate na-ám-. . .-a as "because of" since, to our knowledge, the expected construction would be na-ám-. . .-šè or even just na-ám. . . .

(4–5)For the possible significance of ki- before a city name, see W. Römer, Königshymnen 252.

(6–7)The construction ù . . . ù . . . is ambiguous. Perhaps in this passage ù means "woe" (cf. Krecher, *Kultlyrik* 115), thus "Woe, the fate of her spouse! Woe, the fate of her child!" Another possibility is that ù . . . ù . . . is a construction signifying "not only . . ., but also . . ." (cf. Poebel, *GSG* p. 152 and cf. eršemma 171:88). Our preference for this latter interpretation is based upon all three variant texts writing simply ú/ù, none having the more common forms of "woe," i.e., ù-a, ù-u_8-a etc.

(13)For the reading of É.NUN in our passage, see R. Caplice, *Studies Gelb* p. 304 wherein the alkali of the É.NUN is discussed.

(15)For zé-b, "to pull out, to pluck," see *MSL* 4, Emesal Voc. III 110 with note. For zé, "to pull out, to pluck," see CAD B 97 sub *baqāmu,* AHw 749 sub *nasāḫu(m)* I. We assume that -zu- in text A is merely a variant for zé-.

In lines 15–17, we have assumed the locative to be a mistake for the ergative. Note line 51, text B below wherein ᵈDumu-zi-da is a mistake for ᵈDumu-zi-dè.

The form uru^ki-ni-gin$_7$ in text A is syntactically difficult. Perhaps this is but a variant for the sound uru-na-ka/ke$_4$, having been influenced by ama-ni-gin$_7$ in the previous line.

(16)Is the sa-sign a result of the scribe miscopying the gaba-sign, or is sa to be understood as "sinews, muscles?"

(17)For kur-gar-ra, see W. Römer, *Königshymnen* 166 wherein our passage is quoted. Note CAD K 559 sub *kurgarru:* ". . . the mention of daggers seems to suggest that they were devotees of Ištar performing some sword dance."

(18)S. N. Kramer in his translation has understood ì-lum as being a variant for e-lum. Clearly ì-lum is a variant form for e-lum in line 47 wherein, ì-lum parallels ᵈDumu-zi in line 48. It is also possible that ì-lum here denotes a mourning song. For ì-lum as a variant for e-el-lu see J. Krecher, *Kultlyrik* 148 n. 433. Perhaps -sag modifies ì-lum in the same way as it modifies šìr (see Krecher, *ibid.,* 162 n. 462 for šìr-sag). Perhaps the line means "Over him for whom mourning songs were not precious."

(19)We expect the ergative ga-ša-an-an-na-ke$_4$.

(20–21)If we have here a clause meaning "when . . .," we expect ba-gin-a.

(22–23)Note *MSL* 13 194 295–297 for ú-sag = ŠU-*gu,* GAR.[ME]Š *ri-iš-tu-u, bīl-tu ri-iš-ti-tu.* For ú-sag note line 27 below, as well as the incipits of eršemmas nos. 92 and 93 and the balag incipit eden-na ú-sag-gá-ke$_4$ (*4R*^{2} 53 i 52). We have followed Jacobsen's translation "early" and "later pastures" in this passage.
For other examples within our eršemma corpus of the infix -e- reflecting the locative, see the commentary to eršemma no. 60:37.

(24)We have translated gi$_4$ as "to kill" on the basis of the lexical equations gi$_4$ = *dâku* (CAD D 35) and gi$_4$ = *šabāṭu(m)* II (*AHw* 1119). Note, however, that in all bilingual passages cited by the CAD sub *dâku* the reduplicated form gi$_4$-gi$_4$ occurs. W. Heimpel, *Tierbilder* 3.55, suggests that the form im-gi-ra-a might be translated on the basis of gi$_4$ = *dâku.*

(25)The nuance of the commitative infix is unclear to us. For the root sum occurring with the commitative infix, where the infix -da- does not mean "with" or "able," but rather seems untranslatable, see Gragg, *AOATS* 5 pp.

40 and 61. We don't expect the suffixed sign -mà, since the verb ba-an-zé-èm is the preterite.

(35)Text B does not tend to be syllabic. Thus, the orthography ma-aš is surprising. Could ma-aš be for amaš or máš?

(38–39)If the verb in 39 is merely -bal, then we might translate "all seven demons argued with the lad" (CAD D 4 sub *dabābu* for bal meaning "to argue"). Another likely restoration is the compound inim bal. Although inim bal frequently has the meaning "to translate," it also may simply mean "to speak." Cf. Bird and Fish 103: INIM lul-la bala-zu "deceitful words you've spoken"; see J. vDijk, *SGL* II 100 for (KA lul) bal-bal "to speak." For bal meaning "to speak," see line 73 below.

The syntax wherein imin-bi follows guruš/Dumu-zi rather than gal_5-lá seems very awkward.

(40′-46′)The suffix -e after ku_4-ra should be the ergative for this nominal phrase. Note the puzzling verbal form mu-un-ku_4-re-en-na in line 46 of text A. From context we are unable to suggest any interpretation of the suffix -en-.

(47)ù-am-mi- in text A is a sandhi-writing for ù-a mi- as in text B. ì-lum appears to be a variant for e-lum, *kabtu* (see commentary to line 18 above).

(50)im-me-e-zu seems to be a rather far-fetched syllabic rendering of gin-mu-e-da. The verbal form mu-e-da- contains the first common plural infix (see A. Falkenstein, *Das Sumerische* E. J. Brill, Leiden, 1964, 49 for *mu-me-da› me-da-.)

(51)We expect the vocative as in text A.

(53)Based on the context of lines 54–55, we have presumed text B to be a variant for text A, although elsewhere text B tends to be more reliable. For u_8 lu, "to tend sheep," see Å. W. Sjöberg, *TCS* 3 96 commentary to 214. ú-lu-lu could, of course, mean "who makes vegetation flourish."

(54)Our translation of rig_7 as "to ravage" is based upon the equation rig_7 = *akālu* (CAD A/1 245).

(56–59)For su, "naked," see CAD E 320 sub *erû*. We expect -za in text A, since "to put on" is gál plus the locative. The form um-te-gál ‹um-ta-e-gál.

In line 59 we expect me-ri, not me-ra.

(61)For šu TU.TU (*ekēmu, ḫarû, maḫāru*), see Å. W. Sjöberg, *AfO* 20 173a; *ZA* 65 242; B. Alster, *Dumuzi's Dream,* line 55.

(62–65)Could -BI-gub in these lines be a mistake for gub-bé? For an infix -BI- directly before the verbal root cf. eršemma 163.2:a+15; J. Krecher, *Kultlyrik* 174 n. 496; M. E. Cohen, *JAOS* 95 599 line 37.

In syllabic text A, gi$_4$ - seems to be a variant for ḫé-, ka- for ga- and gú- for ḫu-. However, note line 97 below, wherein text A has gi$_4$- whereas text B has ga-.

(68–77)For parallels to this passage, see B. Alster, *Dumuzi's Dream,* lines 164–182, 191–217, 226–238 with commentary wherein our passage is discussed.

(69)B. Alster, *ibid.,* p. 116 chose to restore [a-a], thus, "You are my father." Utu, as the parallel passages quoted by Alster state, was the brother-in-law of Dumuzi, not his father. This would then be the only reference to a father-son relationship between Utu and Dumuzi. Alster's restoration is presumably based upon line 73 below. To say the least, we are uncomfortable with his reading: a-a-ni-šè, which would, despite all other texts, indicate Utu was Dumuzi's father. To avoid this dilemma, perhaps we might suggest a transliteration for line 73 as [ka]r-kar-a-ni-šè, "because of/concerning his flight."

(78)šu bi-il$_5$-lá appears to be an orthography for šu bí-in-lá.

(80)For šu ak see E. Gordon, *SP* 1.186 and W. Heimpel, *Tierbilder* 7.8.

(81)Note the homonymous variant in text A: "A frightened dove was quiet(?)/ placed(?) at the bush." For tu^{mušen} ní-te-a / *summatu parittu,* see W. Heimpel, *Tierbilder* 58.11. For giš-ú-GÍR = ^{giš}ú-šeg$_x$, see vDijk, *Falkenstein Festschrift* p. 240 with n. 38.

(86–87)The suffix -na in text A is unexpected.

sa ab-ra-mu-ni-du apparently is an orthography for sá ba-ra-mu-ni-du$_{11}$. Our translation "to succeed" is somewhat free.

(88)We have understood e-ri-a as a variant for é-ri-a, "desert."

We have also interpreted di-bé as an orthography for dib / *ṣabātu, aḫāzu,* "to grab." Kramer in his translation suggests that dib in this passage may mean "to follow." Cf. dib = *ba'û, etēqu,* "to pass by/ through." However, dib = *redû,* "to follow," is unattested.

(89)Note *MSL* 12 165 262–263: [lú é-r]i-a = *ša*⌜*x x*⌝*-a-tim,* [lú]⌜é⌝-ri-a = *ša na-me-e,* "he of the steppe."

(90)Although pa$_4$ is not attested with an Auslaut -r, pa$_5$ / *palgu* has an Auslaut -r, (for example *STT* 156 rev. 11 and duplicate *SBH* 57 rev. 3). Perhaps this led to the variant in text A, parimria, for pa$_{4/5}$(r)-e-ri-a. We expect pa$_4$-e-ri-a-ka/ke$_4$.

(91)We expect double genitive construction: lú-pa_4-e-ri-a-ka-ke_4. The syntactical problem in this line and in line 90 can be resolved if we read pa_5-ri-a, "of that ditch" and lú-pa_5-ri-a-ke_4, "the man of that ditch." However, the fact that we have the term lú-e-ri-a attested as *ša namê* (see commentary to line 89) makes this solution unlikely.

(93, 95, 97)Note that text A consistently writes ku-li-na in lines 93, 95 and 97. Yet in line 97, text B has ku-li-ni in apposition to ga-ab-ús = *murteddû, rē'ûm, kaparru* A, "shepherd." We have translated according to text B since B tends to be less syllabic and more reliable. ku-li-na in text A could merely be a variant for ku-li-ni, or "of his friend" or even "no one's friend." However, in light of line 97, we believe a genetive construction to be rather unlikely.

We are unable to reconstruct the verbal root from the orthography gi_4-me-e-da-LI-na.

(96)We assume that udu-dul_4 is a variant orthography for udu-udul.

(101)This line is highly problematic. If (e-)ne is indeed the dative third plural infix, then -š- cannot be the terminative infix.

Although a-aš-ši might well be for aš-a, "alone," it might also be for A.ŠI, IŠI, $eš_9$, "crying, tears" Cf. J. Krecher, *Kultlyrik* 88–91 and note in particular p. 88, wherein Krecher suggests the possibility of a reading a-ši for A.ŠI. If this interpretation is corect, then ú-lu-lu in text A might be a variant for e-el-lu, "a cry of woe" (Krecher, *ibid.,* 148 n. 433). If a-aš-ši is indeed "crying, tears," then DU might be a variant for du_{11}, be read $ša_4$ (see Krecher, *ibid.,* 90 n. 232 for $še_8$-$še_8$ and even $ša_6$ with isiš) or even be read du/gin, "to go (in tears)."

(102)For tur-tur as an orthography for dur_x-tur, see B. Alster, Dumuzi's Dream 85. Perhaps the verbal root is šu ti, "to seize." Throughout text A, the suffix a/en-na occurs where unexpected (46, 86, 95(?), 116–117). Thus, we hesitate to reconstruct the root as šu a_5 for which cf. CAD A/2 527 sub *azāru* for šu a_5, "to help, forgive."

(104–105)We expect úr-. . .-a-na-ke_4

(113)For the sign $banšur_2$, see SL 458 no. 227.

(116–117)for the unexpected form nu-me-en-na cf. commentary to line 102.

(119)For sa lá, see most recently Å. W. Sjöberg, *ZA,* 65 220.

Eršemma no. 88

(1)For e-en, *kīam,* "How!," see CAD K 326. The restoration gig-ga-[bi] is based upon the incipit of eršemma no. 97: [e]-en gig-ga-bi with catalogue entry B_2 39: e-en gig-ga-bi.

(4–9)This list of epithets also occurs in A) *SBH* 37 obv. 13–18; B) *4R*^{2} addition to pl. 27:5–10; E) *BA* 5/5 30 5–10; F) *VAS* 2 35 2–4; G)*JCS* p. 80 (*HSM* 7522 2–4, 18–19). This list consists of deities associated with the netherworld and, therefore, ultimately with Dumuzi.

(4)For Damu as a netherworld deity, note the composition "Damu in the Netherworld." (*VAS* 2 35,*JCS* 16 p. 80 *HSM* 7522).

(5)Note the variants: A, B, C, D: du_5-mu umun-mu-zi-da E: du_5-mu ^{d}Umun-mu-zi-da For ^{d}Umun-mu-zi-da as the Emesal form of ^{d}Nin-giš-zi-da see *MSL* 4 Emesal Voc. I 105. For Ningišzida as the child of Ninazu and Ningirda, see J. vDijk, *SGL* 2 71 ff. Curiously in the fifth tablet of AN = ^{d}A-nu-um, we have Ninazu listed, then his wife, and then seven gods summed up as the seven children of Girda. Ningišzida is missing from these seven. However, the very next entry is Ningišzida. It would appear that An = ^{d}A-nu-um here combined two traditions, for most certainly the occurrence of Ningišzida directly after Ninazu, Ningirda and their children, reflects the tradition of his being their son. There appears to be no reason to assume a tradition wherein Damu was considered to be the son of Ningišzida as Tallquist, *Götterepitheta* 279 suggests. According to AN = ^{d}A-nu-um, Damu was the son of Ninisina and nowhere there is there any connection between the Ninisina/Damu tradition and that of Ninazu/ Ningišzida. Nor are there any literary texts which prove a connection. Therefore, we choose to translate dumu umun-mu-zi-da as "the son, Ningišzida," the two being in apposition. Moreover, were the epithet "son of Ningišzida" we should have a double genitive: dumu-umun-mu-zi-da-ka. The epithet "son," therefore, refers to Ningišzida's being Ninazu's son. In "Damu in the Netherworld," ^{d}Nin-giš-i-da is used interchangeably with Damu. We would hardly expect this were Damu, the son of Ningišzida. Rather the two become identified because they are male deities, sons, who are identified with the netherworld.

(6)Note A) ^{d}Ištaran-i-bí-šuba^{ba}. Ištaran is listed in the fifth tablet of AN = ^{d}A-nu-um, a tablet which consists of deities associated with the netherworld. Note *CT* 25 pl. 6 9–10: [^{d}KA$^{iš-ta-ra-an}$].DI

^{d}IGIMIN(=ištaran)-i-gi-šu-ba-ku.ŠUBA

Thus, Ištaranigišuba is to be understood as the actual name of this manifestation of Ištaran.

(7)The reading of ^{d}Alla is shown in the syllabic orthographies in G), *PRAK* 2 D 41 i 30: al-la mu-un-sa-bar, and *VAS* 2 26 vi 36: [d]Al-la ù-mu-un-sa-pàr. ^{d}Alla occurs in AN=^{d}A-nu-um Tablet 6.

Note *MSL* IV Emesal ^{d}Umun-sa-pàr = ^{d}Lugal-sa-pàr. ^{d}Lugal-sa-pàr occurs in AN = ^{d}*A-nu-um* Tablet 6 as a god identified with Nergal. There does not appear to be any special relationship between ^{d}Alla and ^{d}Lugalsapar, other than both being netherworld deities here identified with Dumuzi.

(8)Note the variant E) li-bi-ir ^{d}Umun-šud$_{x}$-dè. See *MSL* IV Emesal ^{d}Umun-šud$_{x}$-dè = ^{d}Lugal-šud$_{x}$-dè. ^{d}Lugal-šud$_{x}$-dè occurs in AN = ^{d}A-nu-um Tablet 6, as a god identified with Nergal.

(9)-šír- in our text is a variant for -šìr- as in A, B, C, D, E: mu-lu-šìr-ra-an-na. For mu-lu-šìr-ra, "singer," see J. Krecher, *Kultlyrik* 117. The relationship of the epithet mu-lu-šìr-ra-an-na to Dumuzi is unclear to us.

(11)Since ì-sìg-ge is *marû,* we expect im-mi-íb-d[u$_{7}$-du$_{7}$] to be *marû.* Perhaps then the infix -b- is the accusative referring to "the land."

(12)For other references to the phrase a šà-ba-ni a bar-ra-ni, see J. Krecher, *Kultlyrik* 145.

(16)For the reading ì-du-du, note eršemma 171:63–64 for im-dù-dù-e parallel to ì-tuš-en in a similar type of passage.

(22)R. Kutscher's reading of igi-du$_{8}$ in *YNER* 6 *25–*26 is unwarranted. Rather read simply umun-bi. Our translation of gaba-ri gíd is based upon a literal interpretation "to move opposite."

(27)For ka-ab-gaz, see the commentary to eršemma 191:10.

(28–29)šu-da-a is an elision of šu-dù-a. For šu-dù-a and á-lá in parallel, see B. Alster, *Dumuzi's Dream* 112–113 wherein our passage is quoted.

For ul$_{4}$ "to fear," see Å. Sjöberg *Afo* 24, Commentary to Nungal 75. We have interpreted the dative e-ne-ra as reflecting the causitive.

(30)We expect im-da-šub-bu-uš im-da-zi-ge-eš.

(32)The meaning of the term ge-em-ge-em is unclear to me. Possibly speaking against interpreting ge-em-ge-em as being syllabic for gam-gam, is Krecher's discussion in *Kultlyrik* 197 wherein a syllabic orthography gi-gi-ru-ma is attested for GAM.GAM.

(44)For šà-šè gíd *ana libbi šadadu,* "to consider, to ponder," cf. Bird and Fish (MS. Sjöberg) 55: ku$_{6}$-e a-na mu-ni-in-dúb-ba šà-šè nu-mu-un-gíd-dè "he did not consider the insults the fish hard hurled."

(46–47)For gaba- as an orthography for ga-ba- in the verbal form cf. *CT* 15 pl. 8:39 for gaba-da-zah$_{x}$ (PEŠ) with the following lines containing ga-ba-da-zaḫ$_x$: eršemma no. 171:69 gaba-ra-è. Note the form ga-ba-e-da-DU at the end of these lines.

(49–50)For these lines, see B. Alster, *Dumuzi's Dream* p. 86.

(53)For these lines, see B. Alster, *ibid.*, pp. 120–121.

Eršemma no. 165

(2)Rather than translating tab-an-na as "heavenly companion," we have interpreted tab-an-na as a variant for dab$_5$-a-na. Were tab-an-na (an epithet nowhere else attested for Dumuzi) actually an epithet, we expect it to occur directly after a guruš and before the apparent beginning of the refrain šeš-e.

(4)For sù(-sù) = *riāšu(m),* "to rejoice," see *AHw* 979 f.; for nu-sù-ga-mu referring to Dumuzi cf. *4R*^{2} 27 no. 1 8–11 (CAD I 70): ^{giš}ildág šità-na-ba nu-sù-ga-mu ^{giš}ildág úr-ra ba-ab-su$_x$-ra-mu / *ildakkum ša ina rāṭišu la irīšu ša išdānuš innasḫu,* "(My Dumuzi) who is an *ildakku*-poplar which did not rejoice in its caisson, which was torn out by the roots." In our verbal form we don't expect the infix -n-, unless we have a direct object. It is, of course, possible that é-gal-a-ni is the direct object, thus, "did not rejoice over his palace" or "did not make his palace rejoice." But note *4R*^{2} 27 no. 1 8–11 above for the object being rejoiced over taking the locative. Moreover, from context we expect a *marû* verbal form, since Dumuzi is being described in his present unhappy state. Previously he did rejoice at his palace (and this is what got him in trouble). Perhaps nu-mu-un-sù-ga is an elision for nu-mu-ni-sù-ga, this locative-terminative infix reflecting é-gal-a-né. Note, however, that throughout this eršemma we have a large number of verbal forms containing an unexpected -n- infix.

(8)The meaning of the term lú-ka-ba-ra-ke$_4$ is unclear. For KA ba ra BI, see W. Heimpel, *Tierbilder* 5.71 who suggests that perhaps the term means "sein Hirtenjunge." (Cf. CAD K 176 sub *kaparru* A "shepherd of low rank" for the orthographies ga-ab-ra, ga-ab-bar, gáb-bar, ka-[ba]r in lexical texts and a literary text with ka-pár.)

(9)The meaning of bára-KA is unclear to us. Since the ka-sign occurs in the copy directly above and below other ka-signs, perhaps dittography has occurred.
The reading and identification of ŠITA$_x$^{ki} is unknown to us.

(10)Posibly ka-aš-ka-sa is a variant for kas-kas = *kaškaššu,* "overpowering, (CAD K 290). A. Falkenstein, *CRRA* (1952) p. 58 had interpreted *CT* 15 20 27 as also referring to the kaskas-demon, apparently transliterating ka-aš$_6$-kàs. However, in this instance, the term is probably to be transliterated ka-ab-gaz, being a variant for kab-gaz, "murderer" (see CAD D 36 sub *dâku* wherein CAD reads tún-gaz).

(18)For šub, "to leave," governing the locative cf., for example, 'Curse on Akkad," 61: ki-sikil ama_5-na šub-bu-gin_7 "like a maiden leaving her cella."

(19–25)These lines have been translated by B. Alster, *JCS* 27 (1975) 223.

(20)For the use of ba meaning "to offer" in the sense of "to bribe," see B. Alster, *Dumuzi's Dream,* lines 131–132 with commentary.

(22)The infix -n- may be for dè-mu-ni-til-le, the infix -ni- reflecting é-kaš-a-ka etc.

(24)Perhaps the verbal suffix stems from -ba-an, an interchange of the liquids 'n' and 'l' having occurred.

(25)For sag-tuk in a similar context, note *VAS* 2 79 obv. 12–15:

gu_4-lu-lu-a-ba na-an-né-ku_4!-ku_4-dè
gu_4-a gu_4-sag-tuk nam-ba-ra-ab-è
e-zé-lu-lu-a-ba na-an-ne-ku_4-ku_4-dè
e-zé-ta e-zé-sag-tuk nam-ba-ra-ab-è

* * *

Do not enter among its numerous/grazing oxen!
Do not drive out the superb oxen from among the oxen!
Do not enter among its numerous/grazing sheep!
Do not drive out the superb sheep from among the sheep!

(26)Cf., "Curse on Akkad" (A. Falkenstein, *ZA* 57 43 ff.) 63: ur-sag ^{giš}tukul-e sag-gá-gá-gin_7 "like a warrior who goes out to battle."

(30)The meaning of the line is unclear. Based on context, it seems highly unlikely that gada-gu-bi could be an orthography for ga-da-gub. Therefore, gada gu-bi is presumably an anticipated genitive, "threads of linen." Could the *maštakal*-plants, the linen threads and the *ardadillu*-plants be intended for some type of magical or medical potion to revive Dumuzi? We could find no such formula in šà-zi-ga.

Eršemma no. 60

(1)On the basis of the orthography am-mu-ra in our line, we have transliterated the catalogue entry K_1 iii 31 as am-mur-ra. Our translation "beaten" is according to the suggestion of S. N. Kramer, who has suggested that mu-ra is the Emesal form of giš-ra/ *maḫāṣu,* "to smite," (*AHw* 580; C. Wilcke, *Das Lugalbandaepos* lines 228, 329a). (For še-mu-ra as Emesal for še-giš-ra, "threshed grain," see eršemma no. 168:36). For a similar description of Dumuzi using sag(-a) ra / *maḫāṣu,* see Th. Jacobsen, "Inanna and Bilulu" (*Image of Tammuz,* p. 64) 74–76.

The infix -n- actually necessitates the translation: "He/she did not let the beaten(?) bull live," a translation which is somewhat obscure in implication, since there is no subject of the verb in our text. We prefer to disregard the infix -n- in our translation.

(5)For the epithet ama-ušum-mu said of Dumuzi cf. *VAS* 10 123 rev. ii 10.

(7–15)This same list of Dumuzi epithets occurs in *VAS* 2 34 5–12; cf. *CT* 42 15 i 24–30 and note, in particular, lines 29–30: [i-bí-lum-l]um-ka-na-ág-gá / [ù-mu-un-gì]r(?)-ka-na-ág-gá.

(12)For the Emuš as the temple of Dumuzi in Badtibira, see Å. W. Sjöberg, *TCS* 3 95.

(14)For i-bí-LUM.LUM as a description of Dumuzi cf. *VAS* 2 27 v 11 (A. Falkenstein, *ZA* 48 89): šeš-i-bí-LUM.LUM-mu šeš-i-bí-lá-lá-mu, "Mein Bruder mit den ge . . . en Augen, mein Bruder mit den 'gebunden' Augen." A meaning of LUM.LUM in our passage as "to be poor" (CAD L 252 sub *luppunu*) is unlikely. As for the meaning "to be twisted" or "to be defective" (CAD K 142 sub *kanānu;* CAD Ḫ 60–61 sub *ḫamāšu;* 235 sub *ḫummušu;* 214 sub *ḫubbušu*), none of the Akkadian equivalents is ever attested as being said of the eyes or face. Moreover, such a description of Dumuzi's eyes hardly seems appropriate, for Dumuzi is described as having igi-sa_6-sa_6, "beautiful eyes" (Th. Jacobsen, "Inanna and Bilulu" (*Image of Tammuz,* p. 62) 30). Note that LUM.LUM has a reading lu_4-ḫum (*AHw* 1056 sub *sullunu* II). For the Akkadian derivative *luhummû* said of the eyes, see CAD L 239 sub *luḫummû* and note the syllabic orthography lu-ḫu-um-ma (Å. W. Sjöberg, *JCS* 21 227 quoted CAD L 239). Perhaps LUM.LUM in our passage is another orthography for luḫum(GIŠ.MI) and thus, should be transliterated lu_4-ḫum. See CAD Ṣ 190 sub *ṣillu* mng.3) for the references to *luḫummû* with *īnu,* translated as an obstructing shade growing on the eye, a cataract. Yet once again this interpretation would be unexpected and obscure for Dumuzi who, as stated above, had "beautiful eyes." An interpretation of ḫum-ḫum as "flowing" (M. E. Cohen, *JAOS* 95 601) does not seem fitting either.

If the meaning of the term lá-lá in VAS 2 27 v 11 (quoted above) were clear, then the meaning of the parallel ḪUM.ḪUM might be known. In view of the fact that the *VAS* texts frequently contain syllabic or unusual variants, perhaps lá-lá is a variant for la-la, for which see CAD L 49 sub *lalû* A, noting in particular mng.4) "pleasant appearance, luxury objects, abundant vegetation." For LUM.LUM, "luxuriant, fecund" cf. lum-lum = *unnubu, uššubu* (CAD E 352 sub *ešēbu*), *sullunu* (*AHw* 1056). Perhaps i-bí-LUM.LUM and i-bí-lá-lá would then refer to a mystical power inherent in Dumuzi's appearance which produces fecundity in his herds. (Cf. the story of Jacob and Laban's flocks, Genesis 30). Perhaps read i-bí-LUM.LUM in *CT* 36 pl. 36 obv. ii 11.

(15)Note the syllabic orthography ù-mu-un-ki-ri-ka-na-ág-gá in *VAS* 2 34 12.

(16)The writing a-gin$_7$-nú-dè-en may be sandhi for a-gin$_7$ ì-nú-dè-en.

(23)Th. Jacobsen has interpreted ki-sikil-ša$_6$-ga-mu and guruš-ša$_6$-ga-mu as referring to men and women who had disappeared with Dumuzi. These two phrases recur in lines 32 and 33. We suggest that Inanna, seeking her partner in love, calls Dumuzi by the frequently paired terms, her "man and woman," "man and woman" representing the totality and gamut of love-making. For the use of opposites or both extremes to represent the entire range of activity, cf. S. N. Kramer, *PAPS* 107 497–8 obv. ii 7–8:

i-gi$_4$-in šul! a-a-zu na-[nam]
i-gi$_4$-in šul! ama-zu na-nam
Lo, the youth, he is your father.
Lo, the youth, he is your mother.

Obviously, in this passage, Dumuzi is not actually Inanna's mother and father, but rather this expresses the totality of the care Dumuzi will show to Inanna. We suggest that the same type of imagery occurs in our text.

(27)For igi-gùn-gùn-nu = *ša panī banû,* see CAD B 81 sub *banû;* = *sarriqum* (CAD I 154 sub *īnu*).

(28)For ḫu-tu-ul note CAD Ḫ 264 sub *ḫutūlu* (meaning unknown) for im-ḫu-tu-ul(var.:-lum) lexically attested only; CAD Ḫ 151 sub *ḫatû* A: ḫu-tu-ul = *ḫa-tu-ú šá* GIG, "to strike (said) of a disease." For munu$_4$-ḫu-tu-ul, a stage in the germination of malt, see CAD B 244 sub *biqlētu*.

(29–41)Eršemma no. 175: a+1 to a+9 is a syllabic parallel of our lines 29–41:

a+1. ki-sikil-ša$_6$-ga-mu ga-na-ab-du
a+2. guruš-ša$_6$-ga-mu ga-na-ab-du
a+3. alim mu-lu ù-da ù-da
a+4. ù nu-gú-a-mu ù-da
a+5. é na-gá-mu ù-da
a+6. ám-ba-ra-ga-na ur bi-nu

a+7. mu-lu-mu ⌈da-ga⌉-na ù-ga bi-dúr
a+8. gi-di-da-na tu-mi a-mi
a+9. mu-lu-mu en-du-ni tu-⌈ni⌉-mi-ri a[m-mi]

(29–33)Although the word umun, "lord," may be pronounced 'u' (A II/4 17 (Cad B 192 sub *bēlu*): ú U = *be-lum*) and thus, ù-da in no. 201 quoted directly above could be a variant for umun-da, "with the lord," in our context, such an interpretation would be quite unlikely, since ù-mu-un clearly could not refer to Dumuzi (note no. 201 :a+3,(quoted above) in which mu-lu must refer to Dumuzi and therefore, ù-da cannot sensibly be interpreted as "with the lord (Dumuzi).") Rather, we suggest that ù- is the verbal prefix. If this interpretation is correct, then da must be the verbal root. The verb da is attested in E. Sollberger, TCS 1 no. 77 3–5: še gi-zu-na^{ki}-ta mu-tùmu-da Nibru^{ki}ḫa-bí-íb-da-e ki-na-me-šè na-an-tùmu, translated by E. Sollberger, "Let him leave(?) at Nippur the barley which he is to bring from Gizuna; he must not take it to any (other) place." Supporting Sollberger's translation of da as "to leave" is J. Krecher, *AOAT* 1 193 n. 59 for da_x/TAKA meaning "to leave" based upon Proto-Ea 204. We suggest, however, that da in *TCS* 1 no. 77, rather than meaning "to leave at," means "to leave from," thus, "Let him leave Nippur that he may bring here the barley from Gizuna; he must not take it to any (other) place." In our eršemma a translation of da as "to leave from, depart" is appropriate, for ever since Dumuzi has left, all the events in lines 36–41 have occurred.

(34–35)For ḫa-lam, "to forget," see *AHw* 631 sub *mašû(m)* II. Cf. to our line eršemma 171:68: mu-lú-zu-da-mu mu-da-ab-ḫa-lam-ma "He who used to know me has forgotten me." For the reading of the name ^{d}Aba$_x$(AB)-ba$_6$, see Th. Jacobsen, *OIP* 58 298.

(36)Since ga-ga is *marû,* the verbal infix -e- (nam-ba-e-ga-ga) must be the locative-terminative (see W. Römer, *Königshymnen* 227; Th. Jacobsen, *Image of Tammuz* 444–445 sub (b)). Therefore, we have transliterated i-bí-bar-ša$_6$-ga-né, literally "at his beautiful glance."

(37)See J. Krecher, *Kultlyrik* 190 for ka-bar-ra / *pû petû, pû uššuru.* For mud$_5$ / *qūlu,* "silence," see C. Wilcke, *Das Lugalbandaepos* 138. Note that mud-me-gar is attested as a variant for mud$_5$-me-gar. According to context, mud appears to mean "silence." Thus, mud-bar appears to be a contrived compound verb to contrast with ka-bar, thus, "at his beautiful open mouth he opens up silence" or "silence is let loose at his beautiful utterance."

(38–39)All the verbs in lines 36–37 and 40–41 are singular *marû* and thus, so, too, are the verbs in lines 38–39. Therefore, the infix -e- reflects the locative. Other examples within our eršemma corpus of the infix -e- reflecting the locative are 97:22–24; 32:43; 166.1:1; 166.2:1,25,26.

Ersĕmma no. 164

(2)We suggest the likely restoration [e-lum] on the basis of a similar pattern in the opening lines of the lamentation of Nergal a-gal-gal $buru_x$ su-su (*ZA* 10 276 K.69, collated) 1–3:

a-gal-gal-la $buru_x$ su-su mu-lu ‹ta›-zu mu-un-zu
bu-tuq-tu mu-ṭe-eb-ba-at e-bu-ru ⌜*gat-tuk*⌝ *man-nu i-lam-mad*
e-lum a-gal-gal-la $buru_x$ su-su mu-lu

(3–6)These lines have been restored on the basis of the work to Nergal *VAS* 2 79 obv. 2–5. For mu-lu-ám-gi-ra, "killer," see *SBH* 37 rev. 11–12: mu-lu-ám-gi-ra-na/*da-i-ki-šú*, "his murderer."

(10)For another reference to IŠ-bar-ra, note Gudea cyl. A xxx 7: gu_4-gal-gin_7 IŠ-bar-ra gub-ba, "like a great ox standing on . . . mountain."

For sa ak, "to net," see A. Falkenstein, *SGL* 1 11:17.

(11)The gloss tu-bar-ri-ma at the beginning of the line is according to the collation of E. Leichty. The glosses indicate that túg-parim-ma is one term not two; therefore, it is a type of garment. The significance of KI.MIN, "ditto.", is unclear to me.

For KU-KU possibly "to lie down" in a context other than ù-ku-ku, "to lie down to sleep," cf. Lamentation over the Destruction of Sumer and Ur (Ms. S. N. Kramer): na_4-arà-gaz giš-gan-na ì-ku-ku lú nu-um-ši-gam-e, "the mortar and pestle lie inert; no one stoops (to use them)."

(14)For zíb possibly meaning "scar," see CAD I 304 sub *ittu* A for zíb=*ittu*, "a mark, sign;" CAD E 13 sub *ebēru* B for zíb-zi-lá=*ebēru ša usukki*, zíb-du_{11}-ga=MIN *šá MIN, "to paint the cheek."* In the ensuing discussion sub *ebēru* B, the CAD states "meaning based on the Sumerian equivalent zag and zíb, both = *šimtu*, "paint," and on etymology, comparing Arabic *ḥibr*, "beauty mark, paint," *ḥibār*, "scar," and Heb. *ḥabbûrā* "wolt, wound." Note also MSL 9 54 80–81: unú-gíd-mu, unú-zíb-mu.

Interpreting gíd as *urruku*, "to make long," we have translated "to gash," literally "to make a long scar."

(15)For another reference to the eye being filled with blood, see *BRM* 4 9:43 (quoted CAD I 154 sub *īnu*).

(20)For zà-si denoting an area about the sides, note MSL 9 57 169.

(22-23)For u_4-šú-a = *berû*, "hungry," see *MSL* 12 181 31 (read as lú-UD.BAR.A in CAD B 207 sub *berû*). For enmen = *ṣūmu*, "thirst," see CAD Ṣ 247. Note J. Krecher, Kultlyrik 216 wherein the expressions u_4-šú-a and nigin-na are contrasted in a couplet whose meaning is unclear. Perhaps nigin (ni-me-en in syllabic texts, e.g., eršemma no. 79:37; *MSL* 2 127 ii 1) in this couplet is a variant for enmen, "thirst."

(24)We have restored šu-dù-a-na both from context and from its paralleling ám-gi-ra in the lamentation eden-na ú-sag-gá-ke_4 (*SBH* 37 rev. 9–12).

We have chosen to read KU as mu_x(= mu_x) on the basis of context and from the clear mu_4 in line 28. Our translation has assumed that the second singular dative infix -ra- indicates the causitive, "I have caused you to wear," thus, "I have dressed you." However, the use of the third singular dative in the first half of each line makes this interpretation tenuous.

(25)For túg-tán/tan_x, see Alster, *Dumuzi's Dream* 107 with previous literature.

(27)The compound verb may be kin ak *šipra epēšu*. However, we are unaware of any attestation of the form kin-šè ak.

(28)For i(-i), "to cry out," see *AHw* sub *nâqu(m)*.

(30)For the epithet EN-bànda referring to Nergal's spouse, Ereškigal, see eršemma no. 79:37.

(34)The phrase bar zal-la-ge (= zalag) in our text might be analogous to the Akkadian *kabattašu ipperdû* "her heart rejoiced" in W. G. Lambert, *BWL* 46 118.

Eršemma no. 171

Portions of this eršemma were transliterated, partially translated and commented upon by J. Krecher, *WO* 4 252 to 259. We have tried to avoid duplicating his commentary.

(3–6)For these epithets of Ninisina, see J. Krecher, *Kultlyrik* II 8–10, 15 with commentary.

(8)For ám-ma-al, Emesal for nì-gál = *būšu*, see J. Krecher, *Kultlyrik* 215 and note, in particular, ám-ma-al-ma-al-la-ta = *kīma būše šaknūti* (*RA* 33 104:23) quoted therein. See also Krecher, *WO* 4 254.

(11)For ge_{16}-le-èm as the Emesal form of ḫa-lam, see Krecher, *Falkenstein Festschrift*, Rome Biblical Institute Press, 1973, 103. For ḫa-lam "to forget," see *AHw* 631 sub *mašû(m)* II and BL 16 iii 12–13 (collated): me-bi [ba(-da)-ḫa]-lam-me-eš mu-ḫur-bi ba-da-kúr-re-eš / *par-ṣu-šu [it]-tam-šú-ú ú-ṣu-ra-ta-šú [it]-tak-kir*, "Its me's have been forgotten; its plans have been altered." We have suggested a restoration [me-e] at the beginning of the line, since we have na-ám-tar in the previous line and since ge_{16}-le-èm, "to forget," is frequently said of the me, (see G. Farber-Flügge, Inanna and Enki, *Studia Pohl* 10, p. 151). Moreover, note *CT* 42 no. 19 obv. 27: me-e urú-a ta i-ni-íb-ge_{16}-le-èm-mèn-na.

(16)For á-sìg éš, sling-stone and rope, see A. W. Sjöberg, *JCS* 21 275.

(18)For this line, see J. Krecher, *WO* 4 254.

(22–23)Krecher (*WO* 4 254) observes that me-na- here is possibly an interrogative used as a prefix, thus, "How long will he (Enlil) . . .?" However, now note the variant me-e in text A, this variant further complicating the situation.

(26)For the phrase a-gin_7 im-da-an-ku_4-re-en elsewhere, see Emeš and Enten 120 (Gragg, *AOATS* 5 60). On the basis of the first singular clausal form -mu-dè in line 25, we expect a-a-mu-ta, not a-a-zu-ta. We have translated accordingly.

(29)For su-bar-ra, "adoptive child," see CAD L 208 sub *liqûtu* (Is the poet referring to the house as the "adopted child of the nation" (as suggested by the parallelism), or could this even refer to Ninisina herself?); for su-bar, "body," see CAD Z 157 sub *zumru*.

(30)We expect šu-mu.

(33–38)Perhaps KU = *šūšubu*, "to place objects," in our line, thus, "I confront him with . . ." We have interpreted mu-e as being a variant for mà-e.

(35–36)We suggest a possible interpretation of these lines: i-bí-mu and bar-mu may contain the locative-terminative (-mu-e›mu). al-tar-re might be translated on the basis of al-tar, a-tar-di, a-tar-du_{11}-du_{11} = *(epeš) namūtu*, "derision." The orthography al-tar-re may simply be a variant for al-tar above.
Thus, perhaps we can interpret the line: *ana paniia namūtu iššakin*, "at my face derision has been placed," or in more colloquial English, "I have been mocked to my face."

(37–38)We assume that Ninisina is referring to herself, thereby stating that Enlil helped in arranging her marriage and in enabling her to have children. After all, she was the daughter-in-law of Enlil (see commentary to line 108 below).

(39)Were na-ám-tar referring to Enlil in this line, we would expect the ergative. Therefore, we prefer to assume na-ám-tar to be the object of the verb and thus, "fate."

(40)For kéš-da, "to close," said of doors cf. *ZA* 59 116 33: ki-sikil-e ^{giš}ig gál-tag$_4$-a nam-mu-un-kéš-dè, "then the girl will not close the open door (in your face)." Could kéš-da meaning "locked" said of a house be fitting for Instructions of Šuruppak 18? (Alster, the Instructions of Šuruppak Copenhagen Akademisk Vorlag, 1974, p. 35 l. 18.

(41–43)na-ám-tar-ra ki-pél-pél-la-bi could be an anticipated genitive formation. However, based upon the context, we suggest that ki-PÉL-la, ki-ur$_5$-ra and ki-mu-lu-da-ba-an-da-šub-ba are in apposition with úr, "lap" (note, line 44 wherein the term na-ám-tar-ra is not genitive or locative). One indication that these terms might refer to the lap, is that the term ki-mu-lu-da, as in line 43, occurs elsewhere denoting an area of the body around the lap (B. Alster, *Dumuzi's Dream* 244): ki-lú (var.:-mu-lu)-da nu-di ḫaš$_4$-gal, "the buttocks, the 'secret' place." The problem of PÉL and ur$_5$ in parallel has been discussed by Krecher, *Kultlyrik* 103. Note now K.4954 wherein pél-la-bi ga-an-du$_{11}$ (cf. *Kultlyrik* commentary to II 4 for pél-la-bi àm-me / ur$_5$-ra-bi àm-me) is rendered as *ḫum-mu-ṭiš lu-uq-bi*.

(44)For the compound zà-da gub, note *EWO* 430 (G. Gragg, *AOATS* 5 p. 60): enkar-šibir ^{giš}má-nu-nam-sipa-da zag-da ḫé-em-dè-gub, "the *enkar*-weapon, the *šibir*-weapon of *manu*-wood (like) shepherds (use) you have placed by your side." Cf. also Ur-Ninurta Hymn (HU) 10(Gragg, *ibid.*). We don't expect the -n- infix, if Enlil is still talking. Moreover, in the previous lines, Enlil states that he has the tablets by him; thus, we cannot assume this line to be narration to the effect: "He placed by him . . ."

(45)The meaning of the phrase šà im-ta-ab-è-dè in our context is unclear to us. Could this correspond to the English idiom "His heart went out to her" which would indicate that Enlil had sympathy for Ninisina? However, the possible interpretations are great in number. Could šà refer to the contents of the tablet?

(47)We have suggested a meaning adversity for na-ám-di-bi-dib-ba on the basis of context and its somewhat parallelism with nì-dib-dib = *pariktu* (*AHw* 833).

(51)Our suggested translation is based upon interpreting ma-e-re-da as being an elision of the first singular pronoun mà-e and e-re-(d). See *MSL* 4 Emesal Voc. II 67 for e-ri = ARAD. Although to our knowledge the 'd' Auslaut is unattested for the Emesal form e-ri, it would not be unexpected, since this would indicate an Emesal form ered in contrast to Emegir arad.

(54–55)Perhaps Ninisina is complaining that just as the silver in bracelets and the lapis lazuli in necklaces are manipulated and formed into the desired shape, so has she been manipulated by fate into being treated as a slave.

(56)For mud($_5$)-me-gar, see C. Wilcke, *Das Lugalbandaepos* 138 with previous literature. Cf. *MSL* 12 197 18: lú-ka-mud-gál = *mu-ta-al-ku (mundalku),* Gudea cyl. A iv 13: nin-kur-kur-ra-me ama-ka-mu-ud-da-ma-mu-da.

(60)The exact meaning of šu-šè ba-ab-tuš-en is unclear to us, particularly in light of the infix -b-.

(63–64)For a parallel to these lines, see eršemma 88:16–17:

> ì-du-du ér-gig ì-še$_8$-še$_8$
> ì-tuš-en šu šà-ga-eš im-lá
> I walk—I shed bitter tears.
> I sit down—I stretch (my) hand over (my) heart.

Thus, im-dù-dù-e would appear to be a variant for du-du. If this is the case, then the most appropriate meanings for BÚR.BÚR are *dâmu*, "to stagger," and *dâlu* A, "to wander about in despair." However, in both instances, BÚR.BÚR is read du$_9$-du$_9$ (which would create a nice poetic contrast in our line with -dù-dù). However, the suffix -re in our line would indicate a reading búr-búr, unless, of course, this was a scribal error. If we assume that dù-dù is for du-du or even if dù-dù means "to build, plant," we can suggest no appropriate meaning for a reading búr-búr.

For sag sìg, "to lower the head, to shake," see J. Krecher, *Kultlyrik* 214 with previous literature. However, the occurrence of the suffix -mà is unexpected. Perhaps the line means "When I sit down, I am beaten on my head?" More likely, we believe, dittography with sag-mà in the next line has occurred.

(65–66)We cannot suggest an appropriate meaning for BIZ. We expect a verb meaning "to stand up" (zi-zi, see CAD Z 158 sub *zumru* for (su-) munsub zi-zi) or "to shake."

(67)The meaning of ám-la-LUM is unknown to us. For i-bí-kúr cf. *AHw* 686 igi/AN-kúr = *muštaptu*, "unverschämt"?; *AHw* 692 an/igi-kúr-kúr = *muzzapru*, "sehr schlecht."

(69)The meaning of mu-lu-su-za is unknown to us. Cf. Å. W. Sjöberg, *JCS*

25 110 51: nam-lú-ulù su-zu(var.:-za) nu-ub-zu-a-ta. Without context we cannot be sure of the meaning of gú-mu gaba-ra-è.

(79)We assume that the suffix -e after nu-un-tar-ra is the vocative.

(81)Perhaps ensi-ma is a variant for ensi-na, "no interpretess."

(91–94)For commentary to these lines, see J. Krecher, *WO* 4 256 ff.

(95)If our reading gá-ág-da is correct, this might indicate a duplicated verb gad-gad. The only solution we can suggest is based upon $kad_{4/5}$ = *kaṣāru*, "to tie;" thus, perhaps "Tie on the lapis lazuli (beads of jewelry)."

(96–97)J. Krecher, *WO* 4 258 is quite reluctant to read tuš/ "to sit." Yet tuš/ "to sit" makes good sense in our context and therefore, we have translated "to sit."

(98)Perhaps i-LI_9-na is a syllabic orthography for iri_x-na, "roots?" We expect dar-a-mèn as in line 99, rather than dar-a-e.

(104–5)Perhaps we could read díb as a variant for dib/ *ba'û, etēqu*. Thus, "I shall come! I shall come!"

(108)For Ninisina as é-gi_4-a-en-^{d}Nu-nam-nir-ra, see W. Römer, *AOAT* 1 282. We have therefore interpreted egí, "princess," as being a variant for é-gi_4-a.

(109)We have no explanation for the reference to Gilgameš and its connection with Ninisina or Enlil.

Eršemma no. 159

(2–8)For variants and commentary to these lines, see J. Krecher, *Kultlyrik* 120–134.

(15)For ^{giš}banšur íl note Gudea cyl. A x 7–8:

> ^{giš}banšur mu-íl
> šu-luḫ si bí-sá
>
> He has carried the offering table
> and has carried out the lustration rites.

Falkenstein's interpretation is presumably based upon gùr = *malû* (*AHw* 597). However, it is also possible that in this context íl/gùr = *našû*, "to carry." Cf. Å. W. Sjöberg, "Nungal Hymn," *AFO* 24, lines 92–93 which, according to the traces we suggest, be restored as follows:

> 92. ^{d}nin-ḫar-ra-ana_x KA ⌈x⌉ba-da-gub igi-mu-šè bí-ib-dab_5-bé
> 93. [^{giš}ban]šur im-gùr-ru ki-nú-a mu-gá-[gá]

Ninḫarrana gives me satisfaction; he goes in front of me.
He carries the [offering ta]ble; he sets up the bed.

If our suggested restoration is correct, then the parallelism with setting up the bed suggests that íl/gùr in relation to $^{gi\check{s}}$banšur means "to carry," rather than "to fill."

(20–21)The verb zé-zé-ba may be Emesal for du_{10}-du_{10}-ga, "to be sweet." However, we hardly expect a drum to sound sweet. We expect sìg-sìg/ *maḫāṣu*, "to beat." Also curious is line 21. To "thunder forth" does not seem appropriate for a flute. We wonder if possibly the verbs in lines 20–21 had been inverted at some point in the text's transmission, thus originally:

My holy manzu-drum which does not thunder forth!
My reed pipe which does not (sound) sweet!

Since the me-zé instrument is a drum, an interpretation of zé-zé-b as "to pluck" (cf. eršemma 97:15) is not possible. The meaning of the variant ḪUR is unclear to us, but perhaps somehow it denotes the making of noise as in the compound GÙ-mur (Å. W. Sjöberg *TCS* 3 84 f.).

(24)Stylistically the variant nu-mu-un-du_{11}-ga-mu is more in keeping with the verbal forms of the other lines.

(29–30)For this difficult verbal form cf. J. Krecher, *WO* 4 259 n. 10.

Eršemma no. 166.1

(1)For bar-. . .-a, "for . . . sake," see A. Poebel, GSG 141 and cf. Gudea cyl. B ii 6: a-nun-na bar-mu-a $\check{s}ud_x$ ḫé-mi-sa_4-za, "Anunna, may you offer a prayer for my sake!" Note 166.2:1 wherein the locative suffix -a is present, thus bar-mà, and is reflected in the verbal chain by the infix -e- (cf. commentary to eršemma no. 60:38–39). In 166.1:1, however, the suffix -a has been omitted, but is still reflected in the verbal chain.

(9)For sùḫ-sùḫ, "to be blurred, dark," see CAD E 378 sub *ešû* mng.2); W. Römer, *Königshymnen* 97–98. Note 166.2:12 for SÙḪ.SÙḪ›si-is-ḫe.

(11)For the Lama of Girsu, see Å. W. Sjöberg, *JCS* 26 158 ff.

(12–15)Note that lines 14–15 omit the prefix na-, whereas 166.2:17–18 include na-, indicating that na- here is the presumptive volitive rather than the vetitive.
Perhaps the infix -n- is for -ni-, thus for šà-ba. It is, of course, possible that this is another instance of the unaccountable -n- infix, seemingly a mistake. But the fact that all four lines in both recensions contain the infix makes it rather difficult for us to ignore it. Therefore, we have interpreted

this as the third singular *ḫamṭu* since this interpretation fits in well with the context. Noting once more the contrast of positive versus negative, we have assumed that the subject of the verb is Ninsun, whom Baba therefore describes as providing her and her spouse Ningirsu with all the accoutrements of lordship. Yet in the next passage, Ninsun deserts the very city she has made so fitting for the gods. It is also possible that the subject of the verb is Enlil. But the fact that Enlil is not mentioned until several lines later, makes this possibility minimal.

(13)Eršemma 166.2:16 has mu-duru$_5$-u$_4$-sur-ra instead of mu-dúr-ru-na-mu as in our passage. We have chosen to interpret mu-dúr-ru-na as an orthography for mu-duru$_5$ *ḫaṭṭu*. However, note *ITT* 5 6875 for a piece of furniture giš-durun-na (CAD Ḫ 42 sub *ḫalḫallu* A). We also wonder if the -na-mu after mu-dúr-ru might be an error, having been the result of a confusion with the na-mu- at the beginning of the verbal form. This passage is quoted by Falkenstein (MSL 4 p. 39).

(14)For àm-mu-uš, Emesal for eš$_5$ "three," see J. Krecher, *Falkenstein Festschrift* 107 wherein are cited variant orthographies for eš$_5$.

(19)For the relationship of Ninsun to Lagaš and Girsu after the Old Sumerian period, see A. Falkenstein, *AnOr* 30 108.

(20)For DI.DI governing the terminative cf. *SRT* 5 41 (*ZA* 45 169): ur-mu-ti-in-na-šè DI.DI-dè, "going to the lap of the man." Perhaps reading sá-di, (see C. Wilcke, Das Lugalbandaepos line 21 for sá-di as a variant for sá-du$_{11}$) note S.N. Kramer, "Inanna's Descent," *JCS* 5, lines 190, 204: me-kur-ra me-al-me-al ki-bi-šè sá bí-in-du$_{11}$. (For di governing the terminative note, for example, *VAS* 10 123 rev. i 10).

For im-du$_8$-⌜x⌝ = *pitiqtu*, "mud wall," see A. Sjöberg, *Falkenstein Festschrift* 207 with previous literature.

(21)The break is most probably to be restored with either the verb rig$_7$ or the verb sì. For sag-rig$_7$-ga-šè rig$_7$, see A. Shaffer, *Gilgameš*, lines 13 and 56; Th. Jacobsen, *JNES* 5 144. For sag-rig$_7$-eš sì, see A. Falkenstein, *NG* 2 88 3–6.

(23–27)The meaning of gú-KU-a is unclear. Cf. 166.2:31–33 for gú-gú-bé.

(28–29)There are several possible interpretations of these two lines. sipa-šub(-šub)-bé may mean "cowering (*rabṣu*)/fallen shepherds," referring to the shepherds of the destroyed cities who have fled their flocks or whose flocks have been decimated. Perhaps sipa, "the shepherd," refers to Enlil and šub-bé for lú-šub-bé, "fallen (of the cities)" te-en(-te-en) could be either "to cool oneself" (*pašāḫu*) or "to extinguish life" (*bulluæ*) (cf. W. Heimpel, *Tierbilder* 285; Å. W. Sjöberg, "Nungal Hymn," *AFO* 24 line 103). Some possible translations are:

> "The fallen shepherds are killed in the grass(lands)."
> "The cowering shepherds are cooling themselves in the grass" (referring to there no longer being any flocks to tend)
> "The shepherd (i.e., Enlil) wipes out the fallen in the grass(lands)."

The preserved portions of the parallel lines 166.2:34–35 are difficult to interpret and do not shed light on our two lines.

(30)The orthography gál-lu-bi in our passage is probably a scribal error for gál-la-bi. For the expression a-na gál-la-bi, see W. Römer, *Königshymnen* 275.

Eršemma no. 166.2

(1)See the commentary to 166.1:1.

(6)We expect é-tar-sír-sír, the sanctuary of Baba in Girsu (see A. Falkenstein, *AnOr* 30 147).

(7)For the ma-gú-en-na, "Haus des Thronsaals," see A. Falkenstein, *AnOr* 30 161. Another possible restoration is kisal-gú-en-na, "courtyard of the throneroom" (W. Römer, *Königshymnen* 167; B. Levine and W. W. Hallo, *HUCA* 38 55).

(11–12)See the commentary to 166.1:9.

(13–14)In 166.1:10–11, there is the contrast of the locations inside and outside. Perhaps the term an-zu also denotes a location. The orthography an-zu may be for an-šà, "midst of heaven" (cf. W. Römer, *Königshymnen* 131 82 for an-šà-ta); or the term may be for an-zà, "horizon" (cf. M. Civil, *JAOS* 92 271 wherein anzu-dè occurs as a variant for an-zà). Also note *MSL* 11 17 4–5: anzu-babbar^{ki}, anzu-gi$_6$^{ki}; 45 34′–35′: ^{d}IM.BABBAR^{ki}/*na-aš-bi-ti*, ^{d}IM.MI^{ki}/*ki-bi-ri-ti*. The parallelism with babbar suggests that gi$_6$-ga means "black" not "sick" in our context. For gi$_6$ with a g-Auslaut cf. MI = gikki$_x$(-g) (Krecher, *Falkenstein Festschrift* 98 n. 14) and the term sag-gi$_6$-ga. Despite the Eninnu having the epithet anzu^{mušen}-bar$_6$-bar$_6$, "the white anzu-bird," (Falkenstein, *AnOr* 30 62) line 14 does not appear to refer to this epithet.

(15)The orthography šà-bar$_6$-bar$_6$-ba-ra appears to be an orthography for šà-ba bára-babbar-ra as in 166.1:12.

(16)Note the homonymous variant mu-dúr-ru-na in 166.1:13. The orthography mu-duru$_5$ also occurs in YBC 9862 (Old Babylonian recension of the balag-lamentation urú àm-i-ra-bi)20: sipa-ra mu-duru$_5$ mu-na-ab-zé-èm-mèn "I, the one who gives the crook to the shepherd," (with First Millennium B.C. recension (*ASKT* 21 rev. 3): sipa-ra mu-du-*he-pí* mu-un-na-ab-zé-èm-mà.) For mu-du-ru-u$_4$-sù-du as *ḫaṭṭi ūmī rūqūti*, see Å. Sjöberg, *Mondgott* 51.

(17) For mi-úš, "third," see J. Krecher, *Falkenstein Festschrift* 107.

(19–20)For šu zu-zu, see A. Ferrara, Nanna-Suen's Journey to Nippur Nippur, Biblical Institute Press. Rome, 1973 line 278 wherein the meaning of šu zu-zu is unclear. Cf. šu zu in E. Gordon, *Sumerian Proverbs* 1.38. Note also the balag-lamentation abzu pe-el-lá-àm 97–98 (*SBH* 57 14–15):

97. ur-šu-zu-⌜mu⌝[lú-kúr-ra] ba-an-[zu-zu]
ka-al!(LA)*-bi šá ut-ta-*⌜*ad*⌝*(?)-du-[u] ana na[k-ri . . .]:*
kal-bi šá ut-t[a-ad-du-u ana nak]-⌜*ri*⌝ *[ú]-di-[i-ni]*
98. ur-šu-[nu-zu lú-kúr-ra ba-ni-in-ús]
ka-[al-bu šá la ut-ta-ad-du-u] ana nak-ra⌜*x*⌝*-[. . .]*

and the duplicate line in the balag-lamentation urú àm-i-ra-bi 91–92 (Old Babylonian recension NCBT 688): ur-šu-aka-mu lú-kúr-ra nam-mu-un-na-zu-zu / ur-šu-nu-[aka] lú-‹kúr›-ra ba-ni-in-ús.

The dogs which know me have made me known (to) the enemy.
The dogs which do not know me follow the enemy.

(25–26)For šu-dab$_5$/díb governing the locative cf.
Lamentation over the Destruction of Sumer and Ur (Ms. S. N. Kramer): giš-ḫur-kù-ga . . . šu-dib-bé (line 17); pad-u$_4$-sikil-la šu-dib-bé (line 24). The locative is reflected in our verbal chain by -e- (cf. commentary to eršemma no. 60:38–39). This line apparently refers to the abundance of precious stones there had been in times of plenty.

(29–30)Perhaps me gú im-me is a variant orthography for mè gú-è *ša tuqunta ḫalip* (see Å. W. Sjöberg, *TCS* 3 145). Since the term a-a, "father," occurs in line 23, rather than interpreting ad as "father," perhaps ad-[. . .] is a syllabic orthography for adda$_x$ (LÚxBAD), "corpse," see *AHw* 809 sub *pagru(m)*.

For the pronunciation of the sign URUxUD, see CAD A/1 sub *abūbu* lexical section: ú-ru URUxUD = *a-bu-bu*; *MSL* 2 73 541: URUxUD / u$_4$-ru.

(Curiously, in bilingual Emesal texts, the Sumerian URUxUD is translated into Akkadian by the sign URU, indicating that the difference between URUxUD and URU is not one of meaning.) The value eri(m)$_x$ for URUxUD has been demonstrated by J. Krecher, *Kultlyrik* 115–116, wherein URUxUD-ma occurs as a variant for erìm-ma, *išittu*, "treasure house."

Krecher reads URUxUD as $erim_x$, yet a reading eri_x (thus, eri_x-ma) is just as possible. For URUxUD seemingly read eri_x when meaning "city," see Å. Sjöberg, *Mondgott* 89 2 and 5 for e-re possibly being a syllabic writing for URUxUD; ibid., 97 33 for the orthography URUxUD-ri perhaps to be transliterated as URUxUD^{ri}. Note also *PBS* 10/4 13 2: egí-re egí-re gù-àm-me-URUxUD in-ga-àm-me ù-li-li. This line occurs n *SBH* 19 rev. 28, *SBH* 46 rev. 32 and *SBH* 47 obv. i. In each of these latter references, the text has omitted the -me-, thus, . . . gù-àm URUxUD . . . The writing gù-àm-me-URUxUD appears then to be sandhi, indicating a reading gù-àm-me-eri_x. However, there are a large number of passages which indicate a reading urú rather than eri_x. A few of these passages are *SBH* 11 rev. 10: URUxUD-^{d}Suen for ^{d}Ur-^{d}Suen; *SBH* 24 10: URUxUD-an-na, a variant for uru_x-an-na, (see Å. Sjöberg, *Mondgott* 135–136 wherein, Sjöberg reads en-an-na). For URUxUD, read urú meaning "city" cf. eršemma no. 35.1:2, 7, 12; *VAS* 17 57 rev. 25: ^{d}Dam-gal-nun-na am-mu-URUxUD-zé-eb-ke_4, a variant for ama-urú-zé-eb-ba; *PRAK* C 72 top edge: am-ru-zé-ba for am-URUxUD-zé-eb-ba; the pronunciation of URUxUD a-še-er-ra in *CT* 42 21 obv. 14, rev. 11: URUxUD-u-a-še-. . .; *UET* 6/2 205 obv. 9: URUxUD^{uru-u}-ni; *BE* 30/1 no. 5 obv. ii 4: ú-ru-zi for uru-zi. And lastly, note that our passage has the syllabic writing ú-ra ad-[. . .], a sandhi writing for URUxUD ad-[. . .] as in the previous line 29. Thus, the vast number of texts support a read urú. Yet noting the great number of inconsistencies in Emesal orthographies (as described by J. Krecher, *Falkenstein Festschrift* 110), it is not inconceivable that an alternate pronunciation eri_x existed side by side with the pronunciation urú for the sign URUxUD when meaning "city."

(31)For gú-gú = *napḫaru*, "entirety," see AHw 737. For gú-gú as "(Ufer)fluren," see W. Römer, *Königshymnen* 257–258.

F(34–35)See 166.1:28–29 for the apparent parallel lines. From the preserved portions of our lines we are unable to translate the passage. For u_4-tur cf. *Ur Lament* 95 (*AS* 12 26); M. Civil, *JNES* 23 2 12; E. Gordon, *Sumerian Proverbs* 1.13; *KAR* 111 i and ii 5; Å. W. Sjöberg, *JCS* 24 126:11 wherein u_4-tur means "childhood." The reading sipa is based upon our collation.

Eršemma no. 1.1

(1)We prefer to transliterate bí-du_{11} rather than Kutscher's transliteration dè-du_{11}, the latter apparently being based upon the orthography gá-e-du_{11} in the late redaction no. 1.2. Against Kutscher's interpretation are three factors. First, the profix ga- is not a variant for dè-; thus, it does not follow that we assume a form dè-du_{11} based upon the much later form gá-e-du_{11}. Secondly, in the singular dè- governs the *marû*, not the *ḫamṭu*, therefore, a form dè-du_{11} should be impossible. Cf. eršemma no. 13:25 dè-ra-ab-bé; no. 13:23 dè-em-mà-ḫun-gá; SBH 21 rev. 27–28 dè-en-gu_7-e / *līkul*; no. 165:22 dè-mu-un-ti-le. And thirdly, Kutscher translates, ". . . look at your city! let me say." the verb "to look at" is u_6-di/du_{11}, thus, the verb -du_{11} in this passage is part of this compound and, therefore, cannot at the same time be translated as "to say."

(11–18)For a discussion of these buildings, see J. Krecher, *Kultlyrik* 80–84.

(21)For e_4-gi_4-a and e_4-gar-ra, "to destroy by flooding," see R. Kutscher, *YNER* 6 138–139; S. N. Kramer, *AS* 12 54 317; and AHw 1167 sub *šanû* VI and add the reference *SBH* 27 obv. 22:[e_4-du_{11}]-ga e_4-gi_4-a-bi / *[. . .] ù(-)šá-nu-[. . .]*

The translation *aḫulap tūršu* in the late redaction is based upon a = *aḫulap* and gi_4 = *târu*.

(22)For e_4-gar, "to flood," see *AHw* 942 sub *raḫāṣu(m)* I; cf. no. 1.2:29 for e_4-ta-gar = *ina mê salû*. For a similar usage of the ablative, see E. Gordon, *Sumerian Proverbs* 1.196 (G. Gragg, *AOATS* 5 31): kaš-sur-ra nu-zu e_4-ta al-s[ì], "He who had no experience with brewing beer was hurt(?) by the water."

(23)ki-lá = *sanāqu ša šuqulti* for which see AHw 1021 sub *sanāqu(m)* I. See 1.2:36 for ki in ki-lá interpreted as *udditum*.

(25–29)Presumably the infix -ni- refers to "in the city."

(30)The implications of the suffix -e- after tur and gal are unclear to us.

(32)See the commentary to no. 1.2:48–49.

(34)See the commentary to no. 60:38–39 for the infix -e- reflecting the locative, in our line ešemen-ba.

Eršemma no. 1.2

(1)Although we assume -dè to be a variant for -di, the syntax of the verbal form gá-e-dè/du_{11} is unclear. For u_6 di/du_{11} governing the locative-terminative, see A. Falkenstein, *AnOr* 29 127, the verbal infix -e- in our line reflecting this locative-terminative. Although the form is cohortative, all six Akkadian renderings interpret the Sumerian as an imperative, perhaps basing their translation upon context. A translation using the cohortative "Let me be amazed/bewildered!" or "I shall be amazed/bewildered!" makes no sense in our context. A corruption of no. 1.1:1, which contains the form bí-du_{11} has occurred.

(28)See the commentary to no. 1.1:21.

(36)For *udditum* as a "ground cover consisting of young reeds," see CAD L 232 sub *lubšu*. We are unaware of any lexical equating of ki with *udditum*. Since, however, *udditum* is a ground cover, its equation with ki, "earth, ground," is understandable.

(48–49)Reading the Sumerian as gal_4-la-bi, instead of sal-la-bi (note the variant sil-la-bi in text J), the scribe translated *qallu*, "penis," and accordingly translated lá as *šuqallulu*, "to suspend, hang," thus, "the dog caused its penis to hang down," a translation that makes little sense in our context. A translation of line 49 assuming *ušaqlil* to be from *šuqallulu* makes no sense, "the wolf caused its scattered to hang down." If, however, we assume *ušaqlil* to be the Š-stem of *qalālu* (although unattested according to *AHw* 893), the translation makes sense, "the wolf caused its scattered to be diminished." Moreover, the fact that the verbal form *ušqallil* in line 48 and *ušaqlil* in line 49 are different, suggests that they might stem from different roots. Lines 48 and 49 are parallel, ur "dog" / ur-bar-ra "wolf," as well as each having the identical Sumerian verbal form. Therefore, we expect sal-la-bi to parallel sig_{11}-bi, its scattered one." For sal = *muṣṣû*, "to strew, scatter," see J. Krecher, *Kultlyrik* 184 n. 525. The Akkadian variant *ittaši*, "carried off," seems most appropriate for lá. We have interpreted ur as "dog" rather than "enemy" on the basis of its paralleling ur-bar-ra "wolf."

(51)Akkadian: "the street with whose beauty I was not sated"

Eršemma no. 35.1

In general, for commentary to no. 35.1, see the commentary to the corresponding line in 35.2.

(1)Note that both mi-na (35.1:1) and en-šè (35.2:1) are equated with Akkadian *adi mati* (*AHw* 632 sub *mati/e*).

(3)ši-bi-kur-ra is for še-eb-é-kur-ra

(5)For ši-bi-du-du-ba cf. *JCS* 29 p. 9 rev. 12': igi-še-eb-tu-tu-ba-šè.

(6)e-si-kur-zi seems to be an orthography for èš é-kur-zi, "the shrine Ekurzi" or "shrine, the faithful Ekur."

Eršemma no. 35.2

(1)The line has been restored on the basis of the catalogue entry B_2 57 and K_1 iii 2. Note the pronunciation guide in *CT* 42 21 rev. 11: urú-u-a-še-e-e-er-ra-a urú-u-a-a-a. The second part, urú-u-a-a-a is probably a repetition of the opening words and not an indication of additional words after urú a-še-er-ra.

(15)For ši gi, "to be quiet," cf. the incipit of the balag-lamentation ušum-gin$_7$ ní si-a (*SBH* 20a 1–2; *MLC* 1862 1; *UET* 6/2 206 obv. 1): ušum-gin$_7$ ní si-a(-⌈àm⌉) ši èn-šè (var.: ši-in èn for ši èn-še) ì-gi / [*ki-ma*] *ba-aš-mu pu-luḫ-tu$_4$ ma-lu-ú mi-na tuš-ḫar-ra-ar*, "Like a serpent full of fear, how long will you keep silent?"; the balag-lamentation u$_4$-dam ki àm-ús (*VAS* 2 17 obv. ii 7; *SBH* 1 rev. 10; *SBH* 2 rev. 31–32) 67: ur$_5$-mu(var.: -gu$_4$) šà-ba:-mu ši-zu(?) ì-gi / *ka-bat-ti lìb-bi-ia [. . . uš-ḫa-r]i-ir* (translation unclear); *SBH* 34 obv. 9: ši èn-šè ì-gi / *[a]-di ma-ti tuš-ḫa-ra-ár*; K.5173 and duplicate BM79037 (courtesy, E. Sollberger and the Trustees of the British Museum) 9–10: [. . .]-eden-na-ra ši mu [. . .-gi] / *[. . .]-ni-šá ina* É *uš-qa-ma-am*; NBC 11433 (courtesy, W. W. Hallo) 10: [. . .]-eden-na-ra ši mu [. . .-gi] (NBC 11433 and K.5173 are not duplicates); the balag-lamentation abzu pe-el-lá-àm (BM 54745, courtesy, A. Shaffer) 43–44: ši ma-dè-gi / *uš-taḫ-ri-ir*; BM 82–7–14, 1818 (courtesy, E. Sollberger and the Trustees of the British Museum) 7: guruš uru-na ši in-še i-[gi], "How long will the young man be quiet in his own city?": BM 79–7–8,75 [. . .] ši èn-šè i-⌈gi⌉ / [. . .] *it-taš-kan a-di ma-tim* [. . .]. Note the variant ka-bi for si-bi in 35.1:7–10. Perhaps the fact that ka "mouth" and ši (Emesal for zi *napištu*) "gullet," refer to areas of the body in the same general region, is responsible for the variant expression with ka.

(19)For ^{u}šumun$_x$(GUG$_4$)-bur-re, ^{ú}numun-bur = *elpet mê purki* and for ^{ú}šu-mu-un = *elpetu*, see CAD E 108; W. Römer, *Königshymnen* 188–189.

(26–31)We have translated these lines with the help of variant Text E. This interpretation explains the genitives ḫa-zí-in-na and ab-ba-a in 35.2:28–29. Lines 28 and 29 also occur in *PRAK* B 471b obv. 19–20:

19. urú gu-ḫa-zi-in! še mi-ni-ib-gi tú-re-eš ba-tu$_9$-ba
20. urú ab-a-e ba⌈x x x⌉ ib(?)-gi ba-tu$_9$

We have translated "like the whir/roar of the . . ." on the basis of gù/mu/gú-. . .-gin$_7$ in Text E. The verbal form ba-da-pad (E:8 (26)), parallel to ba-ra-è in 35.2:24 may be for ba-da-bad (bad = *nesû*, "to remove oneself," (*AHw* 781)). Perhaps the gloss kum-me is somehow related to nigìn = *kummu*, "cella," (CAD K 533).

(27)For du-lum "misery," see Gordon, Proverbs 1.83 and 2.14; Civil in Lambert and Millard *Atra-Ḫasis* p. 140 1.86.

(33)We have not translated the compound verb gú lá in our passage. There is no translation which clearly fits our context. For literary references to gú lá, "to embrace" without the commitative -da, see CAD E 29 sub *edēru*. For gú lá, "to prowl," see *AHw* 774 sub *ne'ellû*.

(39)For Enlil as a fowler, see the incipit of eršemma no. 160.
The word nu-tuk/sík-la seems to be a combination of nu-tuk/sík and nu-la, "the orphan and the widow." For nu-tuk/nu-sík, "orphan," see CAD E 72 sub *ekūtu*; for nu-la, "widow," see *MSL* 12 142 6': nu-la = *al-ma-tu*.
We expect a plural verb form mu-n(i)-gub-bé-eš, but the confusion in the term nu-tuk-la may have induced the scribe to copy a singular form.
As we have suggested throughout this manuscript, the infix -n- directly before the verbal root may possibly be an elision of the locative-terminative infix -ni-. To demonstrate this possibility, we note C. Wilcke, Das Lugalbandaepos, lines 294–295:

> ki-u_4-ba nin_9-e_5-mu kù-[d]inanna-ke_4
> kur-MÙŠ-ta šà-kù-ga-ni-a ḫé-em-ma-ni-pà-dè-en (var.: ḫé-em-ma-an-pà-dè-en)
> This passage occurs again in lines 360–361 with the verbal forms ḫé-em-ma-ni-pà-dè with variant ḫé-em-mi-in-pà-dè.
>
> "Einst hat meine fürstliche Schwester, die reine Inanna,
> mich vom . . . -Bergland her ihr reines Herz berufen."

In this line the prefix ma- indicates, "to me" so that in this example we can see that the -n- infix occurring in the variants cannot be the accusative nor the third singular *ḫamṭu*. It would appear to be a shortened form of the infix -ni-

Eršemma no. 163.1

(1)For sá mar-mar, "arbiter, counselor," see Å. W. Sjöberg, *Or. Suecana* 19–20 168. Note the reference no. 163.2:a+2 sá mu-e-mar / *tuṣammerma*.

(3)Note that no. 163.2:a+4 has [ù-tu]-ud-da-urú-zé-eb-b[a-. . .]. We do not expect any reference to Eridu in Ninurta's geneology. Quite possibly urú-zé-eb-ba is an error, since it is somewhat homonymous with ḫur-sag-gá.

(5)Cf. no. 163.2:a+6 wherein [bulùg-gá] is rendered into Akkadian as *ṣāpīt*, "tower," (see CAD Ṣ 97). This equation, only attested in this line, may derive from bulùg-gá denoting something growing up (for bulùg-gá, see W. Römer, *Königshymnen* 79–80).

(6)For peš(-peš), "to disperse," see AHw 736 sub *napāšu(m)* I; AHw 955 sub *rapāšu(m)*; ŠL 347 41. Note the homonymous variant in no. 163.2:a+7 $peš_6$-$peš_6$ / *qemû*, "to grind (flour)" (*AHw* 913).
Note the Akkadian loanword šip-ri in text C, instead of kin as in text A.

(7)Note variant text C: "Plotting, you have approached the land rebellious against your father (as) a flood."

(9)Note variant text C: "You have trampled down the mountains of cedar like a single planted reed; (but) verily you have (re)planted (them)."

(10)For téš-a sì-ga, see *AHw* 661–662 sub *mitḫariš*, "in gleicher Weise."

(12)For sag-an-ta cf. CAD E 111 [sag-a]n-ta = *pu-tum e-l[i-tum]*, "upper forehead." For sag-an cf. Gudea cyl. B ix 3 and for denoting a person of importance note *MSL* 12 94 35: SAG$^{ti-ri-gi}$.AN = *šarru*. Presumably gù-an-ta-dé is a variant for gú-an-ta-dè, which also denotes something raised high. Cf. gú-an-ta in *SRT* 11 44 and 50; CAD E 99 sub *elītu* mng.8); *ZA* 53 116 for gú-an-ta; and now no. 163.2:a+13 for gù-[an-ta-dè] / *le-a-um*, "powerful one."

(13)For ^{giš}ig gub possibly meaning, "to tear out a door," see Å. W. Sjöberg, *JCS* 24 107 12 wherein our passage is quoted. Note that no. 163.2:a+14 translates gub by *tušbalkit*, "you dislodged." Note that -an-na is translated *šá-qa-ti*, "high," not "heaven" in no. 163.2:a+14.

(17)We expect a verbal prefix for the form sal-sal-e-en.

(18)Perhaps ni-ba in text C is for ní-ba "by itself." Note 163.2:a+19 for the Akkadian translation, "You have demolished and overthrown the land which does not hearken." This translation appears to be based upon bal = *naqāru* (*AHw* 743) and bal = *nabalkutu* (*AHw* 694 ff.).

(19)We have read enmen(KAxA) in text C following the suggestion of J. Krecher, *Falkenstein Festschrift* 97.

For the difficult phrase gù-téš-a-sì-ga, see Å. W. Sjöberg, *JCS* 24 111 with n. 6. Note no. 163.2:a+20 for the variant gug, translated into Akkadian as *sunqu*, "hunger," (for ú-gug, "hunger," see *AHw* 1059).

More literally, the line means, "How long will you cause the harmony you have instilled not to go away?"

(24)We do not expect the first person singular suffix -mu. In fact, text C omits -mu. Perhaps -mu is an error, somehow caused by an aural confusion with the next word mušen.

(25)The úru-sign after engar appears to be an erasure.

(26)This line has been restored on the basis of no. 163.2:a+22.

(28)The English translation of this line is based upon no. 163.2:a+24.

(31)For the probable restoration [dib]-bé cf. the passages quoted by J. Krecher, *Kultlyrik* 93 f.

(33)For á sù-sù, "to swing the arms, to move quickly," see Å. Sjoberg, *Mondgott* 173; C. Wilcke, *Das Lugalbandaepos* 180; G. Pettinato, *Menschenbild* 112; J. Cooper, *ZA* 61 16 30.

Eršemma no. 160

(1)For kur-úr "base of a mountain," see C. Wilcke, *Das Lugalbandaepos* p. 151. For gu-lá, "to spread a net," see A. Falkenstein *ZA* 56 79 commentary to lines 277–279.

(19–29)For the restoration and commentary to these lines, see J. Krecher, *Kultlyrik* VIII 5*–14* and pp. 204–208.

(30)For the reading gúr-gurum, see J. Krecher, *Kultlyrik* 197 and note the numerous instances wherein this verb occurs in the same line as the verb di-di(-di), another instance of what B. Alster calls "word-groups," (*Dumuzi's Dream* p. 23). If our interpretation of this passage is correct, then we shouldn't have the suffix -in. Curiously, note that this same problem with -di-di-in occurs elsewhere (Krecher, *Kultlyrik* p. 196).

(33)Cf. *SBH* p. 130:20–21: a in-lù-lù-e ku_6 in-dib-dib-bé / *mê tadluḫma nūnu tabâr*, "having disturbed the water, you (Enlil) have netted the fish" (CAD D 43 sub *dalāḫu*). Note that the Old Babylonian version has a negative verbal form.

(34)For $laḫ_x$(DU.DU), "to snare," see CAD E 8 sub *ebēlu*. Note SBH p. 130:22 f. and *KAR* 375 ii 15 f. (both quoted CAD A/2 425 sub *ašāšu* B) for the line sa in-ga(-an)-nú-e $buru_5$ in-ga-ur-ur-re/in-ga-an-ur_4-re, "you cast the net and caught the birds" which parallels our Old Babylonian version.

(36)For the restoration of this passage, cf. SBH p. 131:48–49 (quoted CAD A/2 101 sub *anāḫu* A) for i-bí-zu èn-šè nu-kúš-ù and *SBH* p. 53 rev. 23 for èn-še ì-kúš-ù.

Eršemma no. 34.1

(1)Presumably zi-gi-mi-en is syllabic for izi-gin_7-me-en; zi for za-e; ši-ga-ne-na for ši-in-ga-me-en-ne (34.2:1). 34.2:1 has mú ki-ta, whereas 34.1:1 has ki gi-ba; the meaning of gi-ba is unclear to us.

(3)e-gi is syllabic for egí, "princess."

(4)We are puzzled by the first person singular gub-ba-mu-dè, this form occurring also in lines 6 and 7. 34.2:2 contains the expected gub-ba-zu-dè, referring to Inanna's standing upon the earth.

(5)ki-gi is syllabic for ki-gin_7; ri-ba for rib-ba.

(8–9)kur-kur-ra is an orthography for ku_4-ku_4-ra (34.2:5). Quite possibly line 9 should be restored as [é]-zi-de. We have interpreted the suffix -e in si-la-zi-de as the locative-terminative rather than the ergative due to the verbal prefix im-mi-.

Eršemma no. 34.2

(1)For sù-DU-ág with variants referring to the moonlight, see Å. W. Sjöberg, *Or. Suecana* 19–20 163–164. In our passage an-sù-ud-da-ág refers to Inanna, the planet Venus. For mú/ *napāḫu*, see *AHw* 732; for mú-mú with sù-DU-ág, see Å. W. Sjöberg, *op. cit.*, 166–167.

(4)The Akkadian translation differs: "For you, the just street blesses you."

(6)Were *šūluku* a correct rendering of the Sumerian, we would expect an orthography túm-ma, not túm-a. Rather, we prefer to interpret DU-a-mèn as in line 7 below, *ittanallaku*. The Akkadian translation states: "You are a wolf worthy of catching lambs."

(10)For unú-lá šuba-lá, see Å. W. Sjöberg, *TCS* 3 112.

(11)For nì-ú-rum cf. A. Falkenstein, *Gerichtsurkunden* 2 17 n. 8. For Enlil-bani as the "devoted one" of Ninlil, see A. Kapp, *ZA* 51 122–123; for Šulgi as the "devoted one" of Nanna, see *CT* 36 27 9.

(12)The Akkadian translation differs from the Sumerian: "I stand (ready) to discuss the oracles; I stand as an equal." For mu = *têrtu*, "oracle," see *ŠL* 61 52; for giš = *têrtu*, see *ŠL* 296 21. However, there seems to be no Sumerian word in our passage corresponding to *šūtabulu* (although túm = *abālu* A, gub-ba in our line corresponds to *azzaz*). A further complication in our line is that the Sumerian verb gub-ba is not finite in contrast to Akkadian *azzaz*. Due, then, to the many discrepancies between the Sumerian and Akkadian translations, we have interpreted mu-ni-šè simply as *ana šumišu*, "in regard to him."

For AŠ.DU = *gitmālu*, "equal," see CAD G 110. For additional occurrences of AŠ.DU, see Å. W. Sjöberg, *Or. Suecana* 19–20 wherein, Sjöberg draws attention to the "verbal character (-AŠ.DU-dè) [in CBS 11168 rev. 15]."

(16)The Akkadian translation *ina šamê eddešūti*, "in the constantly renewing (or 'ever brilliant') heavens" is based upon giš/mu = *šamû* (*AHw* 1160 (attested twice) and presumably upon $gi_{(4)}$-$gi_{(4)}$-ra being an Emesal form of gibil/*edēšu*, *eššu*. However, aside from this line, there is no attestation of $gi_{(4)}$-$gi_{(4)}$-ra being Emesal for gibil. Thus, it is possible that gi-gi-ir-ra in our line is neither Emesal nor equal to *eddešu*. If, however, $gi_{(4)}$-$gi_{(4)}$-ra is Emesal for gibil, then, perhaps mu-gi-gi-ir means "new year," thus, "at the new year."

(17–27)Throughout these lines the Akkadian scribe has misinterpreted the text as being in the first person, thus, uttered by Inanna. It is obvious from the word za-e in line 27 that the text is addressed to Inanna. Therefore, ár-re-mu means, "my praising (Inanna)."

(24)The Akkadian of the last half of the line differs: "whose name is famous throughout the known world."

(25)Note the Akkadian: "May 'Queen of Heaven' be said above and below!" We are unaware of any other equating of ušumgal and *šarratu*.

(26)The first person singular *asappan* is another example of the scribe misinterpreting the text as being recited by Inanna.

Parallel to Eršemma no. 13

(15)Note that no. 13 has umun-urú-mu instead of u$_4$-urú-mà. At some point in the transmission of the text leading to the redaction in *STT* 155, a scribe interpreted the sound UURUMU as meaning "lord (of) my city" rather than "storm of my city," thereupon, copying u-urú-mu (for the umun-sign having a value 'u' when meaning "lord," see commentary to no. 60:29–33).

An interpretation of ur-sag-gá-me-en as "you are of the warrior" seems rather unlikely. Noting the use of the presumptive volitive in the succeeding lines and, in particular, the form na-me-en in line 17, perhaps ur-sag-gá-me-en is an orthography for ur-sag na-me-en.

(16)For šuba, "bright (one)," see Å. W. Sjöberg, *TCS* 3 96 commentary to 216 and note the syllabic orthography šu-bi, similar to šub$_x$-bi in our passage.

(18)See the commentary to no. 13:13.

(19)See *AHw* 769 sub *nawāru(m)* for šu-$^{\text{su-us-lu-ug}}$sulug = *nawāru*; *AHw* 732 sub *napāḫu(m)* for $^{\text{bu-ur}}$búr = *napāḫu ša ūmi*, "to shine (said) of light."

(20–24)See the commentary to no. 13:16 ff.

Eršemma no. 13

(4)Perhaps the epithet ^{d}Sukkal-maḫ-àm should be restored in our passage. For the epithet ^{d}Sukkal-maḫ-àm occurring in god lists directly before the epithet Nabû, ^{d}Mu-zé-eb-ba-sa$_4$-a, see *SBH* 6 obv. 11–12; *OECT* 6 pl. xxvii obv. 12–13; BL 73 obv. 42–43; *TCL* 15 pl. 32 obv. 26 f. For Nabû as *sukkalu ṣīru*, see K. Tallquist, *Götterepitheta* 148. MMA 81.11.351 (courtesy, I. Spar) has a list similar to our lines 2–7 and in this position is: umun-Tin-tir^{ki} / *be-lum* URU$^!$MIN.

(9–10)These lines enable us to restore *SBH* 22 obv. 3–6.

(13)For zé-zé cf. CAD E 304 sub *erpu* s. for zé-[(x)]-x, zé-[(x)]-id, zé-x-a zé-[x]-id = IM.DIRI = *erpu*. For zé-bi-da (Emesal) = dugud *kabtu* and dugud "cloud," see Th. Jacobsen, *JNES* 2 p. 119.

Cf. the following excerpt from a Ninurta balag-lamentation *SBH* 83 rev. 36–37: ^{d}Utu-gin$_7$ IM.DIRI-na na-an-ku$_4$-[ku$_4$-dè-en]/ *ki-ma* ^{d}UTU *ana ú-pe-e la tir-ru-u[b]* (Akkadian: "Like the sun you do not enter the clouds.") The Akkadian verb *erû* in our passage appears to be the same verb attested in Gilgameš XI 154 and in the gloss to *Dumuzi's Dream* 67: $^{e\text{-}li\text{-}šu}$ $^{i\text{-}ru\text{-}ú}$an-na ma-ra-nigin-e, translated by B. Alster, *Dumuzi's Dream* 61 as "(My hair) will whirl around in heaven for you." Alster in his commentary draws attention to *ŠL* 529 2:[NIG]IN$^{ni\text{-}gi\text{-}in}$ = *e-ru-[u]*?.

It is clear that the profix na- in line 12 is the presumptive-volitive. Stylistically, we expect the profix na- in the following lines 13–18 also to be the presumptive-volitive rather than the vetitive. Moreover, note that according to context, the profix na- in line 19 of the forerunner to no. 13 should also be the presumptive volitive. Therefore, na- in the corresponding line no. 13:14 must also be the presumptive volitive rather than the vetitive as the Akkadian scribe has consistently rendered the profix in the Akkadian translation of lines 13–18. An additional factor suggesting that the Akkadian interpretation of the Sumerian verbal form may be incorrect is the large number of obvious errors in the Akkadian translation of lines 18–21, making the validity of the entire Akkadian translation suspect.

(14)The orthography -bu-re is probably for -búr-re as in the Old Babylonian forerunner, for which see the commentary to the forerunner line 19. The Akkadian scribe apparently read bu as sír, thereby translating *šapû*, "to cloud up" (CAD E 302f. sub *erpetu*).

Perhaps the infix -na- indicates the causitive for which, see C. Wilcke, *Das Lugalbandaepos* 140, 153 and 205.

(16)For inim sum, "to give one's word," governing the dative, see E. Sollberger, *TCS* 1 no. 161:8. A. L. Oppenheim, *Eames Collection* 240, interprets inim sum as "to give notice." We have continued for stylistic reasons to interpret the profix na- as the presumptive volitive, rather than the vetitive. However, both interpretations are appropriate. For Ninurta to give the rebellious notice implies that Ninurta informs them that they shall be punished. A translation "he does not give notice" could be interpreted to mean that Ninurta summarily executes the punishment without forewarning.

(18)For EN(-na)-nu-še-ga, "insubordinate and unsubmissive," see S. Cohen, *ELA* commentary to line 154. Our scribe has not interpreted en as part of a hendiadys, but rather on the basis of EN = *bēlu*. Note 185:11 wherein the form en-šè nu-še-ga occurs, thus, "disobedient to the lord." Curiously, the form umun/ù-mu-un nu-še-ga is not attested in Emesal literature, as would be expected were en = *bēlu*.

(20)For a-mú-sar-ra cf. Laḫar and Ašnan (G. Pettinato, *Menschenbild* 87 f.)

25: a-mú-sar-ra-ka i-im-nag-nag-ne. The translation *e-mu-qí-šú ra-ba-a* is not correct. Perhaps the scribe read á-mú-mú-ra, interpreting this to be a variant for á-gur_4-gur_4-ra for which cf. the eršaḫunga *OECT* 6 iii obv. 3–4: am ⌜á-bi⌝ gur_4-gur_4-ra / *[be]-lum ša e-mu-qa-a-šú* GAL-⌜*x*⌝.

(21)The Akkadian scribe misinterpreted the Sumerian as being an epithet of Asarluḫi and so neglected in his translation what to him was the puzzling element ki.

Eršemma no. 10

(3)For the reading of the name ^{d}Aba$_x$-ba$_6$, see Th. Jacobsen, *OIP* 58 298.

(6)For ^{d}Nab as Baba, see Å. Sjöberg, *Falkenstein Festschrift* 215.

(8)For ^{d}Nin-MAR^{ki}, see Å. W. Sjöberg, *TCS* 3 109 and addenda 153.

(10)We are unaware of any other references to the Eudul. Perhaps this building is to be identified with the é-dul_4-la, "Magazingebäude," (see A. Falkenstein, *AnOr* 30 125–126; CAD E 38 sub *edulû* with the translation "administration building(?)."

(19)The compound ki-mar-mar-ra as *kanšu* or *kanāšu* is a hapax legomenon. The compound ki-gar is commonly "to found" (see A. Falkenstein, *SGL* 1 41, 42, 69; Å. Sjöberg, *Mondgott* 39 f.; W. Römer, *Königshymnen* 14; J. Krecher, *Kultlyrik* 139).

(24–25)The Akkadian translation differs: "My destroyed house brought me wailing; its heart brought me sighs. My ruined city brought me wailing; its heart brought me sighs." Presumably the translation *ub-lam-ma* is based upon interpreting na-ám-mà-ni as a verbal form of gá/mà. However, the only other equating of gá with *abālu* is Lugale XI 10 (CAD A/2 11 sub *abālu* A).

(28)The Akkadian translation differs: "My house in destruction brought me wailing."

(31)For the reading é-rab-di_5-di_5, see J. Krecher, *WO* 4 266.

Eršemma no. 45

(1–9)We have transliterated ut-u_{18}-lu on the basis of the syllabic pronunciation guide in CT 42 12:ut-tu-lu-u. This appears to be a variant for the well attested epithet of Ninurta: u_4-ta-ulu$_x$ (cf. B. Alster, "Ninurta and the Turtle," *JCS* 24 120 line 12; Å. W. Sjöberg, "Hymn to Ninurta," *Or. Suecana* 22 (1973) 19'.) ut-u_{18}-lu "southstorm," is an epithet of both Nergal and Ninurta, (see K. Tallquist, *Götterepitheta* 391 and 422. In line 45:3, we have the Emesal form of the name Nergal (*MSL* 4 Emesal voc. I. 106). For

^{d}Lú-ḫuš (line 8) as Nergal of Kiš, see *KAR* 142 rev. iii 33. The epithets umun-Kiš^{ki}-a-ta and umun-é-kišib-ba (line 4) and umun-é-me-te-ur-sag (line 5) originally referred to Zababa of Kiš (for Zababa as the lord of the Ekišibba, see Å. W. Sjöberg, *TCS* 3 135 with previous literature; as the lord of the Emeteursag in Kiš, see *RlA* 2 361). For the Eunirkitušmaḫ (line 5) in Kiš cf. *2R*^{2} 50 12a: é-u$_6$-nir-ki-tuš-maḫ /MIN (*ziqquratu*) Kiš^{ki}.

For ^{d}gi^{š}Ig-alim-ma (line 6) as the offspring of Baba and Ningirsu, see A. Falkenstein, *AnOr* 30 76–77 with n. 11. Falkenstein states: "mit seinem Namen hängt die Bezeichnung als ig-gal, 'grosse Tür' zusammen." Perhaps we may transliterate the epithet as gi^{š}ig-gu-là-ra (line 6). For gi^{š}ig-gal being identified with Papsukkal (line 7), see K. Tallquist, *Götterepitheta* 436 and AHw 688 sub *mutērtu* for ^{d}Ig-gal-la = ^{d}Pap-sukkal *ša muterrēti*. The syntactical significance of the suffix -ra in the names ^{d}gi^{š}Ig-alim-ma-ta-ra and gi^{š}ig-gu-NU-ra is unclear to us.[209] Although in the case of -gu-NU-ra, perhaps a connection with ^{d}Gu-nu-ra exists, (see J. Krecher, *Kultlyrik* 123). For Papsukkal as *sukkalu ṣīru* (thus, ^{d}Sukkal-maḫ-àm in line 7), see K. Tallquist, *Götterepitheta* 148. Thus, all four epithets in lines 6–7 are interrelated. The reason for the inclusion of these epithets in our text is most likely that Papsukkal is the vizier of Zababa (*CT* 25 pl. 1 18–20; pl. 29 Rm 11, 289 6–9; *CT* 24 pl. 49 obv. 7–8).

Thus, the epithets in lines 4–7, at least originally, are related to Zababa of Kiš and his vizier Papsukkal. The epithet Nergal and Luḫuš clearly refer to Nergal. The epithet ut-u$_{18}$-lu may refer to Nergal or Ninurta. Apparently by the First Millennium B.C.E., Zababa had become identified with Nergal/Ninurta. In the case of Nergal, perhaps it was the fact that ^{d}Lú-ḫuš was identified with Nergal of Kiš, which led to Nergal's assumption of the epithets of Kiš's chief deity, Zababa.

On the basis of the names umun-irigal-la and ^{d}Lú-ḫuš, it could be reasonably argued that this eršemma is of Nergal and that the subscript indicating it to be of Ninurta is an error based upon the epithet ut-u$_x$-lu (which could apply to either). However, complicating the picture is the fact that the epithets of Zababa (lines 4–5) occur in First Millennium B.C.E., recensions of Ninurta balag-lamentations: gu$_4$-ud-nim (-é)-kur-ra 13–16 (*SBH* 18 14–17) and ušum-gin$_7$ ní si-a 9–12 (*SBH* 20 10–13).

(4)Note the peculiar orthography for "lord of Kiš": umun-Kiš^{ki}-a-ta. This same orthography occurs in *SBH* 20a 10 and *CT* 42 no. 24:22. Perhaps the writing Kiš^{ki}-a-ta is a play upon the words Kiš and *kiššatu*, "universe." Curiously, the genitive of Keš can also be Kèš^{ki}-a(m)-ta for which see G. Gragg, *TCS* 3 162–164.

(12)See no. 59:11 for the Akkadian translation *[. . .] u-mu lu-nu-uḫ*, "May I pacify [the insides of] the storm!" However, ḫun-e-ta can hardly correspond correctly to the cohortative *lunūḫ*. For ḫun-e-ta cf., J. Krecher, *WO* 4 272.

(16–23)This list of goddesses includes Baba of Girsu and the two closely identified goddesses Ninisina and Nintinugga. These two goddesses are distinct during the neo-Sumerian and Old Old Babylonian periods, cf. *TCL* 16 75 33: "In Isin I am Ninisina and in Nippur I am Nintinugga." However, by the First Millennium B.C.E. the two are nearly fused for cf. *SBH* 5 rev. 12 wherein Nintinugga is weeping over the Egalmaḫ of Isin. Next in line are the wives of Nabû, Tašmetum and Nanâ, followed by two epithets of Inanna. Lastly is Ṣarpanitum.

Eršemma no. 53

(1)The incipit has been restored on the basis of the instruction for the repetition of the end of the incipit in the left margin of lines 21 and 24 in *CT* 42 12: zag-ga-dib-ba-a-ni-ír-ra and by -ne-ra in text C.

(9–13)For these epithets, see commentary to 45:1–9.

Eršemma no. 59

(6)For the Eḫuršaba as the temple of Nanâ or Lisi in Babylon, see *RlA* 2 304;K. Tallquist, *Götterepitheta* 386 sub Nanâ.

(7)This line has been restored on the basis of NCBT 688 7 and 66; BL 62 6; BL 71 63; *PRAK* C 74 5?. See CAD L 190 sub *lilû* for the demon ^{d}Líl-lá-en-na. See Lu III iv 55 for ama-è-a = *li-li-tu*. Also note our text B variant ama-é-a and *MSL* 12 p. 127 55 for ama-é-a. Apparently the *lilû*-demon was a servant of Ištar, cf. *CT* 28 38 K.4079a:13 (CAD L 190 sub *lilû* mng.b): *Ištar* LÍL.LÁ *ina [bīt] amēli i-[. . .]*, "Ištar will . . . a *l.*-demon in the house of that man."

(8)For ama-é-a, see the commentary to line 7. For ^{d}Dada as the messenger of Inanna, see K. Tallquist, *Götterepitheta* 278.

(9)For Nanâ's identification with Inanna, Ištar in Uruk, see K. Tallquist, *Götterepitheta* 385.

Index of Sumerian Terms in the Eršemmas

This index consists of Sumerian terms indexed according to the catalogue number of the eršemma. The following is a list of the eršemmas with the appropriate page number in the book:

a ("oh!")   10:15–16; 13:23;
  32:5–9; 34.2:18; 79:30–31;
  88:4–9,12–13; 106:22(?);
  164:29,36; 165:2–3;
  166.1:1–7,30; 166.2:2–10

a-a   1.1:29; 1.2:42; 13-parallel
  :24; 23:7–9,13,22,28;
  34.2:13,15; 53:1–4,6–7;
  79:15,22–23; 159:29–30;
  160:36; 163.1:4,7,26;
  163.2:a+5,a+8,a+22; 166.1:21;
  166.2:23; 168:6,8; 171:31,33;
  23.2:5,7–9; 184:2,13,26,45;
  185:5,21

a-a-ka-na-ág-gá   1.1:5

a-a-ka-nag-gá   1.2:5; 53:5

a-a-tu-ud-da   29:17

a-a-ù-tu-ud-da   29:a+29

a-a-ugu   23:22,27; 171:85;
  184:24

a-ab-ba   35.2:29

a-aš-ši   97:101

a-ba   10:1,28; 23:21–24;
  97:79–80; 163.1:20,22;
  163.2:a+21; 168:9–12,41;
  184:50–51

a-ba-a   163.1:22

a-gal-gal   1.2.:41 (variant for
  ama-gan)

a-gi₆-a   184:12

a-gin₇   32:57–60; 60:16–17;
  171:26–29,31–32

a-ma   35.1:16 (for ama₅(?))

a-mú-sar-ra   13-parallel :23;
  13:20

a-na   165:20; 171:87–91,94

a-na-àm 160:20; 165:14,17,24
a-na gál-lu-bi 166.1:30
a-ne 171:70–71
a-nir 88:25; 164:32
^{d}a-nun-ke$_4$-e-ne 163.1:35,37
a-ra 171:82
a-ra-li 60:7; 165:29; 171:1–2
a-ra-zu e 13:25–31
a-šà 171:74
a-še-er 10:18; 35.2:16; 79:28
a-še-r 35.1:1,3–8
á ág 23:15; 168:8; 184:13
á-bàd 13:9
á-gáb-bu 163.2:a+24
á-lá 88:29
á-nu-gál 163.1:4
á-nun-gal 163.2:a+5
á-nun-gál 163.1:4
á-sàg 171:79–84
á-sìg 171:16
á sù-sù 163.1:33
á-sum-ma 163.1:2
á-tuk 184:46
á-zi-da 163.1:27; 163.2:a+23; 184:23
a$_5$/ak 32:56; 79:10;164:26–27
ab-ba 35.2:29; 184:39
aba$_x$(AB) 163.1:24
^{d}Aba-ba$_6$ 10:3; 60:35
abgal 168:34; 184:42; 185:30
ad ša$_4$-ša$_4$ 159:19
al-tar-re 171:35–36
alim(-ma) 1.1:2; 1.2:2; 13:2,4,6,8; 45:2,9; 60:19,25–29; 23.2:2,4
^{d}Alla 88:7
am 60:1–3,16–17; 97:101
^{d}Am-an-ki 1.2:10; 23:6; 29:2; 168:4
am erén-na di-di 1.1:8; 1.2:8; 53:7
ám 171:1–2,6–8
^{túg}ám-bàra-ga 60:38
ám-du$_{11}$-ga 160:4
ám-gal-la 171:1–2,6–7
ám-GAM-ma 171:58–59
ám-gi-ra 164:5–6,25
ám-gig 166.2:27; 171:52
ám-gu$_7$ 1.1:24; 1.2.:37
ám-i-bí-ur$_5$ 166.2:28
ám-la-LUM 171:67
ám-ma-al 171:49
ám-ma-al-ma-al 171:8
ám-me-e-gá-ar 79:10
ám-ú-rum 34.2:11
àm-mu-uš 166.1:14
ama 10:3,37; 79:11; 88:14,48–50; 97:14; 166.1:19; 171:77–79; 185:7
ama-arḫuš-a 97:103
ama-é-a/e 59:8; 159:6; 171:6
ama-é-šà-ba 159:4; 171:77
ama-gal 23:14; 168:7
ama-gan 1.1:28; 1.2.:41
ama-$^{(d)}$mu-tin-na 60:13; 88:23; 97:53
ama-ù-tu-ud-da 29:a+28
ama-ubur-zi-da 79:5
ama-ugu 79:29; 97:102–103; 164:21
ama-urú-sag-gá 159:3; 171:4
ama-ušum 60:5
$^{(d)}$ama-$^{(d)}$ušumgal-an-na 60:6; 88:3
ama$_5$ 32:13,43,50; 35.2:20–24
amalu 97:14
amar 25.2:22–23; 165:18
amar-sag-tuk 165:25
amaš 10:27; 88:20–21; 97:34,40–46,60–61; 106:6–7; 171:86
ambar 171:76; 184:27
an 13:10,23; 23:30; 32:10,21; 34.2:8–11,18–20,22–23; 45:10; 53:14; 59:5; 79:8,15; 97:107; 163.2:a+2; 168:1,3,5

an-bir$_{x}$ 32:52
an-eden-na 168:33
an-gal 34.2:29; 168:8
an-gu-la 35.2:25
an-pa 184:5,17
an-su-da-ág 34.1:1–4
an-sù-ud-ág 34.2:1
an-sù-ud-da-ág 34.2:1
an-ta-sur-ra 32:17
an-ta zi-zi 184:30
an-úr 32:11; 184:5,17
an-usan-na 34.2:19
an-zà 23:1–10
an-zu 166.2:13–14
an-zu-babbar-ra 166.2:14
an-zu-gi$_{6}$-ga 166.2:13
ár-re 34.2:17,21–27
arḫuš e 97:103–104
ás e 171:18
^{d}Asar-lú-ḫi 1.2:11;
13:2,11–12,21,24; 29:3
asila ak 163.1:24
^{ú}aš-ta-al-ta-al 165:30
aš tar 171:80,85–86
aš-te 159:35
^{d}Asnan 23.2:21

ba 23:19; 159:22; 165:20,24
túgba 97:57
ba-an 32:56
^{d}Ba-ba$_{6}$ 10:2,36–38; 45:16;
53:20; 59:15
babbar 166.1:12
bad(-bad*) 163.1:19;
163.2:a+20*; 160:35
bàd-gal 34.2:27; 163.1:11
Bàd-tibira^{ki} 60:8
bal 97:39,73,116; 163.1:22;
168:33
bala 106:20–21
balag 97:26; 159:18; 171:96–99
$^{(giš)}$banšur 97.113; 159:15
bar 59:11; 88:12; 97:57;
166.1:11; 164:34,36–37;
171:36,66
bar(-ta) gál 97:57
bar ḫun 45:12; 53:16
bar-mà 166.2:1
bar-mu 166.1:1–7
bar-mu-uš 171:21
bar šed$_{7}$ 10:29; 13:22; 29:a+27;
34.2:30,32,34,36,38,40
bar-ús 185:13
bar$_{6}$-bar$_{6}$-ba-ra 166.2:15
bára 166.1:12
bára-KA 165:9
Barsip^{ki} 1.2:23; 13:8; 29:9;
35.2:10; 160:14
bi-ib-re 166.2:11
^{d}Bil$_{4}$-ga-meš 164:35,37; 171:109
billudu 106:20
bir-bir 166.1:8
BIZ 171:65–66
bu-bu-ra 10:27
bu-r 13:14–15
bulùg-gá(-bulùg-gá*)
13-parallel:24*;13:21*;
163.1:5,26; 163.2:a+22
bur 159:13
bur gul 106:8
bur-gul 106:8
búr(-búr*) 13-parallel :19;
171:23*,63*
buru$_{5}$^{mušen} 160:34; 171:76

da 60:29–33; 97:62–66; 171:46
^{d}Da-da 32:7; 59:8
^{d}Da-mu 88:4
dab$_{5}$ 88:2–3;
97:8,10,72,120;165:1
dab$_{5}$^{tab}-ba 97:85
DAB$_{5}$-bé-eš 171:90
dagal 79:15; 184:12
dal 32:55
dal-dal 184:36
dam 1.1:25; 1.2:38; 10:16;

35.2:30;
97:1–6,8–10,20,22,24,49,52,115;
106:15; 159:25; 160:26–27;
166.1:15; 166.2:18; 171:37
dam tuk-tuk 171:58
dam-tur-ra 1.1:25; 1.2:38
dar 171:98–99
darmušen 184:35
dé(-dé*) 10:17*-18*;
97:114–115; 160:23
di 45:11; 53:15; 171:85;
184:26–27
DI 164:29
di-b 97:88,90,92,94,96,120(?)
di-di 88:33; 166.1:20; 171:103;
184:30
di-di-di 160:30
di-di-lá 35.2:28
^{d}Di-ku_5-maḫ-à(m) 1.2:14; 10:30
29:6; 45:15; 53:19; 59:14
di-ri-ga 35.1:11–14
di_4-di_4-lá 35.2:28; 166.2:25;
168:36; 184:40; 185:16,32
dib(-dib*) 97:54–55,62*–63*;
159:27–28; 160:33; 171:86;
88:10
dib_4 97:94
dili 35:56; 184:31
dili-du 34.2:12–16
dili-maḫ 45:8; 53:13
dilmun$^{(ki*)}$ 1.1:1–2; 1.2:1*–2*
dím 106:9
dìm-me-er 34.2:39
dìm-me-er-maḫ 163.1:5;
163.2:a+6
dingir 88:56; 163.1:34; 171:101
dingir-maḫ 163.1:5; 184:45
diri 35.2:24–26; 168:11(?); 184:7
diri-g 185:13
du 23:20; 34.2:6–7,18;
97:100–101
du-du 23.2:16; 88:16; 165:30;
184:18–20,32
du-lum 35.2:27
dù(-dù*) 97:41,45b,118;
106:4–5,13; 163.1:9; 168:35(?);
171:63*; 184:11*
du_5-mu 164:16
du_6 60:18; 166.2:8
du_6-alim-ma 60:19
du_6-du_6 163.2:a+25(?); 184:1–6
du_6-kù 1.1:13
du_6-Nina^{ki} 166.1:5
du_6-su_8-ba 60:10
du_7-du_7 184:12
du_7-du_7-du_7 23:11
du_8(-du_8*) 79:11–14,16–17;
97:36*,37; 168:34; 171:89*;
184:42
du_{12} 159:18
du_{13}-mu 97:8–9
dub-dub 32:47; 171:23
dub-sag 97:40′
dúb(-dúb) 34.2:22,23*; 59:5;
79:35; 171:21
dul(-dul*) 23:12; 97:26*-27*
dumu 1.1:26–27; 1.2:39,41;
10:16; 23:15; 88:5;
97:6,9,21,23,25,52; 106:16;
159:26; 165:4,22,25; 171:38,87;
23.2:3; 184,4; 185:3
dumu-an-na 23:3; 168:2; 184:3
dumu-an-uraš-a 185:4
dumu-bàn-da 1.1:29; 1.2:42
dumu-é-e 159:7; 171:5
dumu-kù 10:8
dumu-maḫ-di-dè 163.1:32
dumu-maḫ-di-di 163.2:a+28
dumu-sag-an-kù-ga 168:3
dumu-sag-an-na 10:6
dumu-sag-an-uraš-a 13:27
dumu-sag-é-a 59:9
dumu-sag-^{d}En-ki-ke_4 13:3
dumu-$šag_5$-é-e 32:8
dumu-tur-ra 1.1:26; 1.2:39
^{d}Dumu-zi 60:9; 88:2,13,25,44;

gi-ba 34.1:1
gi-di(-da*) 60:40; 159:21*
gi-dili-dù-a-gin$_7$ 163.1:9; 163.2:a+10
ge-em-ge-me 88:32
ge-en 23:21(for gin$_7$)
gi$_4$(-gi$_4$*) 1.2:51*; 32:42; 88:48*; 97:70–71,74–75,78; 106:1*,18; 160:4*,37*; 164:16*–18; 171:20;
gi$_4$-g 32:37
gi$_4$-in 171:60–62
gi$_4$-ra 32:11
gi$_6$ 10:17–18
gi$_6$-par$_4$ 32:6–9
gi$_6$-par$_4$-imin 32:14
gi$_6$-ù-na 32:51
ge$_{16}$-le-èm 10:28; 171:11
gi$_{16}$-sa 166.1:1–8; 166.2:2–11
gešpú 164:6,17
^{d}Geštin-an-na 165:13,18,23,27
geštu 160:20–21
geštúg ḫur 88:54
gíd 164:14
gidim 171:83–84
^{giš}gidri 97:58
gig 35.2:27; 88:18–19; 171:77–78,104,106–107
gig-ga-bi 88:2–3; 97:1
^{giš}gigir 184:28
gin 23:21; 79:30–31; 88:26; 97:14,20–25,50–59,79; 168:9; 171:70,75,81–82
gír ak 97:17
Gír-suki 166.1:2,9,11,24; 166.2:12,14,20,24,32
gìr 60:15; 164:6
gìri 97:59
gìr ak 97:17
gìri(-ta) gál 97:59
gis-sa-al ak 184:24
giš 184:10
giš-gi$_4$ 79:14–15
giš tuk 79:36
giz-zal ak 23:27
gu 165:30
gu-ba 34.1:4,6–7
gu-l 35.1:2,7–10; 163.1:8
gu-la 97:113; 166.1:17
gu lá 160:1,6–18
gu ra 166.2:21–22
gu-sa-ra 184:39
gú 35.2:30; 171:55
gú-ab-ba 166.2:10
gú dab$_5$ 166.2:26
gú e 166.2:29–30(for gú è)
gú è 171:69
gú-en-na 10:7
gú gar 184:20,37
gú gi 29:a+25
gú-gú 166.2:31–33
gú ki ma-al 184:39
gú ki-šè gar 171:15
gú-KU 166.1:23–27
gú lá 35.2:33–35
gú-téš-a-sì-ga 163.1:19
gù-an-ta-dé 163.1:12
gù dé 88:23,45; 97:84–85; 164:30; 165:19,23; 168:1–5; 23.2:25–26
gù-dé-dé 185:14
gù di 23:19,28; 171:70
gù dúb-dúb 97:106
gù e/du$_{11}$ 32:50; 88:49–51; 165:5,7,9
gù-gar 23.1:30
gù gi$_4$ 32:52
GÙ-mu-ra 184:27
GÙ-mur 23.1:30
gù ra(-ra*) 32:49,51; 88:40*–43*,45*; 97:106*; 166.1:18–19; 171:105
gù-téš-a-sì-ga 163.1:19
GÙ zi 23.2:23

gu$_4$ 23:1–6,10; 166.2:19–20; 23.2:1,29–30
gu$_7$ 1.1:24; 1.2:37; 60:21,30; 97:98,116; 159:9,13; 171:74
gub(-gub*) 1.1:31; 1.2:43; 32:10; 34.2:2,12–16; 35.2:39; 97:62–65,67; 106:19; 163.1:5,13*; 163.2:a+14*
gùd-gi 35.2:23
gudu$_4$ 159:24; 164:30
gug-téš-a-sì-ga 163.2:a+20
gul(-gul*) 10:24,26*; 23:26; 32:57*-58; 35.2:15–18,19–23; 79:20,31–32,34 ; 184:23,33; 106:1,8,14*; 160:35*; 163.1:8,18; 163.2:a+9,a+19; 168:37
gul-gul (for gul-ul-gu-ul) 23.2:31
gùn-nu-gùn-nu 60:27
gur 164:30
gur-gur 23.2:19
gúr-gurum 160:30–32
gùr 184:28
guruš 35.2:29; 60:20,24,26,33–34; 88:4–9,12,57; 97:16,38,86,114; 164:15,30,36; 165:2–3; 184:43; 185:31
gur$_{10}$ su-ub 163.1:6; 163.2:a+7

ḫa-lam 60:34–35; 166.1:23–27; 166.2:31–33; 171:68
^{giš}ḫa-lu-úb 184:7
ḫa-ze 97:76,89,91
ḫa-zí-in 35.2:28
ḫa-zé-la 35.2:28
ḫa-zu-ù 97:77
ḪAR 88:53–55
ḫar-ra-an 88:27
ḫaš$_x$(TUM^{x}EŠ) 23:18; 184:15; 185:12
^{giš}ḫašḫur 97:113
ḫé-du$_7$-ra 34.2:8–11
ḫé-gál 23:5
ḫi-li 32:43
ḫu-bu-úr 34.2:25
ḫu-luḫ 23:14; 168:7
ḫu-tu-ul-ḫu-tu-ul 60:28
ḫul 79:21,29
ḫul-du 164:20
ḫul-gig 23:22; 185:10
ḫul-ma-al 163.2:a+24
ḫúl 10:23; 159:25; 164:33; 171:25
ḫúl-ḫúl 23.2:29–31
ḫúl-la-šè 166.1:14; 166.2:17
ḫun 13:23; 29:18; see sub šá ḫun
ḫur-sag 163.1:3,8; 163.2:a+9

i-bí 160:36; 164:14,19; 171:35,93,100–102
i-bí bar 29:a+24; 60:36; 171:39,50–51,55
i-bí du$_8$ 171:100–101
i-bí du$_8$ ní-te(-en*)-na 1.1:7; 1.2:7*; 53:6
i-bí-gùn-nu-gùn-nu 60:27
i-bí-ḫúl-bar 171:56
i-bí ḫur 88:53
i-bí kúr 171:67
i-bí-LUM.LUM 60:14
i-bí-mud$_5$(?)-bar 171:57
i-i 164:28
i-LI$_9$-na 171:98
i-lu 59:1–2,10; 79:24–26; 171:9
i-lu e 160:26,29
i-lu ra 59:1–2
i-ra 79:23; 171:13
i-zi 165:31
ì-lum 97:47
ì-lum-sag-gá 97:18
ì-nun-na 184:41; 185:29

Ì-si-in^{ki} 1.2:26,35,47
i_7 160:23; 171:73
íb-ba/e 10:13–14; 88:10; 163.1:20
(túg)íb-lá 97:82
íb-si 29:20
ibila-é-sag-íl-la 13:9
idim 168:33
^{giš}ig 171:30
$^{d\,giš}$ig-alim-ma-ta-ra 45:6; 53:1[illegible]
^{giš}ig-an-na 163.1:13; 163.2:a+14
^{giš}ig-gu-NU 45:6; 53:11
igi 97:77–78
igi(-šè) du 23:20
igi-du_8 88:22
igi-ni-šè 79:20–23; 97:112
igi zi 97:83
íl 32:20; 159:15
íl-íl 23.2:24
^{giš}ildág 164:35,37
IM 184:32–33; 185:16–17
im^{im} 166.1:20
im-du_8 166.1:20
IM.MA.A.A 168:40
im-ma-al 35.1:15; 35.2:19
imin 23:18; 97:38; 185:12
in(-šè) dúb 171:17
in-nu-uš 165:30
^{d}Inanna 34.2:9; 97:52,66,105–106; 165:5,7,9,11,19
inim 184:24
inim-du_{11}-ga 23:27
inim e 171:83–84
inim-ka 160:5
inim zé-èm 13-parallel :20–22; 13:16–18
ir 10:13–14,23
IŠ 97:101; 184:29
IŠ-bar-ra 164:10
^{d}Iškur 23:2–3,5,7–10,15,17, 27–28;168:2,4,8,39; 23.2:2,5,7–10,15,24,26; 184:2–3,9,26,51; 185:2,5,8,20–21,25,34
^{d}Ištaran-i-bí-šuba 88:6
izi 34.2:1

ka 35.1:7–10
ka-ab-gaz 88:27
ka-ab-ús 97:97
ka ba 23:19; 163.2:a+25
ka-ba-a-a 163.1:21
ka bar 60:37
KA-ḫu-tu-ul-ḫu-tu-ul 60:28
KA.ḪUR see sub GÙ-mur
KA.KA 35.2:31
ka-me-a 184:37
KA-mud_5 171:56–57
ka-na-ág 32:22; 60:14–15; 23.2:21; see sub a-a-
ka-nag-gá 160:31; see sub a-a-
ka-pa-bu-um! 97:65
ka-ša-an 35.1:7–10
ka-ša-an-é-a-na 34.1:3
ka-ša-na-na 34.1:2
ka-ta è 163.1:21
ka-tar 163.2:a+27; 23.2:31
ka-tar si-il 184:49
ka 106:10
ka-maḫ 32:19
KA sù 184:34
kal 97:18
kala-ga 13-parallel :17; 13:11–12; 168:35
kalam 23:11–12; 163.1:23; 23.2:11–12; 184:49
kar 97:72,76,86–87
kar(?)-kar(?) 97:73
Karkara^{ki} 23:4
kaskal 88:26; 171:75
kaš 184:41; 185:29
ki 1.1:13; 32:10–11,21; 34.1:1,5–6; 34.2:1–3,22; 45:10; 53:14; 79:10; 97:107,114; 159:8;

163.2:a+3; 164:13,27–28; 165:20,24; 184:26
ki-ág 13:25
KI.AN.NI.DA 1.2:50
ki-bal 13-parallel:21; 13:17; 23:22,26; 45:11; 53:15; 163.1:7,18; 163.2:a+8,a+19,a+26; 168:37; 184:23,33–35; 185:10,20
ki-bulùg(-gá)-bulùg(-gá) 13-parallel:24; 13:21
ke-en-ke-ne 97:24
ki-gal 1.1:12; 35.1:4,10,14; 35.2:4; 160:8
ki(-bé) gi$_4$-gi$_4$ 163.1:18,30
KI.KAL 164:26
ki kin 171:80
ki-La-ga-sa 166.2:22,33
ki lá(-lá*) 1.1:23; 1.2:36*
ki-Lagaš^{ki} 166.1:3
ki-lú-da 88:55
ki-mar-mar 10:19
ki-mu-lu-da-ba-an-da-šub-ba 171:43
ki-nú 159:12
ki-pél-la 171:42
ki-pél-pél-la 171:41
ki-sì-ga 23.2:27–28
ki sìg 32:5; 59:6
ki-sikil 1.1:27; 1.2:40; 34.2:9; 60:23,32; 97:15; 168:34; 184:42; 185:30
ki-šu-me-ša$_4$ 106:11
ki-tuš 159:11
ki-u$_6$-da 88:54
ki-u$_6$-di 106:10
ki-Unu^{ki} 97:4
ki-ur 35.1:4,10,14
ki-ùr 1.1:12; 1.2:18; 160:8
ki-ur$_5$-ra 171:42
ki-Zabalam^{ki} 32:4,38(?); 97:5
kin(-kin*) 88:52*; 97:24*; 171:80; 164:27
kiri$_4$ 164:19
kiri$_4$ ḪAR 88:53
kiri$_4$-zal 23.2:23
kéš-da 171:40
KU 171:33–38
KU-KU 164:11
ku-li 97:93,95,97
kù 1.1:13; 32:20; 34.2:21; 79:8,15–16,18,22,34; 97:34–36,49,56–59,64,66,115; 159:8,13–20; 160:29; 165:5,7,11,19,23
kù-an-kù-ga 163.1:23
kù-zu 79:2,38; 165:22,25
ku$_4$(-ku$_4$*) 13-parallel:18*; 13:13*; 32:23*; 34.2:5*; 88:24*–25*; 97:40′–46; 106:22; 159:31–32; 171:26,29; 23.2:27–28; 184:8*
ku$_5$ 1.1:23: 1.2:36; 163.1:31
ku$_6$ 160:33; 163.1:24
Kul-aba^{ki} 32:16; 97:11
kun-sag 32:23
kun-ur4-ur4 184:47
kur(-kur*) 34.2:24*,26*–27*; 60:25–28; 79:38; 88:10; 97:114–115; 106:12*–14,15–16(for kur); 160:22; 163.1:6,10*,17; 163.2:a+8,a+25
kur-erím 163.1:9; 163.2:a+10
kur-^{giš}erin 163.1:9
kur-gal 10:21; 23:13; 34.2:30; 53:1; 166.1:22; 168:6
kur-gar-ra 97:17
kur-gul-gul 59:4; 79:3; 106:3
kur KA kur 184:36
kur-kur-ra 34.1:8–9(for ku$_4$-ku$_4$-r)
kur-úr 160:1
kur(-kur*) 106:20,20*,21; 163.2:a+11*,a+12*; 171:8–10,96,99

kuš-e-sír 97:59
kúš-ù 160:36

la-al 1.2:48–49
la-bar-é-e 79:6,13
la-ga 32:40–41
La-ga-sa 166.2:5,22,33
la-ḫe 184:40
la-la 1.2:51; 32:42
lá 1.1:32–33; 1.2:48–49; 23:18; 88:17; 97:81–82; 171:90; 184:15–16,38,43
lá-lá 23:16–19; 184:14–16
Lagaš^{ki} 10:12; 166.1:3,7,25
laḫ$_{x}$ 160:34
laḫtan 32:18
^{d}Lama-é-an-na 10:4
^{d}Lama-é-šà-ba 10:9
^{d}Lama-ki-kù-ga 166.1:11
Larsa^{ki} 1.1:20
LI 97:93,95,97
li-bi-ir 88:8; 164:26–27
li-li 1.2:50(for líl)
líl 1.1:34; 1.2:50
líl(-e) gar 97:43′,45′
líl(-àm) ku$_{4}$ 106:22
^{d}Líl-lá-en-na 59:7
lirum 164:1–10,16; 184:31
lu-lu 97:53; 106:6–7
lú 13-parallel:20; 34.1:8–9; 163.1:1,31; 165:25
lú-a-nir 88:25
lú-á-lá 88:29
lú-BÀNDA 23:16,21; 185:9
lú-dam 171:37
lú-di 79:11
lú-dumu 171:38
lú-e-ri-a 97:89
lú-eden-na 165:6,14
lú-EN.NA 13-parallel:22
lú-ér-re 88:24
lú-erím 163.1:27; 163.2:a+23
lú-gal$_{5}$-lá 88:22
lú-ḫi 184:9
lú-ḫul-gál 165:12,17
^{d}Lú-ḫuš 45:8; 53:13
lú-ka-aš-ka-sa 165:10,16
lú-ka-ba-ra 165:8,15
lú-ki-bal 13-parallel:21
lú-ki-sikil 34.2:8
lú-pa$_{4}$-e-ri-a 97:91
lú-šu-da-a 88:28
lù 160:33
lugal 97:50; 184:44
lul 171:102–103
LUM.LUM 60:14

ma 32:11,15; 171:51–55
ma-a 171:77–78; 97:79–80(for máš?)
ma-al(-ma-al*) 159:28; 160:19–20,22,25; 166.1:12–15; 166.2:16–18; 171:9*-10*,51,55,70–72,79,93
ma-ám-ma-ra 106:12
ma-aš 97:35
ma-é-gal-maḫ 1.1:18
ma-gú-en-na 166.2:7
ma-la-ra 171:14,16
ma-mu-šú-a 1.1:17
ma-mú-d 106:4–5
ma-ra 34.2:15; 171:40
^{giš}má-gul-gul 97:114–115
mà-e 163.1:11
^{túg}ma$_{6}$ 97:57
maḫ 1.1:30; 1.2:44–47; 23:1–6,10; 32:19; 23.2:1,17,27; 184:31,50
mar-mar 163.2:a+15
mar-uru$_{5}$ 184:30; 185:36
maš-dà 97:71,74–75
maš-tab-ba 23:6; 168:4; 23.2:6
máš 35.2:21; 97:55,79–80
máš-sag 97:93

me 166.2:29; 171:7,11
me ("to be") 23:25; 32:40–41; 97:116–120; 168:34; 171:44,60–62
me-a 32:51–54; 60:20; 164:1–2
^{d}Me-dím-ša$_4$ 23.2:28
me-e 60:18; 79:29–30; 88:40–43, 46–47,52; 159:27,31–35; 163.1:5(for mè-šè); 164:19; 171:96
me-er 10:1–12,20–21; 184:35
me-gal(-gal*) 106:18*; 171:7
me-lám 23:12; 23.2:12
me-na 29:19; 79:11–14,16–17; 106:1; 171:21 (?)–23
me-na-šè 13:31; 29:20
me-ra(-ta) gál 97:59
me-ri 97:75
me-ri gub 184:28
me ur$_4$-ur$_4$ 106:19
me-zé 159:20
mè 163.1:5; 163.2:a+6
men 97:56
mer(?)-sig(?) 32:a+62 to a+63
^{giš}mes 35.2:33–37; 184:7
^{giš}mes-di$_4$-di$_4$-lá 35.2:34,36
^{giš}mes-gal-gal 35.2:35,37
^{d}Mes-lam-ta-è-a 164:4
mi-ir 32:45
mi-na 35.1:1,4,6
Mi-na 166.2:8
mi-úš 166.2:17
mí(-zi*) du$_{11}$ 166.1:22; 166.2:24*
mu 23:1–11; 34.2:24; 35.2:29(for gù?); 168:40–41; 171:94(for mu$_4$); 23.2:11
mu-ba-ra 1.2:49
mu-bar 1.1:33; 1.2:49
mu-dúr-ru-na 166.1:13
mu-duru$_5$ 166.2:16
mu-e 171:33–38
mu-gi-ga 106:22
mu-gi-gi-ir-ra 34.2:16
mu-gi-íb 34.1:2,4,6–7
mu-gi$_4$-gi$_4$-ra 34.2:16
mu-gi$_{17}$-ba 171:107
mu-gi$_{17}$-ib 10:39; 34.2:2,18,31; 59:2,10;79:3; 171:104
mu-gig-an-na 32:13,15,17,19, 21,23,26,32,34,40,42;59:3
mu-gù-di-dè 159:22
mu-lu 13:16–19; 29:14; 32:46,56; 34.2:5,18; 60:20,25(?),34–35,39,41: 79:30–31; 97:47–49; 160:35; 163.1:1; 164:29; 165:20,22; 171:96–97,100–101,104,106
mu-lu-a-ra-zu 29:16
mu-lu-ám-gi-ra 164:5
mu-lu-e-ri-a 97:89
mu-lu-é-kur-ra 35.2:38–39
mu-lu-EN 13:18
mu-lu-ki-bal-a 13:17
mu-lu-pár-im-ri-a 97:91
mu-lu-sizkur-ra 29:15
mu-lu-sún(?) 60:3
mu-lu-šír-an-na 88:9
mu-lu-šìr-ra/e 35.2:36–37; 166.1:30
mu-lú 171:68–69,105
mu-ni-šè 34.2:12–16
mu-nú 159:34
mu-ra 60:1–3; 168:36
mu$_4$ 164:28
mu$_x$(KU) 164:24–27
mu-šè-en 163.1:24
^{d}Mu-tin-an-na 88:21; see sub ama-
mu-ud-na 13:25; 60:4,11; 97:26
mu-ud-na-tur-ra 97:19
^{d}Mu-ul-líl 1.1:5; 1.2:5; 10:22; 13-parallel :24; 23.2:13,22; 32:38; 34.2:30; 35.2:26,31;

53:1–4,6–7; 159:30;
160:5,27,31,36; 163.1:32,36,38;
166.1:22; 166.2:24; 168:6
^{d}Mu-zé-eb-ba-sa$_{4}$-a 1.2:13;
13:6,26; 29:5
mú 34.2:1,24; 160:24
mú-mú 184:7
mud bar 60:37
mud-me-mar 171:58–59
mud$_{5}$-me-mar 171:56
munus-ša$_{6}$ 79:6,13
MUNUS.ÚS.DAM 97:105
muru$_{x}$ 184:17; 185:13
mùš-àm 171:100–103
mùš ga-ga 60:36
mušen 163.1:24
mušen-buru$_{5}$^{mušen} 171:76
mušen-dù 35.2:39; 160:1,30

na-ám 97:13(for naga)
na-ám 97:1–7; 171:97
na-ám-di-bi-dib 171:47,53
na-ám-di-bí 171:78
na-ám-di-bí-dib 171:57,61
na-ám-díb-ba 171:72
na-ám-ge$_{16}$-le-èm 160:22–23;
171:48,71
na-ám-ku$_{5}$ 163.2:a+26
na-ám-lú-ulù 106:11; 171:29
na-ám tar
(-tar*) 171:33*–34*,79
na-ám-tar 171:10,30–31,39,41,
44,46,52,56,60,70(?),77,104,
106–107
^{d}Na-na-a 13:29; 32:8; 34.2:39;
45:20; 53:24; 59:9,19
na rú-rú 32:12
na$_{4}$-di$_{4}$-di$_{4}$-lá 184:21
na$_{4}$-gal-gal 23:24–25; 184:22
na$_{4}$-TUM$_{10}$-tur-tur 23:23
na$_{4}$-tur-tur 23:25; 185:18
^{d}Nab 10:6
nag 60:22,31; 97:117; 159:10,14;
171:73
nam-lú-u$_{x}$-lu 185:28
nam-maḫ 184:49
nam tar 184:38
^{d}Nanna 13-parallel:19;
13:14–15; 79:14
NE 171:24
ne-éš 88:24–25; 171:49
ne te 97:81
^{d}Nè-iri$_{11}$-gal 164:3
Ni-ib-ru 35.1:2,8,12
ni-me-en 79:37(for nigin)
ní 32:57–59
ní-bi-a 166.2:35
ní-ta-na 185:33–34
ní te 32:55
ní-te(-a*)-ni 97:81–82;
168:38*–39*
nì-ga 171:106–109
nì-ki-luḫ 184:38
nì-maḫ 184:45
Nibru^{ki} 1.1:10; 1.2:17,29,45;
35.2:2; 160:6
níg-e-rib-ba 184:44
nigin 1.2:1–17,19,21,23,26;
35.2:22; 165:28–29
nigín 1.1:1–20; 1.2:1–4,17,21
nim 97:26–27; 165:19–20,23–24
nim-gír 23:20; 185:15
nimgir 184:32
^{d}Nin-líl 23:14; 160:27; 168:7
nin$_{9}$ 79:37; 88:20–21,44; 97:104
nin$_{9}$-arḫuš-a 97:104
nin$_{9}$-gal 160:28
Nina^{ki} 166.1:5,27
ninda 88:49–50
nir-gál 163.1:23
nu 79:24–25
nu-gig-an-na 106:2
nu-mu-un-su 23.2:24
nu-nuz$_{x}$-ša$_{6}$ 10:38; 32:7; 45:16;

53:20; 59:8,15
nu-sík 23.2:24
nu-sík-la 35.2:39
nu-tuk-la 35.2:39
nú 35.2:38; 60:16–17,38; 97:47–49; 159:12,31–32,34; 160:34
numun-e-eš 160:25
^{ú}numun-sar-ra 79:35

pa è 13:14–15; 23:1–6,10; 23.2:1
pa-pa-al 79:1,7–9
pà 35.2:26; 165:20,24
pa$_{4}$-e-ri-a 97:90
^{d}Pa$_{4}$-nun-na-ki 13:25
pa$_{5}$ 184:11
^{d}Pap-sukkal 45:7; 53:12
pár-im 97:82,90–91
pe-el 79:22
peš-peš 163.1:6
peš$_{6}$-peš$_{6}$ 163.2:a+7

ra 184:1–2
ra-ra 168:40
ra-ra-ra 163.1:12
ri 160:21; 163.1:24; 166.2:15
ri-ba/i 34.1:5–7
ri-ri 32:56; 34.2:21; 23.2:24
re-re 97:50–51("to go")
re$_{7}$ 97:50–51,100
rib-ba 34.2:3; 45:10; 53:14; 185:35
rig$_{7}$ 35.2:20("hut"); 60:39("hut"); 97:54–55

sa 97:16; 160:34
sa ak 164:10
sa du$_{11}$ 97:86–87
sa ku-ku 164:11
sa lá 97:119
^{dug}sa-ma-(a)n 184:43; 185:31
sa-mar(-mar*) 163.1:1,7*
sa-r 1.2:43
sá 184:50–51
sá [du$_{11}$] 97:86
sá-mar(-mar*) 163.1:1*; 163.2:a+8
sa$_{6}$ 171:87–88
sa$_{12}$-du$_{5}$-maḫ 159:2; 171:3
sag 97:56; 171:65
sag-an-ta-dè 163.1:12
sag(-šè) du$_{7}$-du$_{7}$ 88:11
sag-e-eš rig$_{7}$ 166.2:3
sag gá-gá 165:26–27
sag(-ta) gál 97:56
sag gi 184:31
sag-gi$_{6}$-ga 160:25
sag-giš-ra-ra 184:48
sag íl 184:30
^{giš}sag-kul-an-na 163.1:15; 163.2:a+16
sag mar 163.1:7
^{d}SAG.PISAN-Unu^{ki}-ga 164:9
sag-rig$_{7}$-eš 166.1:21
sag sìg(-sìg*) 23:13; 163.1:9*; 168:6; 171:64
sag sum 168:41
sag-tuk 165:25
saḫar dub-dub 32:47
saḫar-gar-i$_{7}$-da 32:48
saḫar šú-šú 32:47
sal 1.1:32; 1.2:48; 163.1:17; 171:14
sal-sal 163.1:17
sar 1.1:31; 1.2:43
sar-sar 171:76
si 1.2:50; 164:15
si-gar 34.2:21; 163.1:11
^{giš}si-gar-an-na 163.1:16
si-ig 88:10; 165:11
si-il(-si-il*) 163.1:15; 163.2:a+16*
si-is-ḫe 166.2:12
si-la 34.1:8(for sila), 10(for silá)

^{giš}si-mar 34.2:27
^{giš}si-mar-an-na 163.2:a+17
Si-ra-ra 166.2:9
si-sá 184:14
si-si 23:16–17
sì 23:26; 97:112(?); 168:37; 184:23
sì-sì-g 34.2:26
sig 168:1
síg 79:35; 171:65
síg-bar-ra 168:34; 184:42
síg zé-b 97:15
síg zu 97:15
sìg(-sìg*) 32:5; 34.2:22,23*; 88:11,39,41–43; 97:16; 164:7; 171:16
sig$_4$ 1.2:49(?); 97:112
sig$_7$ 171:87–88,91
sig$_7$-i-bí 32:20
sig$_{11}$ 1.1:33; 1.2:49
sig$_{11}$ di 29:23; 163.1:21
sikil 97:41′–42′
sil-la 1.2:48(for sal-la)
sil$_6$-lá 159:24
sila 34.2:4; 164:18; 184:12
sila$_4$ 34.2:6; 35.2:20; 60:16; 97:54; 165:18
silim 185:34
silim-me-eš e 168:38–39
sim^{mušen} 32:55
sipa 13:10; 97:62(?); 166.1:28–29
sipa-sag-gi$_6$-ga 1.1:6; 1.2:6; 13:10; 53:5
sír 184:17
Siraráki 166.1:6,26
sis 164:15
su 1.2:50; 97:56–59; 171:66
SU-bar-ra 171:29
su-d 163.1:16
su-g 165:6,12
su-mu-ug 88:13
su-ru 97:28–31
su-ub 97:13; 163.1:6; 171:92
su-zi 164:13
sù 1.1:34; 184:29,33–35
sù-sù 184:10
sù-g 32:24; 88:31; 165:4,8,10
su$_8$-su$_8$-g 10:19
su$_x$-pa 163.1:6
su$_x$-su$_x$ 163.2:a+17
su$_x$-ud 163.1:16
^{d}Suen 34.2:13
sùḫ-sùḫ 166.1:9
suḫuš 184:32
sukkal 23:20; 45:7; 53:12; 23.2:25–26; 185:15
^{d}Sukkal-maḫ-àm 45:7; 53:12
sukkal-zi 13:26

šà 29:a+28; 32:23; 45:13–23; 53:17–27; 59:11–20; 88:12,17; 159:23; 160:19; 164:33; 166.1:10,12; 166.2:15; 171:91–94,96,98–99
šà-é-dìm-ma 1.1:14
šà è 171:45-50
šà(-šè) gíd 88:44
šà ḫun 10:29-39; 13:22,24; 29:a+26; 34.2:28-29, 31, 33, 35, 37, 39; 45:12-23; 53:16-27; 59:11-22
šà-íb-ba 163.1:20; 163.2:a+21
šà-kúš-ù 10:24-27
šà-ne-ša$_4$ 97:73
šà si-ig 165:11
šà-sù-da-ke$_4$ 160:3
šà-túm 34.2:7
šà-tur 88:51
šà zi-zi 165:31
ša$_6$ 32:7–8; 60:23–24, 32–33, 36–37; 79:6, 13; 106:15–16
(dug)šakan 168:35
ša$_6$ 32:7–8; 60:23–24, 32–33, 36–37; 79:6, 13; 106:15–16
(dug)šakan 168:35

šár 88:14–15
še 1.1:23; 1.2:36; 163.1:6; 163.2:a+7; 171:74; 23.2:20–21
še-eb 1.1:11, 19–20; 1.2:18–19, 21–26; 32:11, 16; 160:7, 10, 12–15; 166.1:3, 6; 166.2:9
še-en 35.2:23
še-er-nu-ma-al 171:62
še(-ga) 13-parallel: 22–22a; 13:18–19; 163.1:17–18; 163.2:a+18 to a+19
še-ga-ra-di-n 184:40
še-garadin 185:32
še-gu-nu 23.2:18
še-gur 32:56
še-mu-ra 168:36
^{d}Šed-dù-ki-šár-ra 13:7
šed$_7$ 10:1, 28; 159:23; 163.2:a+21; see sub bar šed$_7$
šed$_{10}$ 163.1:20; 163.2:a+21
šeg$_6$ -...gi 35.2:27–31(for šeg$_x$ gi$_4$)
šeg$_9$-bar-ra 97:78
šeg$_x$ gi 35.2:27–31
šem$_5$ 159:19
šen(-šen*) 163.1:5; 163.2:a+6*
šen(?) di 163.1:21
ŠÈR-ra 171:44
šeš 1.1:27; 1.2:40; 34.2:14; 60:13; 88:24; 97:53; 165:1–2, 24, 28–29
šeš$_4$-šeš$_4$ 88:16
ši-bi-du-du-ba 35.1:5
ši-bi-kur-ra 35.1:3, 9
ši gi 35.2:15
šilam 35.2:22
šim 171:89
šim-bi-zi 171:93
šip-ri su$_x$-pa 163.1:6
šìr 29:22; 88:19
šìr ra 160:26; 164:21–23
ŠITA$_x$ki 165:9
šu 79:33; 88:17; 97:58, 68, 70, 74; 164:36–37; 171:54
šu bal 160:5
šu-bal ak 106:21
šu-da-a 88:28(for šu-dù-a)
šu dab$_5$ 166.2:25
^{giš}šu-de-eš-an-na 163.1:14; 163.2:a+15
šu du 165:17
šu-dù-a 164:24
šu du$_7$(-du$_7$*) 106:17*; 165:14
šu(?) du$_{11}$ 32:39
šu(-ta) gál 97:58
šu (-ta) gar 171:39
šu-gar-gar-ra 97:66
šu gi 10:20–22
šu ir 32:53
šu lá 32:54; 88:17; 97:78
šu ma-al 166.1:13
^{ú}šu-mu-un 35.2:19
šu mú-mú 34.2:4
šu ni-me-en 79:37(for šu nigin)
šu nigin 32:48
šu pe-pe-el 171:102
šu-si-ga 97:64
šu-sulug 13-parallel :19
šu ta 184:21
šu tag 184:22
šu ti 23.1:23–24; 34.2:6; 97:77
šu tu 34.1:10 (for šu ti)
šu TU-TU 97:60–61
šu(-šè) tuš 171:60–66
šu-um-du-um 171:103
šu ús 171:30
šu zi 97:68
šu zu-zu 166.2:19–20
šú(-šú*) 32:47*; 168:33
šub(-šub*) 13:30–31; 29:1–21; 88:30; 163.1:24; 164:12; 165:13, 18; 166.1:28, 29*; 166.2:27*–28*; 168:35; 184:43
šub$_x$-bi 13-parallel :16
šuba 32:17; 171:90
šuba-lá 34.2:10
^{giš}ukur 97:120
šul 163.2:a+27

^{ú}šumun$_x$-bu-re 35.2:19
^{ú}šumun$_x$-bur-re 35.2:19

ta 163.1:1; 164:1–2
ta-àm 160:19, 21
tab-an-na 165:2
tab-ba 97:85
tag$_4$-tag$_4$ 34.2:21
TÁL 32:a+62 to a+63
tan$_x$(-tá-na*) 164:25, 27; 171:94*
TAR 164:19
^{giš}tašgari 171:99
te 23:21–24; 88:14–15; 160:30–32; 163.1:8; 163.2:a+9; 164:12, 20; 168:9–12
te-en(-te-en*) 163.1:20*; 166.1:28, 29*
téš-a sì-sì-ig 163.1:10
téš-bi 34.2:26
ti 60:1–15; 79:18–19; 168:32
ti-l 29:22; 159:25; 165:22
ti-lim-da 159:16
ti-na gub 163.1:5; 163.2:a+6
til 32:43
TIL.TIL 171:20
Tin-tir^{ki} 1.1:21, 33, 46; 13:31; 29:7; 35.2:8; 160:12
tu 97:12(for tu$_5$)
tu^{mušen} 97:81; 184:36
tu$_5$ 97:12
tu$_9$ 79:16–17
tu$_{10}$-b 35.2:27, 31; 160:35
tu$_{11}$-b 35.2:27
túg 23:12; 88:46–47; 97:81; 164:24–28; 171:94
túg-pa-rim$_4$-ma 164:11
tuk 79:18–19; 164:36–37
^{giš}tukul 165:26; 184:32
tukundi 29:18
TUM-dib-kù 159:4
TUMxEŠ(=ḫaš$_x$) 23:18
túm 88:46–47; 165:31
tum$_{10}$ 60:40–41; 88:10
tum$_{10}$-mi-ir 60:41; 184:6
tum$_{10}$-mu 184:6
tur-e 1.1:30; 1.2:44–47
tur-tur 97:102–103(for ^{d}Zé-er-tur)
tùr 10:26; 35.2:21; 97:118; 106:6; 166.2:19; 171:85
tuš 32:52, 54; 79:7; 88:17; 159:26, 35; 164:31–35; 171:64, 96–97, 104–105; 23.2:27–28

ú 60:30; 97:24, 116; 159:9; 166.1:29
ú-eger-ra 97:23
^{giš}ú-GÍR 97:81; 184:33
ú lu-lu 97:53, 101
ú-ra 166.2:30
ú-ru 35.1:2, 7, 11–14
ú-sag-gá 97:22, 27
ú-téš-nu-un-zu 160:24
ú . . . ú . . . 97:6–7
ù 97:47–49; 163.1:4
ù-da 34.1:12(for u$_4$-da)
ù-dúg 32:10
ù ku(-ku*) 60:16–17; 171:19*
ù-li-li 34.2:18
ù-lú 164:1–9
ù-lul-la ku-ku 1.1:9; 1.2:9; 53:8
ù-mu-un 13-parrallel: 15, 20, 23; 23:6–7; 29:19; 60:15, 29; 88:21; 97:60; 163.1:26; 164:13; 168:4; 23.2:25–26; 184:1–2, 27, 38, 51; 185:19
ù-mu-un-du$_{11}$-ga-zi-da 1.1:4
ù-mu-un-e-a-ra-li 60:7
ù-mu-un-e-Bàd-tibira^{ki} 60:8
ù-mu-un-e-du$_6$-su$_8$-ba 60:10
ù-mu-un-e-é-kur-ra 163.1:2
ù-mu-un-e-é-mùš-a 60:12
ù-mu-un-e-é-ninnu 163.1:3
ù-mu-un-é-nin$_5$-ù 163.1:3
ù-mu-un-guruš-a 13-parrallel 16–17
ù-mu-un-ḫé-gál-la 23:5

ù-mu-un-Karkara^{ki} 23:4
ù-mu-un-kur-kur-ra 1.1:2
ù-mu-un-mu-zi-da 88:5
ù-mu-un-sa-pàr 88:7
ù-mu-un-šud$_x$-dè 88:8
ù-sá 159:33
ù-še-eg 97:81
ù-tu(-ud) 163.1:3; 163.2:a+4; 171:109; 23.2:20
ù . . . ù . . . 97:6–7; 171:88
ù-u$_8$ 10:23
u$_4$ 13-parallel:15; 23:7, 16–20, 28, 30; 32:49, 53; 45:12; 53:16; 59:11; 97:20–21, 106–107; 163.1:4; 166.1:10; 166.2:34–35; 23.2:10; 185:12, 14, 28; 184:15–16
u$_4$ 97:24(for ú)
u$_4$-ba/u$_4$-bi-a* 79:36*; 97:33* 168:33
u$_4$-da 34:2:8
u$_4$-eger-ra 97:23(for ú-eger-ra)
u$_4$-gal 23.1:8
u$_4$-gal-an-na 23.2:14
u$_4$-GÙ-mu-ra 184:27
u$_4$-sag-gá 97:22 (for ú-sag-gá)
u$_4$-sar-ra 34.2:15
u$_4$-sur-ra 166.2:16
u$_4$-šú-a 164:22
u$_4$-ta-àm 97:107
u$_4$-tur 166.2:34–35
u$_4$-zal-la 34:2:20
u$_4$ zal-zal 1.1:24; 1.2:37
u$_5$ 23:7–9; 97:116; 164:13; 23.2:17
u$_6$-da 184:10
u$_6$ dè 1.2:1
u$_6$ di 88:54; 106:10
u$_6$ du$_{11}$ 1.1:1–20; 1.2:1
u$_8$ 35.2:20; 60:16; 97:54
u$_8$ lu-lu 97:53
ub 32:34; 106:19
^{kuš}ub 79:34; 159:17
ubur 79:5
udu-dul$_4$-a 97:96
udu-eger-ra 97:94
udu-sag-gá 97:92
udu-súb-a 97:96
udu-u$_5$-a 97:95
udu-ua$_4$ 97:95
ug 97:98–99
ug-an-kù-ga 163.1:23
ug-ban-da 184:25
úg-an-na 23:10; 168:5
úg-bàn-da 23:29
úg-gal 23:9
ug$_5$ 97:9, 11; 171:106–109
uga^{mušen} 60:39
ugu 23:25; 168:33
ul 23:21; 79:1, 7–9; 184:28
ul-ḫé 34.2:24
ul$_4$ 88:28–29; 168:9–10
um-ma 184:41; 185:29
umun 1.2:10, 12, 14; 10:22; 13:1, 5, 7–8, 11, 23; 29:1, 4, 6–13; 34.2:29–30; 45:7, 15; 53:12, 19; 59:14; 160:19; 163.2:a+22
umun-an-uraš-a 1.2:16
umun-Barsip^{ki} 13:8; 29:9
umun-du$_{11}$-ga-zi-da 1.2:4; 53:3; 160:32
umun-é-dàra-an-na 29:13
umun-é-kišib-ba 45:4; 53:9
umun-é-maḫ-ti-la 29:11
umun-é-me-te-ur-sag 45:5; 53:10
umun-é-rab-di$_5$-di$_5$ 10:31
umun-é-sag-íl-la 13:5; 29:8
umun-é-te-me-an-ki 29:12
umun-é-u$_6$-nir-ki-tuš-maḫ 45:5; 53:10
umun-é-zi-da 13:5; 29:10
umun-irigal-la 45:3
umun-ka-nag-gá 53:5, 8
umun-Kiš^{ki}-a-ta 45:4; 53:9
umun-kur-kur-ra 1.2:3; 53:2; 160:2–3